STERLING
Test Prep

BAR Exam Review

MBE Essentials
Governing Law Outlines

7th edition

www.Sterling-Prep.com

This publication is designed to provide accurate and authoritative information regarding the subject matter covered. It is distributed with the understanding that the publisher, authors or editors are not engaged in rendering legal or another professional service. If legal advice or other expert assistance is required, the services of a competent professional should be sought.

Sterling Test Prep is not legally liable for any mistakes, omissions or inaccuracies in the content of this publication. Sterling Test Prep does not guarantee that the user of this publication will pass the bar exam or achieve a particular level of performance. Individual performance on the bar exam depends on many factors, including but not limited to the level of preparation, aptitude and individual performance on test day.

7   6   5   4   3   2   1

ISBN-13: 978-1-9475564-5-4

Sterling Test Prep products are available at special quantity discounts for sales, promotions, career counseling offices, and other educational purposes.

For more information, contact our Sales Department at:

Sterling Test Prep
6 Liberty Square #11
Boston, MA 02109

©2020 Sterling Test Prep
Published by Sterling Test Prep
Printed in the U.S.A.

Dear Future Attorney,

Congratulations on choosing this book as part of your bar preparation!

MBE Essentials: Governing Law describes the principles of substantive law, which most often governs the correct answers to Multistate Bar Examination Questions. The performance of examinee on individual questions has been correlated with success or failure on the bar examination. Through an analysis of these statistics, we have been able to identify those questions that are best able to predict success or failure on the bar examination and put together the outlines of laws that govern those questions.

You should learn these important governing law principles in order to determine the answers to the questions on the MBE. These rules of law will likely determine the answers to more than half of the questions on each section of the MBE. Learn and review these principles because your decision between two tough choices will depend on knowing the rule of law, and it is important to have that knowledge to get a passing score on the multistate bar exam.

The content of this book was developed by legal professionals and law instructors that possess extensive credentials and have been admitted to practice law.

We wish you great success in your future legal profession and look forward to becoming an important part of your successful preparation for the bar exam!

Sterling Test Prep Team

190730vgr

Table of Contents

Table of Contents (*cont.*)

Table of Contents (*cont.*)

Introduction to The Multistate Bar Examination (MBE)

The Two Components of the State Bar Examination

The Bar Examination consists of the Multistate Bar Examination (MBE) given on one day and the state essay / state multiple-choice examination given on a contiguous day.

Generally, the MBE and state portions are given equal weight in determining a passing score. After each part of the examination is scaled on a range of 1-200, the two scores are combined for a total of 400 possible points.

The Multistate Bar Examination (MBE)

The Multistate Bar Examination consists of 200 four-option multiple choice questions prepared by the National Conference of Bar Examiners (NCBE). Of these 200 questions, 175 are scored, and 25 are unscored pretest questions. Candidates answer 100 questions in the three-hour morning session and the remaining 100 questions in the three-hour afternoon session. The 175 scored questions are distributed evenly with 25 questions on each of the seven subject areas: Civil Procedure, Constitutional Law, Contracts, Criminal Law and Procedure, Evidence, Real Property, and Torts.

Specified percentages of the questions in each subject are devoted to particular topics within those subjects. For example, approximately one-third of the evidence questions test hearsay and its exceptions, while approximately one-third of the torts questions test negligence.

Scoring the Exam

The examinee is first given a "raw score"; a computation of the number of questions answered correctly. No points are deducted for wrong answers, so it is important to answer all questions, even if the answer is a random guess. The raw score is then adjusted by adding points to achieve the "scaled score."

The number of points added is determined by a complex formula which compares the difficulty of the current examination to the difficulty of a prior benchmark examination. The comparative performance of examinee on "control questions" given on previous examinations forms the basis for determining the difficulty of each examination.

Equating Scores Among Candidates

MBE scores are scaled scores calculated by NCBE through a statistical process of equating commonly used for standardized tests. According to NCBE, this statistical process adjusts raw scores on the current examination to account for differences in difficulty compared to previously administered exams.

Since the MBE is a scaled score, equating makes it impossible to know exactly how many questions must be answered correctly to receive a particular score. Equating allows scores from different examinations to be compared since a certain scaled score represents the same level of knowledge from one examination to another.

The Importance of the MBE Score

A passing MBE score depends on the jurisdiction in which the bar exam is given. In jurisdictions that score on a 200-point scale, the passing score is the overall score. Passing scores are usually in the 130s range. For the July 2018 bar exam, the national average MBE score was approximately 139.5, a decrease of about 2.2 points from the July 2017 national average.

How much the MBE is worth depends on the jurisdiction because each jurisdiction has its policy for how much relative weight is given to the MBE relative to other components of the bar exam. For Uniform Bar Examination ("UBE") jurisdictions the MBE component is weighted at 50%. If the bar exam is taken in a UBE jurisdiction, it is easy to figure out a passing MBE score: take the score needed to pass and divide by two. For example, if the required passing score is 266 out of 400, then a 133 is a passing MBE score.

Most state bar examiners use a method of combining the MBE grades with the grades on the state essay examination, in which the performance by the total class of state candidates on the MBE controls the conversion of the raw state essay scores to scaled scores. Because of this, it is essential to achieve a scaled MBE score of 135 to pass the state portion of the bar examination.

What the Multistate Exam is Trying to Accomplish

A working knowledge of the objectives of the MBE, the skills it attempts to test, how it is drafted, the relationship of the component parts of an MBE question, and the limitations imposed on its authors can provide a student with a substantial advantage in choosing the correct answers to MBE questions and passing the examination. Knowing which issues are tested and the form in which they are tested makes it more manageable to learn the large body of substantive law.

The fundamental objective of the MBE examiners is to provide a device to measure fairly and efficiently which law school graduates have the necessary academic qualifications to be admitted to the bar and which do not.

The MBE tests the following skills:

Ability to read carefully and critically.

Ability to identify the legal issue in a set of facts.

Knowledge of the law that governs the legal issues tested.

Ability to distinguish between closely-related principles of law which are frequently confused.

Ability to make reasonable judgments from ambiguous facts.

Ability to understand the way in which limiting words make plausible-sounding choices wrong.

Ability to guess the right answer by intelligently eliminating incorrect choices.

Characteristics of MBE Designed to Accomplish That Objective

The 200-question multiple choice examination that is used to accomplish this objective must be of a consistent level of difficulty. Furthermore, the level at which the pass/fail decision is made must be achievable by a substantial majority of candidates.

Type of Questions Important to Accomplish That Objective

The performance of examinee on individual questions has been correlated with success or failure on the bar examination. Through an analysis of these statistics, those questions that are best able to predict success or failure on the bar examination have been identified.

In general, the hardest questions weren't particularly good predictors of failure, because most of the examinee who missed them passed the examination. However, many of the easier questions were very good predictors of failure.

Preparation and Test-Taking Strategies

Easy Questions Make the Difference

Pay close attention to these questions

Limitations on the examiners lead to the first important insight into preparation for the examination, the kind of questions that make a difference on whether you pass or fail. On the MBE the median raw score ranges from about 60% correct to about 66% correct. In "Myths and Facts about the MBE," the National Conference of Bar Examiners write, "In a 1992 study, expert panelists reported that they believed MBE items were generally easy, correctly estimating that about 66% of candidates would select the right answer to a typical item."

In most states, depending on the difficulty of the exam you take, you can score slightly below the median, that is, miss as many as 80 questions and still pass. The most important questions to determine if you pass or fail are not the very tough ones, but the easy ones where 90% or more of the examinee answer the question correctly.

Characteristics of Easy Questions

These questions usually test a fairly basic and regularly tested point of substantive law in a straightforward way. The wrong choices, the distracters, are usually fairly easy to eliminate. Your first task in preparing for the MBE is to get these questions correct.

Use This Information to Focus Your Study

As you review your performance on multiple choice questions, you should be concerned if you are consistently missing questions where 90% or more of the students answered them correctly. If you continually have problems with these questions and your overall performance on them is 50% or below, then you lack the fundamental knowledge of the law necessary to pass the MBE. You should spend your time reviewing those basic principles and working deliberately on the easy questions that test those fundamentals.

Study Plan Based Upon the Statistics

These statistics show that an excellent performance on either the MBE questions (134 correct) or the state essays (4's on almost every essay) will virtually assure you a passing score. If you fail the MBE by 9 points (a raw score of 121) or the essays by 5 points (a raw score of 29), the probability of you passing the bar exam are in the single digits.

It is our advice that you first put your effort into getting 67% of the MBE questions right for the following reasons. The questions are objective, and there are enough questions which are predictable concerning content and structure that it is possible, through reasonable effort, to answer 134 questions correctly. Studying the MBE first has the added advantage of preparing for the substantive law for several of the state essays.

The essays cover many subjects, the precise subject matter tested is unpredictable, and the answers are graded subjectively by graders who work quickly. Moreover, you have had three years of law school experience with essays, and much less experience with multiple choice questions.

Therefore, we recommend that you should work to achieve an acceptable MBE score (134 raw score or above) before spending much time preparing for the essays.

Historical Factors Relevant to Passing the Bar

Based upon an analysis of relevant statistics from the performance of law school students in the past, the following factors predict the likelihood that you will pass the bar.

- LSAT Score
- First Year Grade Point Average

LSAT Scores

LSAT scores are an important predictor of success on the bar exam because the LSAT requires similar multiple-choice test-taking skills as the MBE.

The LSAT also tests many of the types of legal reasoning which are tested on the MBE.

A poor LSAT can be overcome by a comprehensive study of the governing law of the MBE, but the student must work harder.

First Year Grade Point Average

Most of the subjects tested (e.g., constitutional law, civil procedure, contracts, criminal law, real property, torts) on the MBE are taken in the first year of law school. The first year GPA measures your mastery of these subjects, how well you were able to prepare for exams, and your ability to understand legal principles and apply them to fact patterns.

The MBE measures the same factors, but in a multiple choice format rather than an essay format.

LSAT Scores above 155 and 1st Year GPA above 3.0

Past statistics indicate that law students with an LSAT score above 155 and a first-year GPA above 3.0 are reasonably assured to pass the bar exam. They should study conscientiously and take the practice MBEs to make sure that they are performing at the level needed to pass, but they have little cause to panic.

LSAT Scores from 150-155 and 1st Year GPA from 2.5-3.0

Students with an LSAT score between 150 and 155 and a first-year GPA between 2.5 and 3.0 are in more danger of failing and need to engage in more rigorous preparation. They have to be certain to achieve a scaled score of 135 and should take both released practice exams and understand the reasons for incorrect choices. They should prepare for the state essays by making sure that they have covered all of the governing law in this preparation book.

LSAT Scores from 145-150 and 1st Year GPA from 2.2-2.5

Past statistics indicate that these students have about a 50% chance of passing the bar. These students should not rely on the ordinary commercial bar review. They need intense training, particularly on the MBE component of the bar exam. They must devote 50-60 hours per week for seven weeks to prepare for the bar, by learning the format and content of the substantive law tested on the MBE. They should take both released practice exams under exam conditions and conscientiously study the questions they missed.

LSAT Scores below 145 and 1st Year GPA below 2.2

Students with a GPA below 2.2 have had a failure rate of approximately 80%. They must take this preparation faithfully and conscientiously. They must engage in a rigorous course of study, more than is demanded by the traditional bar review course.

Learning and Applying the Applicable Substantive Law

Knowledge of Substantive Law

The most fundamental reason for missing a question is a failure to know the principle of law which controls the answer or failure to understand how that principle is applied. Before taking the MBE, you must re-learn a large body of law which is taught in your first-year courses.

Governing Law

It is important for you to commit governing (i.e., substantive) law to memory because it is likely that the same principle of governing law will control the answer to a question which you will see on the exam. It is also important to analyze the governing law as it is applied in the context of the question because you must not only know the governing law but you must also know how to apply it.

Where to Find the Law

All of the questions asked on the examination have to be related to the subject matter outlined in the material published by the bar examiners. While that outline is broad and ambiguous, years of experience with the examination has delineated the scope of the material you must learn. You can feel confident that you do not have to go beyond the information provided with this course to find the governing law which is likely to appear on the MBE and to learn how to apply it.

The statements of governing law were compiled by analyzing the questions released by the multistate examiners. The analysis revealed that there are a limited number of legal principles which are tested regularly and repeatedly.

You should review these principles before preparing answers to practice questions and understand how these principles are applied to obtain the correct answer. Just before taking the MBE, you should commit these principles to memory.

Controlling Authority

The examiners have also specified their sources of authority for the correct answers. In subjects like torts or property, it is the generally accepted view of the law in the United States. In substantive criminal law, it is common law. Decisions of the United States Supreme Court control in Constitutional Law and Criminal Procedure. The Uniform Commercial Code is the controlling authority in sales questions, and the Federal Rules of Evidence is the controlling authority in evidence. The large body of released questions and the official answers to those questions determine the controlling law by process of deduction.

Recent Changes in the Law

Because of logistical requirements, the MBE must be printed almost a year before it is given. Therefore, the examiners are not in a position to incorporate recent changes in the law into the questions you will answer. Recent changes in the law will not form the basis for correct answers to questions.

If a recent change makes an answer originally designated as the correct answer to be incorrect, the examiners will credit more than one correct answer. The holding of a United States Supreme Court case will not be tested on the MBE before two years have elapsed since the decision was published.

Lesser-known Issues Tested

Some of the toughest questions on the examination are based upon little-known principles of law. Missing them will not cause you to fail the examination. However, it is easy to learn these principles and answer the question correctly, thereby improving your overall performance and chances of passing the exam.

Unusual Applications Tested

There are some issues where the correct answers are different from the usual rules. For example, hearsay evidence which would be inadmissible at trial is admissible before a judge hearing evidence on a preliminary question of fact. See Federal Rule of Evidence 104 (a).

✝ Which Governing Law Is Being Tested

A common wrong answer or distracter on an MBE question is an answer which is correct under a body of law other than the governing law being tested.

An example of this is a question governed by Article 2 of the UCC, where an offer is irrevocable if 1) it is in writing, 2) made by a merchant, and 3) states that it is irrevocable. One of the wrong answers states the correct rule under the common law of contracts, where an offer is revocable unless consideration is paid (i.e., option) for the promise to keep it open.

✝ Answers Which Are Always Wrong

There are some commonly used distracters which are always wrong and can be eliminated quickly. A simple illustration is a choice in an evidence question which says that character can only be attacked by reputation evidence. This choice is always wrong because both opinion and reputation evidence is admissible under the Federal Rules of Evidence when attacks on character are permissible.

Honing Your Reading Skills

There are several levels at which your reading skills become critical. The basic level is reading to understand the facts and to keep the parties straight. A mistake at this level results in answering the question incorrectly no matter how much law you know.

Reading Complex Transactional Questions

If the question asks about a transaction with many parties, diagram the transaction before you begin to analyze the choices. The diagram should show the relationship between the parties such as grantor-grantee or assignor-assignee, the date the transaction took place, and the relationship of a person to the transaction (e.g., *donee* or *bona fide purchaser*).

Read all of the Choices

Never pick an answer until you have carefully read all four choices. The directions tell you to pick the best answer, but you can't make that determination until you have compared all of the choices. Sometimes the difference between the right and wrong answer is that one choice is more detailed or more precisely sets forth the applicable law. You don't know that until you have carefully read all answers.

Impediments to Careful Reading

The two biggest reasons candidates fail to read carefully are:

1) They hurry through a question. A careful test taker maintains a steady, deliberate pace during the exam.

2) They are fatigued because of lack of sleep or the strain caused by the exam itself. Practice in advance and be well-rested on the test day.

Reading Too Much into a Question

The examiners are publicly committed to designing MBE questions which are "a fair index of whether the applicant has the ability to practice law." Psychometric experts review them to make sure that they are fair and unbiased. Even though you have to read every word of these carefully drafted questions, do not read the question to try to find some bizarre interpretation of the words.

The examiners have an obligation to ask fair questions; they do not rely on "trick" questions. Again, it is the basic, straightforward questions that determine whether you pass, not the occasional very difficult question which tests some obscure point of law. Reading too much into a question and looking for a trick lurking behind every fact will lead you to the wrong answer more often than it will lead you to the correct answer. Therefore, take questions at face value.

Read the Call of the Question First

Before you read the facts of the question, read the call of the question because it tells you what task you are to perform in selecting the correct answer. This focuses your attention before you read the facts. The question contains many words of art such as "most likely," "best defense," or "least likely" which will govern the method by which you choose the correct answer. The call is often phrased in the positive, asking which is the "best argument" or "most likely result."

Be Careful of Negative Calls

However, when the call of the question is in the negative, asking for the "weakest argument" or asking which of the options is "not" in a specified category, you must examine each option with the perspective that the choice which has those negative characteristics, will be the correct answer.

After you have read and fully understood the facts, read the call of the question once more before you read the choices, and analyze each choice in relation to the requirements set forth in the call of the question.

Consistency with the Body of the Question

Read the choices for consistency with the body of the question and eliminate the choices which are inconsistent with the question.

Broad Statements of Black Letter Law Can Sometimes be Correct

When reading an answer choice, do not rule out choices which are imprecise statements of the applicable black letter law. If the examiners always included a choice which was exactly on point, the questions would be too easy. Instead, they try to disguise the wording they use in the correct answer.

For example, the Federal Rules of Evidence contain an elaborate set of rules of relevancy which limit the right to introduce evidence of repairs after an accident. If there was a question where the introduction of that evidence was permissible, and there were no choices which specifically cited the exception to the general rule of exclusion, a choice phrased in terms of the general rule of relevancy, namely: "Admissible, because its probative value outweighs its prejudicial effect" would be the correct answer.

Improving Your Multiple Choice Test-Taking Skills

The previous discussion dealt with knowledge of the law and your reading skills as the vehicles select the correct answer. This discussion shows how to increase the odds you pick the correct answer based upon technical factors which are independent of your knowledge of the substantive law.

Limitation on the Examiners

The greatest limitation on the examiners is that every question must have one demonstrably correct and three demonstrably wrong answers. This limits the way in which they can write choices. When you look at the details of the construction of the questions, you see how this limitation sometimes gives clues to the correct choice. This section explores various techniques for getting to the correct answer.

Process of Elimination

Your task in answering a multiple choice question is not to find the ideal answer to the question asked, but rather to pick the best of the four available options. Most of the time you accomplish this task by eliminating three choices for various reasons and then looking at the remaining choice and choosing it if it is plausible.

Some options can be positively eliminated because they state an incorrect proposition of law or do not relate to the facts. If you can positively eliminate three options and the remaining option is not unacceptable, then pick it and move on to the next question.

Eliminating Two Wrong Answers

Certain questions on the MBE are challenging because of the difficulty involved in distinguishing between two of the four choices when finally picking the best answer. A common comment from examinees leaving the bar exam is "I could not decide between the last two choices." The positive side of that problem is that you have eliminated two of the four choices. The following processes are helpful in eliminating two answers.

Pick the Winning Side

In a question with two choices on one side and two on the other side of a court's decision, first, try to pick a choice on the side you think should prevail. By far the most common choice pattern is the "two-two" pattern - two choices which state that the plaintiff prevails, and two which state that the defendant prevails.

The best way to approach this kind of question is to <u>rely on your knowledge of the law</u>, or on your instinctive feeling as to <u>which general conclusion is correct</u>. Then try to distinguish between the explanations following the general conclusion which you chose and pick the one that best justifies the conclusion.

Distance Between Choices on the Other Side

However, if the justifications following the conclusion on the side you chose seem indistinguishable, then look at the explanations for the choices on the other side. If the reasons for the choices on the other side are readily distinguishable, and one appears reasonable and the other incorrect, then reconsider your initial choice of a general conclusion. Remember that the examiner is required to provide a distinguishable reason why one explanation of a general conclusion is correct, and the other is wrong.

That obligation does not exist if the general conclusion itself is wrong. If choices (A) and (B) on one side both look correct, that is, they sound extremely reasonable and are consistent with the fact pattern, and one of the choices with the opposite general conclusion, answer (C), seems clearly incorrect, or is inconsistent with the facts, and answer (D) with the same general conclusion sounds reasonable, then from a technical viewpoint, the best choice is answer (D).

Playing the Odds

It takes about 125 correct answers to pass the MBE. An important strategy in reaching that number is intelligently eliminating choices. If you are sure of the answer to only one-quarter of the 200 questions on the examination and can confidently eliminate two of the four choices on the remaining 150, then you can randomly guess between the two remaining choices, and the odds are that you will get 75 of them correct. Those 75, coupled with the 50 questions of which you were sure of the answer, will produce a raw score of 125 on the MBE exam and a scaled score above the benchmark 135. Unfortunately, you cannot avoid guessing on some questions, but there are intelligent methods to reduce the viable choices to only two.

Questions Based upon a Common Fact Pattern

On the MBE you will find several instances where two or more questions are based upon the same fact pattern. You should always look at the wording of the second question to guide you concerning the correct answer to the first.

For example, if the first question has two choices which begin with "P prevails" and two choices which begin with "D prevails," and the second question starts with "If P prevails" then it is likely that one of the "P prevails" choices is the correct answer to the first question. If you picked a "D prevails" answer to the first question, go back and think carefully before you select it as your final answer.

Common Fact Pattern

Some questions share a common fact pattern. When you are asked to assume an answer to a first question from a fact pattern to answer the second question, the probability is high that the answer to the first question is in accordance with that assumption.

"Only If" Questions

Be very careful of any choice with the limiting words "only if." If there is any other reason the same result could be reached, the choice is wrong. Sometimes the words are used to make a distinction between the two "affirmed" choices to make one of them wrong.

Multiple True/False Issues

In addition to the true/false question, the exam sometimes states three propositions in the root of the question and tests some characteristic of those propositions in the call of the question. The choices list various combinations of propositions.

The difference between this type of question and the double true/false question is that only four of the eight possible combinations can fit into the options. It is, therefore, possible to reach the correct result if you are not sure of the truth or falsity of all the propositions but are sure of one.

Process of Elimination to Increase Your Odds

Sometimes you might not be able to eliminate all of the wrong answers just because you are sure of your answer to one of the choices.

If you can eliminate with confidence even one choice, you increase your probability of answering the question correctly.

The property questions are probably the most difficult on the MBE. The fact patterns are usually long and involve many parties in complex transactions. In preparing for the MBE it is important to learn basic property principles and apply them, but extensive studying into the depths of property law is not necessary, to score well in these questions.

Correctly Stated, but Inapplicable, Principle of Law

The task of the examiners is to make the wrong choices look good. A clever way to accomplish this is to write a choice which impeccably states a rule of law that is not applicable because of facts in the root of the question. For example, in a question where a person is an assignee, not a sublessee, one of the choices may correctly state the law for sublessees, but it is inapplicable to the fact pattern.

Conjunctions: "Because," "If," "Only If" and "Unless"

These conjunctions are commonly used in the choices in MBE questions. It is important to understand their role in determining whether a choice is correct.

Use of the Conjunction "Because"

The word "because" connects a conclusion and the reason for that conclusion with the facts in the body of the question. There are two requirements for an MBE question using "because" to be correct:

1) The conclusion must be correct.

2) The reasoning must logically follow based upon the facts in the question and the statement which follows the word "because" must be legally correct.

If the "because" choice states the correct result for the wrong reason, it is incorrect.

Use of the Conjunction "If"

The conjunction "if" requires a much narrower focus than "because." When a choice contains an "if," you must determine whether the entire statement is true, assuming that the proposition which follows the "if" is true. There is no requirement that facts in the root of the question support the proposition following "if," or if there are facts in the root which might support the proposition, that such a construction be reasonable.

"Because" or "If" Need Not Be Exclusive

There is no requirement that the reason for the conclusion following "if" or "because" be exclusive. For example, if a master could be liable in tort either under the doctrine of *respondeat superior* or because the master himself was negligent, a choice using "if" or "because" holding the master liable would be correct if it stated either reason, even though the master might be liable for the other reason.

"Only If" – Requirement of Exclusivity

When an option uses the words "only if," assume that the entire proposition is correct as long as the words following "only if" are true. The critical difference, where "only if" is used, is that the proposition cannot be true except when the condition is true. Therefore, exclusivity is required for "only if" questions.

"Unless"

The conjunction "unless" has the same logical function as the words "only if," except that it precedes a negative exclusive condition instead of a positive one. It is essentially the mirror image of an "only if" choice. Thus, the best approach to an option using an "unless" conjunction is to reverse the result and substitute the words "only if" for "unless."

Exam Tip – "Because"

Notice that in an answer choice which would have been correct, the word "because" limits the facts you could consider to those in the body and call of the question where you were told certain facts. The difference between the effect of "if" and "because" controls the answer to this question.

You should be able to quickly identify those limited situations (e.g., where the appropriate standard is strict liability) and distinguish them from those which are satisfactory (e.g., if the standard is negligence).

Limiting Words

Choices can be made incorrect by the use of limiting words which require that a proposition be true in either all circumstances or under no circumstances. Examples of limiting words include: all, any, never, always, only, every and plenary.

Improving Your Ability to Make Correct Judgment Calls

Applying Law to Facts

Most MBE questions give you a fact pattern and ask you to pick the choice which draws the correct legal conclusion required by the call of the question.

The first skill required to answer such a question is to draw inferences from the facts given so that you have placed the conduct described in the question in an appropriate legal category.

The second step in the process is to apply the appropriate legal rule to conduct in that category and finally choose the option which reaches the appropriate conclusion.

The process of drawing inferences from a fact pattern and placing conduct in an appropriate category often requires the exercise of judgment.

Bad Judgment Equals the Wrong Answer

To make the questions difficult, the examiners often place the conduct near the border of two different classifications, and you must decide which side of the demarcation the conduct falls on. Inevitably, reasonable people can differ on these judgments. If your judgment does not coincide with the examiners, you are likely to answer the question incorrectly no matter how much law you know.

You can mitigate this problem to some extent by reviewing released questions which involve judgment calls where the examiners have published the correct answer and thus their judgment call. For example, a death occurring because the parties were playing Russian roulette is considered depraved heart murder, not involuntary manslaughter.

Judgment Calls Happen

Difficult judgment calls occur several times during the MBE, and you are bound to make some close judgment calls incorrectly. While this adds to the frustrations of taking a multiple-choice test, it is part of the exam.

If you narrow most of these judgment call questions to two choices and then guess, you will get approximately half of them correct. You will not fail the MBE solely because you were unlucky on judgment calls. The examiners remove many judgment calls by procedural devices.

The Importance of Procedure

The correct answer may be controlled by the procedural context of the criminal prosecution involved. The question does not ask what a jury should find on the facts given.

For example, it is given that the jury has found the defendant guilty of murder, and the only question on appeal is whether the judge should have granted a motion to dismiss at the end of all of the evidence. This is because a reasonable jury looking at the facts and inferences most favorable to the prosecution should not have found the defendant guilty of murder. The same procedural issues are present when the question asks if a motion for summary judgment should be allowed or if the court should direct a verdict.

MBE Tips and Suggestions

Time Allowed

The time given to complete the MBE is usually adequate if you have practiced enough questions to improve your speed and efficiency to the required level. The examination is divided into two 100-question segments. You are allowed three hours for each set of 100 questions, an average of one minute and forty-eight seconds per question.

[handwritten note in left margin: 1:48 per question]

Before taking the MBE, you should take previously released examinations in two three-hour periods on the same day. Since this examination is approximately the same length as the exam you will take, you will know whether you have a timing problem for the MBE. If you cannot come close to completing the practice exam in the allowed time, then you will probably have the same trouble on the exam. If so, be prepared to adopt the alternative strategies below.

All questions do not require the same amount of time. If you believe that you can complete 100 questions in three hours, you should use the following strategy.

[handwritten note in left margin: 15 mins = 9Q 30 mins = 18Q 36 = 1hr Q]

Standard Timing Game Plan

When the exam starts, you should break the allotted time into 15-minute intervals and write them down. You should set an initial pace of 9 questions every fifteen minutes. Then check your progress at each 15-minute interval. As long as you have completed 18 questions in the first half hour, 36 in the first hour, 72 in the first two hours, and 90 in the first two and a half hours you are on target to complete the exam in the allotted time. At this pace, you should complete 100 questions in two hours and forty-six minutes. If you keep up this pace, it will leave you 14 minutes to check your answer sheet, revisit troublesome questions, or use the extra time to go a little slower on the last group of questions when fatigue is impairing your mental ability.

Difficult Questions

If you find a particularly hard question or one you do not know the answer to, do not spend a disproportionate amount of time on it since each question counts the same in your final score. Mark it in your test booklet, make a shrewd guess within the budgeted time and make a note to yourself to come back if time allows.

Do NOT leave any answer choice blank.

Approach for When Time is Not a Factor

If you find that your natural, *careful* pace is faster than the budgeted target of 9 questions every 15 minutes, then work at your faster pace, but use your extra time on the harder questions or in thoroughly rechecking your work at the end. It is unwise to leave the examination early. However, do not change your original answer choice unless you have a specific reason for the change.

Approach for When Time is a Factor

If you learn from taking the practice test that you may not be able to finish all the questions in the allotted time, then skip those questions with a long fact pattern followed by only one question. If you follow this advice, make sure that you keep your place on your answer sheet by skipping the row for the question you skipped.

Return to those questions at the end and complete as many as time permits. Then, before turning your paper in, guess at the rest. In this way, you can reduce the number of random guesses to a minimum.

Make sure that you answer every question, even if you have not read the question since wrong answers do NOT count against you.

Minimize Fatigue to Maximize Your Score

The mental energy required to answer 200 multiple choice questions under stress on a high stakes exam in two three-hour periods, with only a short lunch break in between, produces fatigue.

Fatigue will slow down the speed at which you can effectively process questions and is likely to impair your reading comprehension.

First, you should take at least two released MBEs under timed conditions so that you know in advance how significantly fatigue affects your performance.

You should be sure to arrive at the exam site on time. If necessary, stay at a nearby hotel, rather than getting up two hours early and risking a long drive the morning of the exam.

You should relax during the lunch break and not discuss the morning session with anyone. You should know enough about your metabolism to eat the correct amount and type of food during the day of the exam and reinforce yourself with appropriate levels of caffeine during the day.

You should process questions more slowly at the end of each session and more quickly at the beginning, before fatigue sets in.

The Answer Sheet

As you decide each correct answer, circle the corresponding letter in your exam book and then mark the appropriate block on your answer sheet. At the pace of 9 questions per 15 minutes, you will have about 14 minutes at the end of the exam. Spend that time proofreading your answer sheet, which is the only paper that will be graded.

Check against the answers you circled in the book to be certain that you marked the appropriate block on your answer sheet. Make sure that there are no blanks on your answer sheet and no questions have two answers marked.

Proofread Your Answer Sheet

The one-page answer sheet is the only document examined and graded by the examiners. If you have erased, make sure that your erasure is thorough; otherwise, the computer may reject your answer because it cannot distinguish between the two marked answers.

Do NOT use this time to change the answer you have already selected unless you have a very good reason to change it. If you have time left after your proofreading is done, go back to the difficult questions and re-think the answers you have chosen.

However, even after careful thought, you should hesitate to change an answer. Do not leave any section of the exam early. Your objective is to use all the allotted time wisely.

Intelligent Preparation

By diligently preparing, in advance, practice questions and intelligently assessing why questions were answered incorrectly, your skills for the MBE will improve substantially during the course of your systematic study.

You can continue to improve those skills by following the advice given in this introduction until you reach a level of proficiency which will enable you to pass the MBE. This proficiency is easily and accurately measured when testing is in the multiple choice format.

Some students will have to work harder than others to achieve the required proficiency, but all the tools are in this study guide, and any law school graduate can be successful in passing the bar exam if they expend the required time and effort to be prepared for test day.

Hard Work Over a Sustained Period

There is no easy way to conquer an examination as difficult and comprehensive as the MBE except through practice and investment of time and effort well in advance of the actual exam.

Best wishes in your preparation!

Overview of American Law

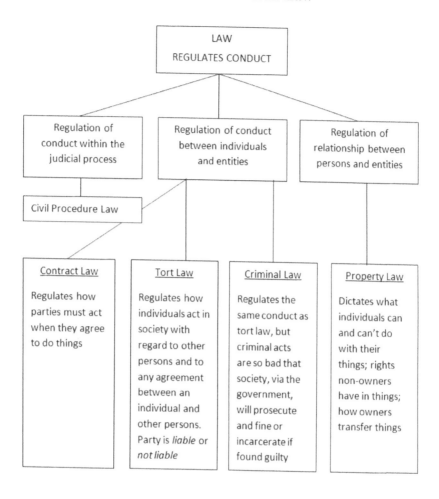

Constitutional Law

The statements governing constitutional law were compiled by analyzing the constitutional law questions released by the multistate examiners and setting forth the principles of law which governed the correct answer to each question.

An analysis of the questions revealed that there are a limited number of legal principles which are tested regularly and repeatedly and that this compilation most likely contains the principles which will govern the majority of the constitutional law questions on the examination which you must answer correctly to pass.

You should review these principles before preparing answers to the practice multistate constitutional law questions and understand how these principles are applied to obtain the correct answer. Just prior to taking the MBE, you should commit these principles to memory.

Constitutional Law – Overview

1. Creates a national government – allocates power among 3 branches

2. Controls relationship between federal and state governments (federalism)

3. Limits government power – protecting individual rights

4. Constitutionalism

Issues: Historically important decisions (*Marbury v. Madison*, *Dred Scott v. Sanford*, *Brown v. Board of Education*) and current cutting-edge issues.

The issue is usually about <u>who</u> gets to decide the merits (executive, legislative, judicial branches – federal or state)

Decisions by a single, multi-justice court: US Supreme Court

- Effects of judicial philosophies and changes in personnel

- Methods of Constitutional decision-making (the basis of the decision in the text/language of the Constitution, original intent, precedent, policy considerations, current societal needs, etc.).

Provisions of the Constitution establish and address these essential characteristics of our system of government:

> Separation of Powers
>
> Limited Powers (or Plenary/Exclusive Powers)
>
> Bicameralism
>
> Checks & Balances
>
> Federalism
>
> Protection of Civil Rights/Individual Freedoms
>
> Judicial Review of Legislative & Executive Branches

Nature of Judicial Review

Federal and State Court Systems
Jurisdiction of the Federal Courts

The most important constitutional bases of federal court jurisdiction are federal question jurisdiction and jurisdiction based upon diversity of citizenship.

States and agencies of a state are not citizens of a state to determine the existence of diversity jurisdiction.

A claim based upon the United States Constitution presents a federal question conferring jurisdiction on the federal courts.

A claim that an agency whose activities constitute state action is discriminating by race raises a federal question arising under the United States Constitution.

If no basis of federal jurisdiction is present, the federal court must dismiss the suit.

A statute which creates a right of action under federal law can require state courts to grant jurisdiction in state courts to litigants pursuing that action.

Eleventh Amendment

The Eleventh Amendment bars a suit in federal court against a state by a resident of that state or the resident of another state for damages against a state.

The Eleventh Amendment does not bar suits permitted by the state in state court.

A private citizen can challenge the constitutionality of a state statute in a federal court by suing a state officer to enjoin the enforcement of the statute on the ground that it is unconstitutional. Under *Ex Parte Young*, such a suit is not barred by the Eleventh Amendment.

Municipalities can be sued in federal court because they do not have Eleventh Amendment protection.

Congress can constitutionally authorize a suit by a citizen against a state without violating the Eleventh Amendment if it acts according to the Fourteenth Amendment.

Supreme Court Jurisdiction and Review

The United States Supreme Court may not review a decision by a state court which has been decided on an independent and adequate state ground, even if the state court has decided on an issue under federal law which is not essential to the outcome of the case.

However, if the state court decides on an issue controlled by state law and declares that it is deciding that issue by federal law, then the United States Supreme Court may review that decision because the state ground is not independent of federal law.

In addition to bringing suit to vindicate a proprietary state interest, a state may sue another state under the original jurisdiction of the United States Supreme Court on behalf of its citizens on claims affecting a multiplicity of citizens. This right is known as the *parens patriae* doctrine.

A litigant may not appeal directly from a federal district court's decision holding an act of Congress unconstitutional to the United States Supreme Court.

If a state court acting under applicable state law renders an advisory opinion interpreting federal law or the United States Constitution, there is no right to appeal the decision to the United States Supreme Court because there is no case or controversy, as required by the United States Constitution for federal court jurisdiction.

Congress cannot expand or contract the original jurisdiction of the United States Supreme Court.

Congressional Control Over Jurisdiction: Article III Courts

Under Article III of the Constitution, within constitutional limitations, Congress can control the jurisdiction of the lower federal courts and can establish or abolish them.

Once it has created a federal court, Congress cannot interfere with its inherent judicial functions by legislation.

While Congress can alter the appellate jurisdiction of the United States Supreme Court according to its authority under Article III, it cannot remove the appellate jurisdiction from the court in a manner which interferes with the Court's constitutional function of preserving constitutional order and the separation of powers.

For example, Congress cannot pass a unconstitutional statute and provide in it that the United States Supreme Court has no jurisdiction to review its constitutionality.

Under its Article I powers, Congress can establish courts such as the United States Tax Court. Judges serving in Article I courts are not guaranteed life tenure and other constitutional protections given to judges of Article III courts.

To be constitutional under the Due Process Clause, a matter decided by an Article I tribunal or an administrative body must have an ultimate appeal to an Article III court.

The Supreme Court and not Congress has the ultimate power to determine the substantive content of the Equal Protection Clause.

Case or Controversy

Federal court jurisdiction under Article III of the Constitution extends only to cases and controversies (i.e., lawsuits based upon existing, not hypothetical facts), where the court has the power to enter a binding judgment in a dispute between litigants.

Standing

Federal taxpayer standing is available only in a suit challenging legislation authorizing federal expenditures on the ground that those expenditures violate specific constitutional limitations on the spending power such as the Establishment Clause.

Standing cannot be maintained to litigate a case in which the plaintiff has a philosophical, ethical or intellectual interest in the outcome but not an interest which affects him personally.

Standing exists in a party whose interests are not directly affected by litigation but who has a close relationship to the party injured if the injured party is unlikely to assert his rights successfully.

A person whose interests are most affected by the outcome of the litigation is most likely to have standing.

Mootness

If the passage of time or changes in the facts or law resolve a controversy so that a party who originally had the standing to bring the lawsuit no longer has a stake in the outcome, the case will be dismissed as moot. If a case by its nature becomes moot before it can be fully litigated and the issue is one who would consistently evade review because of mootness, the case will not be dismissed.

Ripeness

Cases which raise material issues that have not yet occurred will be dismissed as unripe because there is no case or controversy existing at the time the suit is filed.

The federal courts lack the power to entertain a suit that is not ripe for adjudication because such a suit does not present a "case" or "controversy" within the meaning of Article III, Section 2, Clause 1 of the Constitution.

Abstention

If a decision by a state court on an issue of state law, which is pending in a federal court, might eliminate the need for the federal court to decide a federal constitutional issue, the federal court has the discretion to abstain from deciding the issue of constitutional law until the state court has decided the issue of state law.

If a state criminal prosecution has begun in a state court, a federal court will abstain from an action in the federal court asking for an injunction against the state proceeding and asking that the state statute be declared unconstitutional.

Justiciability: Political Questions

The political question doctrine requires the dismissal of suits when the court determines that the Constitution commits the final decision on the matter raised in the suit to another branch of the government. For example, the qualifications of individuals to be members of the House of Representatives are finally determined by the House of Representatives. The conduct of foreign relations is a matter finally vested in the Office of the Presidency.

Burden of Proof in Constitutional Litigation

The burden of proof is on the state to show a compelling state need or meet a similarly phrased burden and to show that no less burdensome method would achieve that objective when constitutional litigation concerns matters assigned to the *strict scrutiny* level of equal protection, the denial of highly protected personal substantive due process rights, or the deprivation of the right of free speech based upon the content and in some cases involving the free exercise of religion.

If it is not clear that discrimination requiring strict scrutiny or the *intermediate standard* of review exists, the plaintiff has the initial burden of showing discriminatory purposes before the state has the burden of showing a compelling state need or compliance with the intermediate standard.

The burden of proof is on the state to show that its classification is designed to achieve important governmental objectives and is closely tailored to achieve those objectives if the statute challenged discriminates by gender.

The burden of proof is on the plaintiff to show lack of a rational basis in constitutional litigation involving economic regulation and other matters than those described above.

The plaintiff never has the burden of proof in cases involving highly protected rights, and the state never has the burden to prove *rational basis*.

Separation of Powers

Congressional Commerce Power

Congress has almost unlimited power to regulate commerce in the United States, both interstate and local, under its power to regulate interstate commerce. It may regulate purely local commerce as long as it affects interstate commerce.

For example, Congress can restrict the power of private individuals to discriminate by race on the theory that such discrimination affects interstate commerce. Congress could not achieve this result under the Fourteenth Amendment because the activities of the private individual would not constitute state action.

The modern limitation on the Congressional commerce power is expressed in *United States v. Lopez*, which held that, where Congress regulates intrastate activities because of their relation to or effect on interstate commerce, the relationship must be substantial. The court did not find such a substantial relationship existed in the banning of guns around local schoolhouses.

Congressional Taxing and Spending Power

As long as a taxing statute does not violate a specific limitation on the power of Congress and it has the effect of raising revenue, there is no limitation on the taxing power of Congress.

Congress cannot require state governments to enact legislation. However, Congress may constitutionally condition the right to receive appropriations upon the performance by the states or individuals of actions which Congress could not require them to perform through regulatory action.

The only limitations on the congressional spending power are the specific constitutional limitations on the power of Congress, such as the prohibition on the establishment of religion.

The power to tax and spend for the general welfare is given to Congress. As an enumerated power of the Constitution (Article I, Section 8).

Even though Congress cannot regulate directly through the General Welfare Clause, it can influence behavior through a taxing statute which will be constitutional if it has the purpose of raising revenue.

Congressional Property Power

Article IV of the Constitution vests in Congress the power to control the property of the United States. It, rather than the Commerce Clause, is the most appropriate source of congressional power to deal with property owned by the federal government.

The executive branch does not have inherent rule-making authority over public lands. Article I, Section 8, Clause 17 gives Congress power to provide for the regulation of activity on such lands.

Congressional Power Over Territories

In the territories, Congress can regulate activities which are reserved to state legislatures in states.

Judges authorized to perform the function similar to state court judges in U.S. territories are authorized under Article I of the Constitution and are thus not entitled to the lifetime tenure enjoyed by Article III judges.

Congressional Investigative Powers

Congress has the power to investigate to obtain information for potential legislation. It can subpoena witnesses and documents to obtain that information.

Congress may question members of the executive branch about the performance of their duties to gather information which might be helpful in proposing legislation. Privilege, either executive privilege or the privilege against self-incrimination, would be the only practically available reasons for refusal to answer.

An individual can defend against contempt of Congress charge for failing to answer a question from a congressional committee by successfully showing that he claimed the privilege against self-incrimination or by showing that the question was beyond the scope of the power delegated by Congress to the committee seeking the information.

Speech and Debate Clause

A member of Congress has absolute immunity for any speech on the floor of either house of Congress which relates in any way to a legislative function. An aide to a member of Congress acting in support of such a member would have the same immunity as a member of Congress if the member were performing a legislative function.

Police Power

There is no specific grant of the police power to Congress. The police power is a source of state power.

Congressional Power to Enforce Thirteenth, Fourteenth and Fifteenth Amendments

Under the Thirteenth Amendment, Congress has the power to regulate individual conduct as well as state activity but only to eradicate slavery or the effects of slavery. Pursuant to that authority to eradicate the effects of slavery, it has the power to affect individual conduct which is detrimental to the African-American race.

Congressional power under the Fourteenth Amendment is limited to "state action" as defined hereafter which abrogates the rights guaranteed by that Amendment.

Congress has power under the Fifteenth Amendment to directly regulate voting procedures in the states to ensure that persons have the right to vote and that their votes are appropriately counted.

Courts can invalidate legislative apportionment statutes if their effect is to deprive minorities of having their votes effectively counted.

Powers of the President

The President has the discretion to refuse to spend funds which have been authorized by Congress unless the authorizing legislation directs him to spend the funds.

The power of the President to pardon for federal crimes, whether or not there has been a conviction, is plenary and cannot be limited by Congress.

The President and his aides have the absolute executive privilege to refuse to answer questions about matters of defense and foreign policy.

Disclosure of confidential communications between the President and advisors concerning all other areas in which the President operates are presumptively privileged. That presumption of privilege can be overcome only when a specific communication is subpoenaed, and a substantial governmental interest outweighs the President's interest in nondisclosure.

The President has the power to enter into executive agreements according to his or her power to conduct foreign policy. State actions or legislation which are inconsistent with the executive agreement are unconstitutional because of the Supremacy Clause.

The constitution reserves the conduct of foreign relations to the President of the United States and not the federal courts.

Ordinarily, the President does not have authority to direct the actions of persons outside the executive branch unless an act of Congress authorizes the President's direction.

The President, as the chief executive officer of the U.S. government, has authority to direct the actions of federal executive agencies, so long as the President's directives are not inconsistent with an act of Congress.

Unless legislation specifically limits the President's authority, the executive power conferred on the Office of the Presidency by the Constitution gives the holder of the office latitude to initiate action relative to domestic affairs.

Inter-branch Checks on Power

By enacting a law by the procedure for enactment set forth in the Constitution, passage by a majority vote of each house of Congress and either a signature by the President or passage over a presidential veto, legislation has the right to delegate, with appropriate standards, the rule-making power to administrative agencies.

However, once delegated, the only way that Congress can nullify a rule made by that administrative agency according to the grant of authority given to it, is to pass a new law which nullifies the rule. It cannot reserve to itself a legislative veto over an administrative rule by vesting in itself the power to negate that rule by the vote of the entire Congress or by a congressional committee.

Only the President has the right to appoint officers of the United States, and an attempted appointment by Congress or by members thereof can render an act establishing the office unconstitutional.

The final authority to decide an issue can be vested in a branch of the federal government other than the Supreme Court. For example, Congress has the authority to determine the qualifications of its members.

While the Supreme Court has the ultimate authority to determine which branch of government has the right to make a final decision on a matter, it will not decide an issue reserved to another branch of the government. It designates such an issue a political question.

The Advice and Consent Clause gives the Senate the right to confirm judicial appointments and other presidential appointments. Except for recess appointments, advice and consent are a condition precedent to such appointees holding federal office.

However, the President can remove federal executives without congressional authorization.

Pursuant to his or her obligation to execute the laws of the United States, the President must execute any provision of law if Congress makes that obligation mandatory instead of discretionary.

Congress can delegate to the President and the executive branch of government authority to determine how a law should be implemented. As long as there are general guidelines, such delegation is constitutional.

Congress may delegate rule-making authority to federal agencies through statutes that provide an intelligible principle governing the exercise of that authority.

The Relation of the Nation and States

Intergovernmental Immunities

States may not impose taxes on property owned by the United States.

States and their subdivisions can impose non-discriminatory taxes on owners of buildings which are leased to federal government and upon contractors doing business with the federal government. Congress, by specific legislation, can exempt such individuals from taxation.

The federal government has the right to tax and regulate the instrumentalities and employees of state government.

Under the Supremacy Clause of the Constitution, the lawful actions of a federal agency may not be regulated by a state or municipality in a manner which impedes its functions without the consent of Congress.

The federal government does not have the power to require officers of the state government to enforce federal laws. In *New York v. United States*, the court held that the federal government does not have the power to commandeer the mechanisms of state government to accomplish federal policies.

The federal government cannot tax essential state governmental functions and cannot single out the states for specialized taxes.

Authority Reserved to the States

Except in rare instances, the Tenth Amendment as the basis to justify state action is the wrong answer to constitutional law multiple-choice questions.

The Commerce Clause (Article I, Section 8, Clause 3 of the Constitution) gives Congress the power to regulate commerce among the states and, by negative implication, restricts the regulatory power of the states concerning interstate commerce.

Any state law that has a substantial effect on interstate commerce must not be protectionist or otherwise impose an undue burden on interstate commerce.

A protectionist law benefits in-state interests at the expense of out-of-state interests. A state law that discriminates against interstate commerce is protectionist unless it serves a legitimate local interest that cannot be served by nondiscriminatory legislation.

The fact that a state activity is authorized by a provision in a state constitution rather than an act of the state legislature is irrelevant in determining its constitutionality.

A state's regulation or taxation of interstate commerce is unconstitutional because of the negative implications of the Commerce Clause if that regulation discriminates in favor of local commerce or against interstate commerce. For example, a state statute requiring state natural resources be sold only to in-state buyers or permitting disposal of refuse in state landfills only for trash which is generated in-state is unconstitutional.

A state's regulation of interstate commerce is unconstitutional because of the negative implications of the Commerce Clause if that regulation, even if non-discriminatory, unduly burdens interstate commerce.

In determining the validity of such a regulation, the court will balance the police power right of the state to provide for the safety of its citizens against the extent of the harm caused by the regulations to interstate commerce. An important consideration in weighing that balance is whether the state used the least restrictive means to achieve a legitimate state objective.

The state as a purchaser or seller of goods and services as distinguished from the state as a regulator is not subject to the negative implications of the Commerce Clause and may discriminate in favor of in-state entities.

Congress is the holder and ultimate arbiter of the power of a state to discriminate in favor of local commerce. It can expressly authorize such discrimination, even if that discrimination has been held unconstitutional by the courts because of the negative implications of the Commerce Clause.

National Power to Override State Authority

The Supremacy Clause (Article VI, Section 1, Clause 2) invalidates any state action that is contrary to federal law.

The Supreme Court will hold state statutes, actions or decisions unconstitutional under the Supremacy Clause because they conflict with the Constitution, laws, or treaties of the United States or acts done in furtherance of them.

For example, the application of the Supremacy Clause will invalidate a state or municipal law in conflict with a federal regulation dealing with standards applicable to federal office buildings.

A state may not regulate interstate commerce if the regulation is contrary to specific federal policy or Congress has expressly or impliedly forbidden state regulation in a particular field.

The Supremacy Clause is a vehicle for invalidating state actions but is not a source of congressional power.

As a general principle when there is a federal action regulated by the state, the federal government wins.

State legislation or decisions which are contrary to a federal policy expressed in an executive agreement between the President and a foreign country are invalid.

Foreign policy is the exclusive province of the federal government. States may not act in that area.

Preemption

Congress has occupied the entire field if it has enacted a comprehensive scheme of regulation in an area. When it has occupied the field, any state regulation (even if complementary to the federal legislation) will be invalid, unless Congress intended to allow state regulation.

Congress can permit state activity in areas in which it has legislated as long as the state regulation is not contrary to federal policies. In many instances, such as civil rights, Congress has permitted states to enact stricter regulation than the Congressional legislation.

Privileges and Immunities

The Privileges and Immunities Clause of the Fourteenth Amendment has been narrowly construed to apply only to the privileges of national citizenship. It is almost universally the wrong answer to a multistate question.

The Privileges and Immunities Clause of Article IV of the Constitution operates like the negative implications of the Commerce Clause. It renders unconstitutional a state statute or action which discriminates on a matter of fundamental interest in favor of the state's citizens and against citizens of other states.

Unlike precedent under the negative implications of the Commerce Clause where a state governmental entity is permitted to discriminate in favor of local commerce if it is acting in its role as a market participant rather than a regulator, the Privileges and Immunities

Clause of Article IV applies to governmental entities even when they are acting as market participants.

The Privileges and Immunities Clause of Article IV applies not only to discrimination against out of state residents but also to discrimination by a subdivision of the state against non-residents of that subdivision.

When there is an abridgment of a fundamental right of a non-resident, the Privileges and Immunities Clause does not automatically hold the governmental action unconstitutional.

Also, if there is a tight fit between the discrimination against out of town residents and the evil which the limitation on non-residents is designed to remedy, the action is constitutional.

Higher fishing and hunting license fees for out-of-staters do not violate the Privileges and Immunities Clause of Article IV.

Full Faith and Credit

The Full Faith and Credit Clause of the Constitution (Article IV, Section 1) prohibits state courts from re-litigating cases in which the courts of another state have rendered final judgment and requires a state to enforce the final judgments of a sister state in its courts as long as the sister state had the jurisdiction to render that judgment.

Individual Rights

State Action

The Due Process Clause of the Fifth Amendment applies only to the Federal Government.

The Fourteenth Amendment guarantees of individual liberties are only applicable to state action and do not apply to actions of private individuals unless they are performing a governmental function or the activity is so entwined with the state that it is deemed state action.

The fact that a state taxes or regulates a private activity does not in itself cause the activity itself to become "state action."

The act of permitting private organizations to make use of public facilities on a non-discriminatory basis without any additional factors does not constitute state action causing that activity of the organization to be subject to Fourteenth Amendment scrutiny.

State aid to a segregated facility which benefits that facility to an extent greater than general governmental services constitutes forbidden state action.

The governmental activities of any political subdivision of a state or a state agency constitute state action.

If a state is an economic partner in a facility, the activities of that facility constitute state action. However, a one-time state subsidy to a private project does not provide a sufficient nexus to constitute state action.

The activity of an entity which performs a governmental function such as performing municipal services can constitute state action. However, activities in a privately owned shopping center do not constitute state action.

The Due Process Clause

The Fourteenth Amendment incorporates within it almost all of the specific provisions of the first eight amendments to the Constitution. The basis on which specific amendments are incorporated is "whether they are essential to an ordered system of liberties."

Substantive Due Process

The rational basis standard of review applies to economic regulations when such regulations are attacked as violating substantive due process.

While the substantive Due Process Clause will not invalidate economic regulation, it can be used as a vehicle to invalidate regulation of fundamental privacy interests unless the state can show a compelling state need. Examples of regulations held invalid are the banning of contraceptives, zoning regulations limiting the right of an extended family to live together, and abortion rights.

Abortion

The Substantive Due Process Clause protects fundamental personal rights. *Griswold v. Connecticut* (1965) held that the right to have access to and use contraceptives is a fundamental right. *Roe v. Wade* (1973) held that until the fetus becomes viable, a woman has a constitutionally protected right to an abortion. The state cannot prohibit the right of a woman to have an abortion prior to the time the fetus becomes viable.

A state can prohibit abortions at state facilities as long as there are reasonable alternatives for abortion at private facilities, and the state does not interfere with the alternative facilities.

In *Planned Parenthood v. Casey* (1992), the Supreme Court held that parental notification requirements violate a minor's right to an abortion unless there is a satisfactory judicial bypass procedure. Such a procedure must allow a court to approve an abortion for a minor without parental notification if the court finds: (1) the minor is sufficiently mature and informed to make an independent decision to obtain an abortion; or (2) the abortion would be in the minor's best interest.

Takings

Requiring the dedication of interest in the property as a condition of a building permit when there is no proportionality between the interest requested and the adverse impact of the permit constitutes a taking.

The government's acquisition of property is sufficient but is not necessary to establish a taking (i.e., eminent domain) within the meaning of the Fifth Amendment, as applied to the county by the Fourteenth Amendment.

A government regulation that eliminates the investment-backed expectation and economic value of an individual's property is a taking for which the government must pay just compensation.

A government ordinance requiring a private property owner dedicate a portion of his building for permanent physical occupation is a taking.

Imposition of the Death Penalty

A court can only order the death penalty when the defendant has committed an act of murder.

When there is a felony murder where several conspirators participated in the felony, the death penalty can only be administered to the individual who caused the death.

A statute which mandates the death penalty for a specific crime is unconstitutional because a jury must have the opportunity to impose the death penalty only after considering mitigating factors.

A death penalty can only be imposed by a jury. A judge can not impose it after the jury has convicted the defendant of the substantive crime.

Procedural Due Process –Applicability

Since the Due Process Clause is contained in the Fourteenth Amendment, the requirements of procedural due process do not apply to the actions of private individuals unless those individuals are engaged in "state action."

The procedural due process applies only when a state or an entity whose activities constitute state action deprives an individual of life, liberty or property without due process of law.

The Due Process Clause of the Fourteenth Amendment generally prohibits states from taking property from an individual without; (1) a hearing, and, (2) an opportunity to be heard. In the context of a government job, where state law provides that state employees can be fired only for good cause, a person has a legitimate claim of entitlement to, and thus a property interest in, her government job.

The right to a hearing when an individual is dismissed from government employment depends upon whether the individual has been deprived of a property right. In the field of education, tenure or a contract which is either continuing or which the individual has an express or implied right to renew is the type of property interest which cannot be taken away without notice and a hearing.

A public employee, even one who does not have a property right in his job, cannot be fired for exercising his right of free speech concerning matters of public concern. If his employment is terminated after he has exercised his right of free speech or association, the public employer has the burden of demonstrating that the exercise of his free speech rights or the joining of the organization were not in whole or in part the reason for his termination.

If the government action is dismissal from employment of an individual possessing property rights, the hearing must be held before the employee is dismissed.

Unlike the rule when there is suspension from protected government employment, procedural due process is satisfied in the license revocation situation when the licensee is afforded an appropriate hearing within a reasonable time after the suspension has occurred.

What Process Is Due Process

The minimum government action necessary to satisfy due process whenever the procedural due process is required is notice of the action taken and an opportunity of the person who is affected by the action to be heard by the governmental entity taking action.

Greater governmental procedural steps are necessary to satisfy due process if the interests infringed are substantial, or there is a substantial likelihood that the governmental actions will be erroneous.

A court will assess the burden on the government in providing an additional process in determining if that additional process is required.

The initial burden in a constitutional challenge to lack of procedural due process in discharge cases is upon the employee to show that he has a property right in his employment. Once the employee shows a constitutionally-protected property interest, the government agency would have to demonstrate that it did not violate procedural due process in the manner in which the employee was discharged.

If government employment was terminated after an employee exercised his free speech rights, the government is required to demonstrate that the employee was fired for reasons other than the exercise of rights of free speech even if the employee does not have a property right in his employment.

Criminal statutes which are so vague and imprecise that they do not give fair warning of the conduct which is criminal are unconstitutional under the Due Process Clause. However, judicial construction of a vague statute which defines the action which is criminal under that statute more precisely will render that statute constitutional concerning persons charged after the judicial decision, but not for any person charged before the decision was rendered.

Equal Protection – Overview

Sources of Civil Rights

- Due Process Clause of the 14th Amendment

- Equal Protection Clause of the 14th Amendment

- Congressional Legislation under the Interstate Commerce Clause

Amendment XIV [1868]

"No State shall… deny any person within its jurisdiction the equal protection of the law."

The Equal Protection Clause of the XIV Amendment prohibits the states from denying similarly situated persons the equal protection of the law. It applies only to public/state action and not to private conduct. While the Equal Protection Clause of the XIV Amendment applies only to state (as opposed to Federal) action.

The 5th Amendment to the Constitution, which applies to Federal action, has been interpreted to include the right to equal protection.

The following test will help you assess when the equal protection clause may be successfully invoked to challenge the constitutionality of a statute/rule/ regulation.

When looking at a statute, rule, or regulation ask the following questions to decide whether the Equal Protection clause is triggered.

Equal Protection Test:

I. Is there a governmental classification which treats similarly situated persons differently? (If yes, see below)

II. Is the classification Discriminatory OR Benign on its face?

  A. Is the classification discriminatory on its face? If yes:

    i. What is the nature of the classification? Is it a suspect classification? A protected class?

- Nature of Classification: Race, national origin, or ethnicity. Any classification based on race, national origin, or ethnicity are considered suspect.

This is a protected class.

- Apply **Strict Scrutiny**: Is the statute narrowly tailored to further a compelling government interest?

        - <u>Burden:</u> *Government holds the burden.*

    • <u>Nature of Classification</u>: Gender. Any classifications based on gender are considered quasi-suspect.

        This is also a protected class.

        - Apply **Intermediate Scrutiny**: Is the statute substantially related to an important government interest?

        - <u>Burden:</u> *Government holds the burden.*

    • <u>Nature of Classification</u>: based on sexual orientation, developmental delay, age, or wealth/poverty.

        Classifications based on the above are not considered suspect.

        These are not a protected class.

        - Apply **Rational Basis Test** (minimum scrutiny): Is the statute rationally related to the legitimate public interest?

        - <u>Burden</u>: *Person (s) challenging the law (plaintiff) holds the burden.*

III. Is there a governmental classification which implicates a fundamental right or interest guaranteed by the Equal Protection Clause?

   A. If yes, apply strict scrutiny (regardless of whether a protected or suspect classification is involved).

       • Fundamental rights have been held to include:

           1. Voting,

           2. Appeals to criminal and quasi-criminal proceedings, and

           3. Travel

The Equal Protection Clause fundamental interest line of cases mandates "equal access" to the particular right or interest.

The Equal Protection Clause

Applicability

Even though there is no constitutional provision guaranteeing citizens equal protection of the laws against action by the federal government, the substance of the Equal Protection Clause is applied to the federal government through the Due Process Clause of the Fifth Amendment.

Fundamental Rights

If the classification by the state involves a fundamental right, then the highest tier of equal protection, strict scrutiny, is applicable.

The Right to Travel

The right to travel is a fundamental right subject to strict scrutiny in Equal Protection Analysis. Discrimination by the state for those newly arrived in the state because they have exercised their fundamental right to travel must be justified by a compelling state need.

To satisfy the legitimate need that voters are *bona fide* residents, states may impose limited residency requirements on the right to vote. A two-month residency requirement has been upheld, while a one-year residency requirement has been held unconstitutional.

The Right to Vote and Have That Vote Counted

The right to vote is a fundamental right and subject to strict scrutiny in equal protection analysis. The state may deny that right only if it can show a compelling state need and that the method chosen is the least restrictive means of achieving that need.

The right to vote includes the right to have that vote counted on an equal basis with all other votes. To accomplish this goal, legislative districts for congressional, state legislative and municipal bodies must contain approximately equal numbers of voters. This requirement is popularly known as the one-man-one-vote rule.

The election of members of a district whose primary function is the management of land or water resources can constitutionally be limited to property owners, an exception to the one-man-one-vote requirement.

Ballot Access

While the right to be a candidate is a right placed in the highest tier of equal protection, to protect against frivolous candidacies, the state may impose reasonable requirements for an individual to appear on the ballot. These include the collection of filing fees, residency requirements, and the gathering of petition signatures to achieve ballot access which may be less stringent for nominees of parties who have demonstrated substantial support in previous elections.

Suspect Classifications

Classifications by the state which are designated as suspect bring about the highest level of equal protection review. The state must show that the classification is necessary to satisfy a compelling state need.

The initial burden in a constitutional challenge for a violation of rights because of the Equal Protection Clause is upon the plaintiff to show that there was a purposeful classification which is subject to increased scrutiny.

Once the plaintiff shows that purposeful discrimination, the burden shifts to the government to satisfy the standards required by the higher tier of equal protection.

Classification by Race

No governmental entity can classify by race or nationality except to satisfy a compelling state need.

The Equal Protection Clause applies to a regular pattern of discrimination in the enforcement of a statute as well as discrimination on the face of the statute.

A regulation or decision which classifies on the basis of race to remedy specific past racial discrimination satisfies a compelling state need and is therefore constitutional.

However, a system of racial quotas by itself does not satisfy the compelling state need standard.

A governmental classification based upon a racially neutral principle such as residence, which indirectly discriminates by race, is only unconstitutional if the classification is made with the purpose of discriminating by race.

In drawing legislative districts, a state may not deliberately use race as a criterion to dilute the voting power of racial minorities. Drawing of compact districts which follow existing municipal boundaries rebuts the inference that race was used improperly.

Classification by Alienage

Alienage is not a suspect classification for the federal government. The federal government may constitutionally discriminate on the basis of alienage in the furtherance of foreign policy.

A state can discriminate against non-citizens in elective governmental positions and non-elective governmental jobs which formulate or execute public policy. Otherwise, states cannot discriminate against non-citizens.

Classification by Gender

Gender-based classification is valid only if it serves an important governmental purpose and is substantially related to achieving that purpose.

Classification by Legitimacy

The state cannot deny worker's compensation benefits, wrongful death benefits, or intestacy benefits based upon illegitimacy where the parent-child relationship has been adjudicated or acknowledged, but can classify by legitimacy where proof of the relationship is difficult.

The Rational Basis Standard

In all cases except where fundamental rights or suspect classifications are involved, such as economic regulation, the court will apply the rational basis standard. In those cases, the plaintiff must show that there is no rational basis for the classification set forth in the legislation.

Since the right to be free from poverty is not a fundamental right, classifications by states which discriminate against poor people are ordinarily judged by the rational basis standard.

Since the right to work is not a fundamental right, classifications by the state which deprive individuals of employment, such as age classifications, are judged by the rational basis standard.

Level of Scrutiny – Litigation

If constitutional litigation involves the strict scrutiny tier of equal protection, the denial of substantive due process rights which are highly protected, or the deprivation of the right of free speech or freedom of religion, the state must show a compelling state need (strict scrutiny) and that no less burdensome method would achieve that objective.

If constitutional litigation involves sexual discrimination, the state must show that the classification has an important governmental objective and is substantially related (intermediate level scrutiny) to achieving those objectives.

If constitutional litigation involves matters other than those described above, the plaintiff must prove that the legislation lacked a rational basis.

The state (defendant) never has the burden of proof when only the lack of a rational basis must be shown.

The plaintiff never has the burden of proof when highly-protected rights (or suspect class) are involved.

Obligations of Contract

The Obligations of Contracts Clause is a limitation on states but not the federal government. State laws or activities which render unenforceable a valid executory contract are invalid unless there is a valid police power reason for the legislation or unless it only alters the remedies for breach of contract and other feasible remedies are available.

The provision applies to both contracts between private individuals and contracts in which the state is a party.

The Contracts Clause (Article I, Section 10, Clause 1 of the Constitution) does not forbid state laws affecting prospective contractual relations between private parties so long as they are reasonably related to a legitimate state interest.

Courts typically defer to state regulations of prospective private contracts as reasonable.

Bills of Attainder

A bill of attainder, a legislative punishment for specific actions, is unconstitutional. This clause applies to both the state and the federal government. Legislation which withholds appropriations for a specific job as long as a named individual holds that job is a bill of attainder.

Ex Post Facto Law

An *ex-post facto* law is a legislative enactment which punishes acts as criminal which occurred before the act became operative. Such a law is unconstitutional and cannot supply the basis for a conviction based upon that conduct.

First Amendment

First Amendment – Freedom of Religion

When an individual defends against a criminal charge on the basis that the statute unconstitutionally restricts his freedom of religion, such as a claim to resist the draft because he is a conscientious objector, the courts have a right to examine the sincerity of his religious belief, but not the belief itself.

Because of the Free Exercise Clause, courts do not have the right to determine the truth or falsity of religious beliefs in litigation, including litigations dealing with the title to church property, even if that determination is necessary to decide the case.

The government may impose non-discriminatory time, place and manner restrictions on religious activity when they are designed to serve important public interests.

A compelling state interest need not justify a statute or rule by the state which has an incidental effect of burdening a particular religious practice but is religiously neutral and of general applicability.

First Amendment – Establishment of Religion

Displays on state property which are solely religious violate the Establishment Clause of the First Amendment.

Officially sponsored prayers as part of public high school commencement ceremonies violate the Establishment Clause.

State activity in aid to religions is constitutional if it satisfies each part of the following three-part test.

> 1) Such aid must reflect a secular purpose,
>
> 2) have a primary effect which neither advances nor inhibits religion, and
>
> 3) there must be no excessive entanglement between church and state.

Even though state activity aid does not discriminate between religions, it will violate the Establishment Clause if it violates any part of the three-part test.

State statutes requiring that the Biblical account of Creation be taught in public schools violate the Establishment Clause.

State statutes or activities which discriminate between established religions and non-established religions violate the Establishment Clause.

First Amendment Rights of the Press to Trials

Absent a compelling state need, the press as a representative of the public has the right to attend trials even if the prosecution and defense want the trial to be closed.

First Amendment – Regulation of Content of Speech

The First and Fourteenth Amendments limit the right of both the states and the federal government to regulate the content of protected speech unless the government can show a compelling state need.

All speech is protected speech for purposes of content regulation except fighting words, defamatory speech, and obscene speech.

Protected speech can also include action which is a substitute for words. However, even if action is intended as symbolic speech, it can be regulated to protect a legitimate government interest divorced from the content of the symbolic speech itself. For example, the federal government can ban the burning of draft cards on public safety grounds.

The state can proscribe the content of protected speech which is directed toward inciting immediate lawless action and is likely to incite that action.

A threat communicated with the intent to intimidate the recipient is not constitutionally protected speech.

Commercial speech does not enjoy the same degree of constitutional protection as non-commercial speech. It is subject to reasonable governmental regulation to prevent it from being misleading to protect consumers and other legitimate government interests.

Outright prohibition of commercial speech is unconstitutional. The regulation of commercial speech must be narrowly tailored to achieve a substantial governmental interest.

There must be a reasonable fit between the interests which the governmental entity desires to protect in the regulation of commercial speech and the means chosen to advance it.

The state is unconstitutionally regulating the content of speech if it requires an individual to display a message prescribed by the state.

The state has an affirmative obligation to protect a speaker before an audience, but the speaker can be required to stop speaking if there is a genuine likelihood of immediate violence which the state cannot prevent.

Meeting rooms at public institutions which are made generally available for student use are a limited public forum.

Students have a First Amendment right to use such a limited public forum for expressive activity consistent with the purpose for which they are made available.

A denial of the use of a limited public forum based on the content of the expression proposed for that forum must be tested by strict scrutiny, which requires the institution to prove that its denial was necessary to serve a compelling governmental interest.

Obscene Speech

Speech is obscene and subject to complete prohibition if it appeals to the prurient interest of an average person applying contemporary community standards, depicts or describes sexual activity in a patently offensive way, and taken as a whole, lacks serious literary, artistic, political or scientific value.

Child pornography is totally unprotected speech even if it does not meet the definition of obscenity.

Even if the communication is not pornographic, communications portraying nudity or sexual activity can be regulated on the basis of its content concerning the time, place and manner of their exhibition.

For example, a zoning ordinance can limit the areas in which sex-oriented businesses are allowed to operate provided that there are alternative sites available.

First Amendment – Regulation of Time, Place and Manner of Speech

As long as the regulation is not based upon the content of the speech, the state can regulate the time, place and manner in which free speech rights are exercised in public forums such as streets and parks. The regulations limiting speech must be narrowly drawn and limit the discretion of public officials administering the regulation.

Speech rights cannot be totally banned in the public forum.

Free speech rights in semi-public forums such as schools, courthouses, and libraries can be limited to prevent the interference with governmental functions conducted at those forums.

In government-owned property closed to the general public, such as jails, military bases, and private offices, the state has the right to prohibit the exercise of free speech rights completely.

Unless the operation of private property is the equivalent to state action, such as the operation of a company town, but not a shopping center, the owner of private property can regulate the exercise of free speech on that property even according to content and can prohibit the exercise of free speech on that property.

First Amendment – Procedural Problems

If a court has issued an injunction banning the exercise of free speech rights, the constitutional issues raised by the issuance of the injunction cannot be litigated in a contempt prosecution for violation of the injunction.

A statute which is overly broad (i.e., prohibits protected speech as well as properly regulated speech) or vague (i.e., a person of ordinary intelligence cannot distinguish permitted from prohibited activities) is unconstitutional on its face and can be successfully challenged even by those who could be regulated if the statute was clear and narrowly drawn.

An individual is entitled to 1) notice, and 2) a right to be heard at a hearing before an injunction is granted limiting the time, place and manner of his expression unless there is a genuine emergency justifying an ex-parte application.

First Amendment – Freedom of Association;
License or Benefits Based upon First Amendment Rights

A public employee cannot be fired for exercising his right of free speech for matters of public concern or for merely joining an organization deemed to be subversive.

If his employment is terminated after he has exercised his right of free speech or association, the public employer has the burden of demonstrating that the exercise of his free speech rights or the joining of the organization were not in whole or in part the reason for his termination.

A public employee can be fired if his speech indicates that he is not performing his job.

The state can condition employment on an employee taking a loyalty oath which requires him to agree to adhere to constitutional processes.

Constitutional Law – Quick Facts

1. Action having the purpose and effect of altering the legal duties, rights, and relations of persons, **including executive branch officials**, MUST be subjected to a **presidential veto.**

2. The Constitution prohibits the impairment of **contractual obligations** by a state EXCEPT in certain <u>narrow circumstances;</u> a self-interest driven choice to reduce the State's contractual burdens generally does NOT constitute such an exception.

3. The 11th Amendment does NOT bar suits against state officials UNLESS **retroactive relief** is sought.

4. Congress's **general welfare power** relates to **Congress's spending power** (i.e., right to expend federal tax revenues).

5. Congress's power to regulate **interstate commerce** is plenary, so Congress has the right to completely ban the transportation of "harmful" substances in the channels of commerce.

6. Statutes violate the **Privileges and Immunities of Citizens** (PIC) of Art. IV—which prohibits discrimination against nonresidents concerning essential activities—UNLESS (1) the discrimination is closely related to a substantial state purpose, AND (2) less restrictive means are NOT available.

7. Congress's power to **regulate commerce** has been construed broadly, so that it MAY regulate *any activity, local or interstate*, that either in itself or in combination with other activities has a substantial economic effect on interstate commerce.

8. The **police power** – the power to adopt regulations for the health, safety, morals and general welfare of citizens – belongs to the states and a police power regulation that conflicts with federal law is **invalid** under the **Supremacy Clause.**

9. For all practical purposes, the power to **regulate foreign commerce** lies exclusively with Congress; therefore, a state that adopts legislation requiring private vendors to favor U.S. products over foreign products may be acting outside the scope of its powers.

10. The **Property Clause** (Art. IV § 3) gives Congress the power to make all needful rules and regulations respecting the territory or

other property belonging to the U.S., which permits Congress to acquire and dispose of ALL kinds of property and to protect its property with relevant laws.

11. The states have NO power to regulate the activities of the federal government UNLESS Congress consents to the regulation; thus, instrumentalities and agents of the federal government are **immune from state regulations** that interfere with their federal functions.

12. The **media** may NOT be punished for publishing a fact once it is lawfully obtained from the public records or is otherwise released to the public.

13. Supreme Court has held, at least in the context of criminal cases, that **trials and pre-trial proceedings** can be closed ONLY if the closure is necessary to preserve an overriding interest and the closure order is narrowly tailored to serve the overriding interest.

14. Congress may NOT appoint members of a body with **administrative or enforcement powers**.

15. Congress MAY by law vest appointment power of **inferior officers** in the federal courts.

16. Congress has the power to levy taxes under Art. II § 2 and a tax measure will usually be upheld IF it bears some **reasonable relationship** to revenue production OR if Congress has the power to regulate the taxed activity.

17. **Supremacy Clause** – whenever a valid federal law conflicts with state law, the state law is inapplicable and the federal law controls.

18. Supreme Court uses a **balancing test** in determining whether a regulation of the electoral process is valid. If the **restriction** on 1st Amendment activities is severe, the regulation will be upheld ONLY if it is **narrowly tailored** to achieve a **compelling state interest.** For example, requiring a political candidate to obtain a percentage of voter signatures to run probably qualifies as a severe 1st Amendment restriction.

19. The **13th Amendment's** prohibition against **servitude** and **involuntary servitude** is NOT limited to proscribing state action and therefore allows Congress to adopt legislation regulating private parties.

Contracts

The statements of governing Contracts were compiled by analyzing the contract law questions released by the multistate examiners and setting forth the principles of law which governed the correct answer to each question.

An analysis of the questions revealed that there are a limited number of legal principles which are tested regularly and repeatedly. This compilation most likely contains the principles which will govern the majority of the contract law questions on the examination which you must answer correctly to pass.

You should review these principles before preparing answers to the practice multistate contracts questions and understand how these principles are applied to obtain the correct answer. Just prior to taking the MBE, you should commit these principles to memory.

Contract Law - Overview

Definition of and Parties to a Contract

Definition: A contract is an agreement that is enforceable by a court of law or equity.

> *Restatement (Second) of Contracts*: A contract is a promise or a set of promises for the breach of which the law gives a remedy or the performance of which the law in some way recognizes a duty.

Parties to a contract:

- The Offeror – the party who makes an offer.

- The Offeree – the party to whom the offer is made.

Requirements of a Contract

To be an enforceable contract, the following four basic requirements must be met:

- Agreement – There must be an agreement between the parties.

- Consideration – The promise must be supported by a bargained-for consideration.

- Contractual Capacity – The parties must have the capacity to contract.

- Lawful Object – The object of the contract must be lawful.

Agreement

- The agreement is the manifestation by two or more persons of the substance of a contract.

- *Requirements of the Offer*

- The offeror must objectively intend to be bound by the offer.

- The terms of the offer must be definite or reasonably certain.

- The offer must be communicated to the offeree.

Termination of the Offer

- Acceptance of the offer creates a contract.

- A counteroffer simultaneously terminates the offer and creates a new offer.

Acceptance is the *manifestation of assent* by the offeree to the terms of the offer.

Express and Implied Contracts

An actual contract may be either express or implied.

- Express contracts are stated in oral or written words.

- Implied-in-fact contracts are implied from the conduct of the parties.

A Contract is a Contract is a Contract

Consideration

- Consideration is the thing of value given in exchange for a promise.

- Gift or gratuitous promises are unenforceable because they lack consideration.

Capacity to Contract

The law presumes that the parties to a contract have the requisite contractual capacity.

Minors do not always have the maturity, experience, or sophistication needed to enter into contracts with adults.

The infancy doctrine allows minors to disaffirm or cancel most contracts entered into with adults.

- The minor has the option of choosing whether to enforce the contract.

- The contract is voidable by a minor.

Minors are obligated to pay for the necessities of life for which they contract.

Mentally Incompetent Persons.

The law protects people suffering from substantial mental incapacity from enforcement of contracts against them.

Intoxicated Persons.

Most states provide that contracts entered into by certain intoxicated persons are *voidable* by that person.

Lawful Object

The object of the contract must be lawful.

A contract to perform an illegal act is an illegal contract.

Illegal contracts are *void*.

Illegality

Certain contracts are illegal because they are contrary to public policy by promoting a breach of the law or the policy behind a law (e.g., murder, prostitution).

The Statute of Frauds – Writing Requirement

All states have enacted a Statute of Frauds.

Generally, for contracts covered by the Statute of Frauds, an executory contract not in writing is not enforceable.

Contracts that must be in writing to be enforceable under the Statute of Frauds (see discussion on page 85).

Contracts requiring a writing:

1) **Land contracts** - all transfers of ownership interests in real property must be in writing.

2) **One-Year Rule** – contracts lasting more than one year: cannot be completed within a year (assuming unlimted resources of money and manpower).

3) Contracts for the **Sales of Goods in excess of $500**.

4) Contracts to be responsible as a **surety** for another's debts.

5) Contracts in **consideration of marriage**.

6) Contracts by the **executor** of a will to pay a debt of the estate from his monies.

Formality of the writing.

Required signature.

Fraud

Material Misrepresentation of Fact

Intent to deceive

Reliance on the misrepresentation

Injury to the innocent party

Formation of Contracts

Offer

To form a contract, there must be an offer which is accepted.

A person makes an "offer" to enter into a bilateral contract by communicating to another person a proposed exchange of promises between the parties, such that the recipient of the communication reasonably believes that he can enter into a binding contract by accepting that proposed exchange of promises.

The more precise the communication, the more likely that it will be characterized as an offer.

Communication is an offer for a unilateral contract if it sets forth valid consideration in exchange for a proposed action by the addressee of the communication, in such a manner that the person to whom it is directed reasonably believes that he can enter into a binding contract by performing the requested action.

UCC Rules: A sale of goods contract may be made in any manner sufficient to show agreement even though the moment of its making is undetermined.

Acceptance

While there are rules which govern how an offer is accepted in the absence of specific conditions of acceptance set forth in the offer, the offeror has a right to specify the manner of acceptance and make the usual rules inoperative.

If the offeror does not specify any conditions for acceptance, an offer may be accepted at a reasonable time and in a reasonable manner.

If the offer is one for a unilateral contract, it may be accepted only by the performance of the act requested, not by a return promise.

Unless the parties have had a course of dealing where the offeree has accepted offers from the offeror by doing nothing, an offeror will be unsuccessful in arguing that silence by the offeree constitutes acceptance.

Unless the terms of an offer or course of dealing permit the offeree to accept by doing nothing, an offeree will be unsuccessful in arguing that he accepted an offer by silence.

For contracts controlled by common law and not the UCC, (i.e., common law contracts) the offeree can only accept an offer by communicating his acceptance of all of the terms of the offer prior to the time the offer expires, is terminated, or revoked.

Unless the offeror requires a different method of acceptance in his offer, an offer is accepted at the time the letter of acceptance is mailed.

Words of the offeree which the offeror can reasonably believe constitute an acceptance will cause a contract to be formed, even if those words do not include the term "accept."

UCC Rules: Under § 2-206, an offer to buy goods for prompt shipment is accepted when the seller ships the goods and a binding contract is formed at that time.

Unless otherwise unambiguously indicated by the language or circumstances,

(a) an offer to make a contract shall be construed as inviting acceptance in any manner and by any medium reasonable in the circumstances, and,

(b) an order or another offer to buy goods for prompt or current shipment shall be construed as inviting acceptance, either by a prompt promise to ship or by the prompt or current shipment of conforming or non-conforming goods. Such a shipment of non-conforming goods does not constitute an acceptance if the seller reasonably notifies the buyer that the shipment is offered only as an accommodation to the buyer.

Where the beginning of a requested performance is a reasonable mode of acceptance, an offeror who is not notified of acceptance within a reasonable time may treat the offer as having lapsed before acceptance.

UCC Rules: Under § 2-207(1) a definite and reasonable expression of acceptance or a written confirmation which is sent within a reasonable time operates as an acceptance even though it states terms additional to or different from those offered or agreed upon, unless acceptance is expressly made conditional on assent to the additional or different terms.

Under § 2-207 (2), the additional terms are to be construed as proposals for an addition to the contract.

Between merchants, such terms become part of the contract unless

    (a) the offer expressly limits acceptance to the terms of the offer,

    (b) the additional terms materially alter the offer, or

    (c) notification of objection to the terms is given within a reasonable time after notice of them is received.

If the proposed additional term materially changes the original offer, there is still a contract, but the additional term is not part of it.

Under § 2-207 (3), conduct by both parties which recognizes the existence of a contract is sufficient to establish a contract for sale, although the writings of the parties do not otherwise establish a contract. In such cases, the terms of the particular contract consist of those terms on which the writings of the parties agree, together with any supplementary terms incorporated under any other provisions of this act.

If a seller under the UCC ships non-conforming goods in response to an offer and indicates that he has not accepted the original offer, then the shipment of the non-conforming goods is a counter-offer, and the seller is not in breach of contract for shipping non-conforming goods.

If the buyer then accepts the non-conforming goods and the counter-offer, then he must pay the full contract price.

Revocation of Offers

At common law, an offer is revocable by the offeror at any time, even if the offeror promises to keep the offer open for a period of time.

At common law, an offer is irrevocable if the agreement to keep it open for a specified period is supported by consideration. Such an offer is an option contract.

The offeror may not revoke an offer for a unilateral contract if the offeror knows that the offeree has commenced substantial performance.

To be effective, the revocation must be communicated to the offeree before the offeree accepts the offer.

A revocation need not be in the express language. Any communication, such as "I have sold it to someone else," which fairly indicates to the offeree that the offer has been withdrawn, is a revocation.

A revocation need not be direct communication between the offeror and the offeree. If the offeree learns from a third party that the offer has been revoked before the offeree has accepted the offer, the revocation is effective.

An offer for a unilateral contract which occurs when the owner of real estate hires a broker and agrees to pay a commission when, and if the broker finds a buyer ready, willing, and able to purchase the owner's property, is automatically revoked without notice if the owner accepts another offer to purchase the property.

A written offer which is required by the Statute of Frauds can be revoked orally.

The death of the offeror terminates an offer.

If a contract has been formed, the death of either party does not terminate the contract, unless the death of a party makes the contract impossible to perform.

UCC Rules: A "merchant" means a person who deals in goods of the kind, or otherwise by his occupation holds himself out as having knowledge or skill peculiar to the practices or goods involved in the transaction, or to whom such knowledge or skill may be attributed by his employment of an agent, broker, or another intermediary who by his occupation holds himself out as having knowledge or skill.

"Between merchants" means in any transaction for which both parties are chargeable with the knowledge or skill of merchants.

An offer by a merchant to buy or sell goods in a signed writing, which by its terms gives assurances that it will be held open, is not revocable, for lack of consideration, during the time stated, or, if no time is stated, for a reasonable time.

In no event may such period of irrevocability exceed three months.

The offeror must separately sign any such term of assurance on a form supplied by the offeree.

An offer by a non-merchant for the sale of goods under the UCC is revocable in the same manner as an offer at common law.

An oral offer by a merchant for sale of goods is revocable in the same manner as an offer at common law.

A written offer by a merchant, which states that the offer will remain open for a period greater than three months, will remain irrevocable for three months.

Rejection

If at common law, the offeree purports to accept an offer but changes the terms of the offer in any way, the communication is a counter-offer, and no contract is formed. For the sale of goods, this rule is qualified by § 2-207 discussed above.

An offer is terminated by rejection or by a counter-offer. After that, the offeree cannot accept the original offer even if the time when it is to remain open has not expired.

If the offeror has made a multipart offer which can be accepted in part, such as "I will sell you any one of these five lots for $5,000 apiece," acceptance of part of the offer can be considered as a rejection of the remainder of the offer.

An inquiry concerning the offer by the offeree about the precise terms of the offer or the willingness of the offeror to modify the terms of the offer is not a rejection.

Mistake, Fraud, and Duress

The defense of unilateral mistake is available when the mistake by one party was so obvious that the other party should have known of the mistake at the time the offer was accepted.

Unilateral mistake is grounds for avoiding a contract if the first party is mistaken about a material fact, and the second party, while not mistaken about that fact, is aware that the first party is mistaken about that material fact.

Mutual mistake is grounds for avoiding a contract, if, at the time of contracting, both parties relied on an untrue material fact.

There is no meeting of the minds, an essential requirement for the existence of a contract if each party to the contract without fault has a different understanding of the meaning of the words which they agreed to. If the contract involves the ship "Peerless," but each party innocently and honestly is thinking of a different ship named "Peerless," there is no meeting of the minds and no contract.

If the parties orally agree on terms of a contract which is then to be reduced to writing and the scrivener makes an error in setting out the terms of the contract, either party can reform the written contract to conform to the actual oral understanding of the parties.

Indefiniteness and Absence of Terms

UCC Rule: A contract is not void for indefiniteness if there is no price agreed to. There is a valid contract for a reasonable price.

Capacity to Contract

A person who has entered into a contract while a minor can disaffirm that contract, even one that has been completed, except a contract for necessities, within a reasonable time of reaching the age of majority.

If a minor, after he reaches majority, agrees to make a payment on a contract which he had a right to disaffirm, for an amount which is less than the full contract price, the agreement is only enforceable without any new consideration to the extent of the promise made after reaching majority, not for the full contract price.

Implied-in-Fact Contracts

An implied-in-fact contract arises out of the conscious action of a party.

Even though no words are spoken or written, a contractual obligation can be implied from the action of a party. For example, accepting services from someone in the business of providing those services, will create an obligation to pay the fair value of those services.

If a landowner watches another party perform work on his land which he knows is not intended to be gratuitous and says nothing, then the landowner has entered into an implied-in-fact contract to pay for the fair value of the work.

Implied-in-Law Contracts

An implied-in-law contract arises even though a party has not acted in word or deed to incur contractual liability.

The law will imply a contractual liability to pay for necessary services rendered to an individual when he lacks the mental capacity to request such services or to agree to be contractually bound to pay for them.

Quasi-Contracts

If parties entered or attempted to enter into a contractual relationship, but the contract is not enforceable because of the Statute of Frauds or other reason, and one party has conferred a benefit on the other party, the party conferring the benefit can sue the other party in quasi-contract for the fair value of the benefit conferred on the other party. Contract measures of damages do not apply.

A person who has a right to pursue a remedy under an enforceable contract does not have the right to sue in *quantum meruit* (i.e., reasonable sum of money) for a benefit conferred.

Pre-Contractual Liability Based upon Detrimental Reliance

If the owner of property puts a construction contract out to bid to general contractors, and a subcontractor submits an offer to perform a subcontract to the general contractor, with the knowledge that the general contractor is relying on the bid when making his bid for the general contract, the subcontract bid is treated as an option contract.

The detrimental reliance by the general contractor is a sufficient substitute for bargained-for consideration so that the subcontractor cannot revoke his bid. The general contractor has a reasonable time after he becomes the successful bidder to then accept the bid.

However, since the subcontractor's bid is an offer, there is no contract between the general contractor and the subcontractor unless and until the general contractor accepts the bid.

Unconscionability

Unconscionability arises when there are unfair terms, coupled with an unfair bargaining process.

A contract is unconscionable, and a court can refuse to enforce such a contract if at the time of the execution of the contract one of its provisions was oppressive.

The concept of unconscionable is part of the UCC and has been applied with increasing frequency to common law contracts.

Consideration

Bargain and Exchange

The concept of the bargain is the essence of consideration.

A promise by one party to perform an act or refrain from acting, in exchange for a counter-promise by the other party to perform an act or refrain from acting, constitutes valid consideration, making the promises enforceable.

For there to be valid consideration, the party making the bargain need not be the person benefiting from it.

An agreement is supported by consideration if the person benefited is a third party for whom the benefit was requested.

As long as a party promises to do something that he is not legally obligated to do, he has given consideration even though the performance of that obligation is not burdensome.

A promise which does not limit the rights of a party in any way is an illusory promise which does not constitute valid consideration, because the promisor possesses a unilateral right to avoid any obligation made in the promise. For example, "I promise to pay you one dollar for that apple if I choose to" is an illusory promise.

If a promise is illusory because its enforceability is subject to a condition precedent which is completely within the control of one party, there is a valid contract once the condition has been satisfied.

The promise to undertake a minor burden imposed on the recipient of property in what is essentially a donative transaction does not transform that burden into consideration. For example, a statement by a mother to her son, "I will buy you a jacket for your birthday if you stop by the store to pick it up," creates a donative transaction because the uncle is not bargaining with his niece about picking up the jacket.

Adequacy of Consideration

In determining whether a contract is supported by consideration, courts do not measure the value of what a party promises in comparison to what he receives.

An agreement to settle a meritless claim is not valid consideration.

As long as an agreement is supported by consideration so that a valid contract exists, a party who performs his side of the bargain is entitled to enforce the contract according to its terms, even if he is getting far more than he has given.

Detrimental Reliance

Even if an agreement is not supported by bargained-for consideration, such as a promise to make a gift, it may be enforceable if there is a substitute for bargained-for consideration, namely, promissory estoppel.

If an agreement is supported by bargained-for consideration, the issue of whether the elements of promissory estoppel are present is irrelevant and the wrong answer to a multiple choice question.

An agreement which is not supported by bargained-for consideration, such as a promise to make a gift, is enforceable if promissory estoppel, the substitute for bargained-for consideration, is present.

Promissory estoppel is present if:

(1) the one party knows that his promise will induce substantial reliance on the part of the promisee, and

(2) failure to enforce the promise will cause substantial hardship, and,

(3) injustice can be avoided only by such enforcement.

Moral Obligations

A service which has already been gratuitously rendered is not valid consideration for a later promise to pay for that service, because the bargain element, which is the essence of consideration, is not present.

Even though there is no new bargain, a unilateral promise in writing to pay a debt which is barred by the statute of limitations is enforceable without new consideration.

If the new promise differs from the original promise, the contract is only enforceable to the extent of the new promise.

A contract which was originally voidable because of the minority of one of the parties is enforceable against that party without any new consideration if he makes a new promise after reaching majority.

If the new promise differs from the original promise, the contract is only enforceable to the extent of the new promise.

Modification of Contracts: Pre-existing Duty Rule

An agreement to totally rescind an existing executory contract is supported by consideration since each side is bargaining to give up the rights they previously had under the contract.

The traditional common law rule is that fresh consideration (a different obligation that already agreed to) is required to support a modification of a contract and that the agreement to modify is unenforceable if the promises of one party are unmodified and the promises of the other party are more burdensome.

At common law, a contract can be modified if each side gives to the other new consideration for the modification.

Consideration is not an issue if one party to an existing contract modifies its promises in exchange for a promise of the other party to modify its promises.

Modern common law contracts cases hold that an agreement to modify an existing contract without fresh consideration is enforceable when the modification is made in good faith. An example of good faith occurs when the circumstances under which the contract is to be performed had changed through no fault of the parties from the time when the contract was executed.

The traditional common law rule was that, if a party to a contract agreed with the other party to perform an act which he was already obligated to perform because of contractual relations with a third person, then the agreement was unenforceable because it was not supported by consideration.

However, under modern contract principles tested on the MBE, the contractual obligation to a third party to perform the act does not prevent the promise to perform the act from being adequate consideration.

UCC Rule: An agreement modifying a contract needs no new consideration to be binding.

Compromise and Settlement of Claims

Forbearance, a promise not to assert a right, is not valid consideration if the agreement is to forbear in asserting a frivolous claim which the party knows is invalid.

However, forbearance is valid consideration if the person seeking to enforce the contract reasonably believes that he has a valid legal claim.

When there is a dispute concerning the amount owed, and one party tenders a check in payment in full which the other party cashes, there is a discharge of the contractual obligation. If the amount and validity of the claim are undisputed, the cashing of the check does not bar a suit for the remainder.

If there is no dispute concerning either the validity, collectability or amount of the claim, an agreement to settle the claim for a lower amount is not supported by consideration.

Output and Requirements Contracts

Output and requirements contracts are not invalid on the grounds of indefiniteness or lack of consideration.

Output and requirements contracts are specifically enforceable if the non-breaching party will have difficulty in obtaining substitute performance.

UCC Rules. A quantity term expressed in terms of a manufacturer's requirements is enforceable. UCC § 2-306 provides that "a term which measures the quantity by the . . . requirements of the buyer means such actual . . . requirements as may occur in good faith . . ."

The definiteness of quantity requirement is satisfied if there is an available objective method for determining the quantity, and the requirements of a manufacturer would generally satisfy that need.

No quantity unreasonably disproportionate to any stated estimate, or in the absence of a stated estimate, to any normal or otherwise comparable prior output or requirements, may be tendered or demanded.

A lawful agreement by either the seller or the buyer for exclusive dealing in the kind of goods concerned imposes unless otherwise agreed, an obligation by the seller to use best efforts to supply the goods and by the buyer to use best efforts to promote their sale.

Third-Party Beneficiary Contracts

Intended Beneficiaries

Third-party beneficiary contracts arise when the performance of the contractual obligations of one of the parties benefits a person, not a party to the contract, instead of the party who furnished the consideration necessary for that obligation to arise. Thus "A" and "B" enter into a contract whereby A furnishes consideration to B who is contractually obligated to render performance to "C," not A.

Where two parties contract for a service that both parties intend to benefit a designated third party directly, both the third party beneficiary and the promisee are entitled to sue upon the promisor's breach.

The victim of a breach is entitled to recover only those damages which could not reasonably have been avoided. Failure to take reasonable steps to mitigate damages defeats a claim for consequential damages.

No contractual rights vest in an intended third-party beneficiary unless the promisor and promisee parties conclude a binding contract.

Third-party beneficiaries are intended beneficiaries when the contracting parties either explicitly or implicitly direct the performance of the contract for their benefit.

One type of intended beneficiary is a "creditor beneficiary," where the performance of the contract for the benefit of the beneficiary, C, is designed to relieve the party who furnished the consideration, A, from a legal obligation.

The second type of intended third-party beneficiary is a "donee beneficiary," where the original contracting party, A, is satisfying no legal obligation by entering into a contract which is designed to benefit C.

Since one of the contracting parties, A, has furnished the consideration which obligated B to perform, the third party, C, need not provide consideration to be able to sue on a third-party beneficiary contract.

A third-party creditor beneficiary, C, does not give up his rights against the contracting party who furnished the consideration, A, which required that performance be rendered to him until the party obligated to render performance, B, completes his obligation.

Intended third-party beneficiaries need not know that a contract has been made for their benefit at the time they become a third party beneficiary to have rights to sue.

If a party to a third party beneficiary contract, B, is obligated to render performance to an intended third-party beneficiary, C, in exchange for performance by the other party, A, he is relieved of that obligation if A does not perform his obligations to B. Therefore B has a valid defense in a suit by C if A fails to perform his obligations to B.

Incidental Beneficiaries

An incidental beneficiary, a person who will benefit if a contract between two other parties is performed but is a person that the original contracting parties did not intend to benefit, has no right to enforce a third-party beneficiary contract.

Modification of the Third-Party Beneficiary's Rights

The two original parties to a third-party beneficiary contract, A and B, can modify or rescind their contract to the detriment of the intended beneficiary, C, up until the time that C's rights in the contract become vested. They become vested when C either assents to the contract at a party's request, sues on the contract, or changes his position in reliance on it.

Assignment and Delegation

Assignment of Rights

An assignee succeeds in a contract as the contract stands at the time of the assignment.

Once a party has fully performed his obligations under a contract, his right to return performance, including his right to sue for breach of the other party's obligations, can be assigned to a third party even if the contract prohibits assignment.

A party to a contract can assign the benefits of the contract which accrue to him without obligating the assignee to assume the burdens of the contract.

An assignee of a contract only obtains rights under it, which are limited by any defenses that the original contracting party has against the assignor. The rule is contrary to the rule when the assignment is in the form of the negotiation of a negotiable instrument. There the assignee, known as a holder in due course, takes free of the personal defenses which the other party to the negotiable instrument has against the assignor of that instrument.

If one contracting party pays a second contracting party an amount due on the contract before he receives notice that the second party assigned his interest under the contract, the first party is not obligated to an assignee, even though the assignment took place before the payment.

However, if the first party has been notified of the assignment before making payment, he can only discharge his contract obligation by paying the assignee.

UCC Rules: Unless otherwise agreed, all rights of either seller or buyer can be assigned except where the assignment would materially change the duty of the other party, increase materially the burden or risk imposed on him by his contract, or impair materially his chances of obtaining a return performance.

Unless the circumstances indicate the contrary, a prohibition of assignment of the contract is to be construed as barring only the delegation to the assignee of the assignor's performance.

Delegation of Duties

A provision in a contract forbidding delegation is valid and enforceable.

A party may perform his duty through a delegatee unless it is otherwise agreed, or the other party has a substantial interest in having his original promisor perform or control the acts required by the contract, or the party wishing to delegate possesses unique characteristics so that the performance by a delegatee would materially alter the bargained-for performance.

No delegation of performance relieves the party delegating of any duty to perform or any liability for breach.

If the parties enter into a novation so that one original contracting party agrees to look solely to the delegatee for performance, in exchange for releasing the other original party from the obligations of the contract, then the original party is no longer liable if the delegatee breaches the contract.

UCC Rule: An assignment of "the contract" or of "all my rights under the contract" or an assignment in similar general terms is an assignment of rights and duties.

Unless the language or the circumstances (as in an assignment for security) indicate to the contrary, it is a delegation of the duties of the performance of the assignor.

The acceptance of the assignment by the assignee constitutes a promise by him to perform those duties.

The promise is enforceable by the assignor or the other party to the original contract.

Statute of Frauds

The exemption of contracts for less than $500 from the requirements of the Statute of Frauds applies only to contracts for the sale of goods governed by UCC-2.

The Memorandum

The Statute of Frauds applies to specific types of contracts discussed below. The contract itself need not be in writing to satisfy the statute.

There need only be a memorandum which contains the essential terms of the contract signed by the party to be charged.

The memorandum sufficient to satisfy the statute needn't be written at the time of the making of the promise, nor need it to be writing addressed to the promisee.

Contract Cannot be Performed within One Year

In measuring the one year to determine if the Statute of Frauds is applicable, the period starts at the time of the making of the contract, not at the time of commencement of performance.

Thus, the Statute of Frauds applies to an eleven-month personal services contract made on January 1 with work starting on April 1, since the contract will not terminate until March 1 of the following year.

The possibility that death could prematurely terminate a personal services contract for more than a year does not cause the Statute of Frauds to be inapplicable.

The Statute of Frauds is not applicable to a personal services contract for the life of the party, because the natural termination of that contract could occur within a year.

Land Contracts

See Property Law for a discussion of the Statute of Frauds as it applies to land contracts.

A real estate brokerage contract is enforceable even if there is no memorandum signed by the property owner sufficient to satisfy the Statute of Frauds.

General Rule for Sale of Goods

UCC Rules: Except as otherwise provided, a contract for the sale of goods for the price of $500 or more is not enforceable by way of action or defense unless there is some writing sufficient to indicate that a contract for sale had been made between the parties and signed by the party against whom enforcement is sought or by his authorized agent or broker.

A writing is not insufficient because it omits or incorrectly states a term agreed upon, but the contract is not enforceable beyond the number of goods shown in such writing.

A memorandum satisfies the Statute of Frauds if it indicates there is a contract, it contains a description of the goods and the quantity and is signed. It need not contain the price.

Exceptions for Sale of Goods

UCC Rules: Between merchants, if within a reasonable time a writing in confirmation of the contract and sufficient against the sender is received, and the party receiving it has reason to know its content, it satisfies the requirement of the Statute of Frauds against such party unless written notice of objection to its contents is given within ten days after it is received.

A contract which does not satisfy the general rule but which is valid in other respects is enforceable if:

(a) the goods are to be specifically manufactured for the buyer and are not suitable for sale to others in the ordinary course of the seller's business, and the seller, before notice of repudiation is received and under circumstances which reasonably indicated that the goods are for the buyer, has made either a substantial beginning of their manufacture or commitments for their procurement, or

(b) if the party against whom enforcement is sought admits in his pleading, testimony, or otherwise in court that a contract for sale was made, but the contract is not enforceable under this provision beyond the quantity of goods admitted, or

(c) with respect to goods for which payment has been made or accepted or which have been received or accepted.

If, as modified, a UCC contract involves a sale of goods for more than $500, it requires compliance with the Statute of Frauds.

Suretyship

An oral promise to pay the debt of another is usually unenforceable because of the Statute of Frauds.

If the primary purpose of the promise to pay the debt of another is to further the goals of the promisor, the promise is enforceable even if there is no memorandum signed by the promisor sufficient to satisfy the Statute of Frauds.

In addition to the writing required by the Statute of Frauds, a party seeking to collect from a surety must give reasonable notice to the surety that he has extended credit to the other party to the contract.

The suretyship provisions of the Statute of Frauds are inapplicable unless there is a contractual relationship between the creditor and the party who is to benefit from the services, and the creditor knows that the defendant is acting in a suretyship capacity rather than in a direct contractual capacity.

Parol Evidence Rule

The parol evidence rule bars evidence of prior or contemporaneous statements which contradict the terms of a written contract.

If the written contract is completely integrated, evidence of any prior or contemporaneous agreements made between the parties is inadmissible.

However, parol evidence for the terms of a contract is admissible:

(a) to prove that there is a condition precedent to a contract's coming into existence;

(b) to explain an ambiguity;

(c) to show that the parties used words in a nontraditional manner or spoke in code;

(d) to prove a mistake in reducing the terms of an oral agreement to writing;

(e) to prove any modification of a contract by evidence of conversations which took place after the contract was formed. At common law, a provision in a written agreement that a writing can only modify a contract is not valid;

(f) to prove, for an oral contract which is not integrated, subjects not covered by the written contract.

UCC Rules: The terms with respect to which the confirmatory memoranda of the parties agree or which are otherwise set forth in a writing intended by the parties as a final expression of their agreement may not be contradicted by evidence of any prior or contemporaneous oral agreement but may be explained or supplemented,

(a) by course of dealing, usage of trade, or course of performance and

(b) by evidence of consistent additional terms, unless the court finds the writing to have also been intended as a complete and exclusive statement of the terms of the agreement.

A course of dealing, when inconsistent with a usage of trade, trumps usage of trade and controls the interpretation of the contract.

Unlike the rule at common law, under the UCC a signed agreement which excludes modification or rescission except by a signed writing cannot be otherwise modified or rescinded, but except as between merchants such a requirement on a form supplied by the merchant must be separately signed by the other party.

Although an attempt at modification or rescission does not satisfy the requirements of the UCC provisions for the Statute of Frauds, or parol evidence rule, it can operate as a waiver.

Interpretation of Contracts

The primary goal in interpreting a contract is to carry out the intent of the parties.

Permanent employment means employment-at-will. In an employment-at-will relationship, either party can terminate the agreement at any time, without the termination being considered a breach unless the termination was to violate important public policy.

When parties attach significantly different meanings to the same material term, the meaning that controls is that "attached by one of them if at the time the agreement was made . . . that party did not know of any different meaning attached by the other, and the other knew the meaning attached by the first party." Restatement (Second) of Contracts § 201.

UCC Rules: A course of dealing is a sequence of previous conduct between the parties to a particular transaction, which is fairly to be regarded as establishing a common basis of understanding for interpreting their expressions and other conduct.

A usage of trade is any practice or method of dealing having such regularity of observance in a place, vocation, or trade as to justify an expectation that it will be observed for the transaction in question.

The existence and scope of such a usage are to be proved as facts. If it is established that such a usage is embodied in a written trade code or similar writing, the interpretation of the writing is for the court.

A course of dealing between parties and any usage of trade in the vocation or trade in which they are engaged, or of which they are or should be aware, shall give particular meaning to, and supplement or qualify, terms of an agreement.

The express terms of an agreement and an applicable course of dealing or usage of trade shall be construed wherever reasonable as consistent with each other.

When such construction is unreasonable, express terms control both course of dealing and usage of trade, and course of dealing controls usage of trade.

Conditions

Express Conditions

If the obligation of one party to a contract to perform his obligations under that contract is subject to an express condition precedent, the other party seeking to establish a breach of contract must either show compliance with an express condition, or that the other party was in bad faith with respect to the condition, thereby excusing compliance with the condition.

A contract condition that performance be satisfactory to the purchaser will mean that an objective standard will be applied and performance must be satisfactory to a reasonable person.

If the contract involves personal taste, the performance must be subjectively satisfactory to the purchaser. However, even when the subjective standard is applied, the purchaser must act in good faith.

If one party to a contract assumes an obligation, the size of which at the time of contracting is unknown, he is entitled to be paid the consideration promised him, even if the obligation is substantially smaller than anticipated.

If a certificate of completion by the architect is a condition of completion of a construction contract, the builder cannot collect in full under the contract until that certificate is obtained, unless he can prove that the architect failed to provide it because he was acting in bad faith.

If it is clear that the purpose of the condition was to benefit or protect one of the parties, that party may waive the condition and insist that the other party perform.

Constructive Conditions of Exchange

If no order of performance is specified in the contract, each party must perform its obligations under the contract as a condition for demanding performance from the other side.

For example, in a sale of goods contract, the buyer must pay for the goods, and the seller must deliver the goods at the same time. Such mutual conditions precedent is constructive conditions of exchange.

The parties to a contract can make the performance by one party a condition precedent to performance by the other.

Absent a special provision concerning partial payment in the contract; a party has no right to be paid until he completes the required performance.

If the time for performance is not made of the essence, a party may perform in a reasonable time.

Divisible Contracts

A divisible contract occurs when performance by one party of less than the full contractual obligation gives that party a right to require partial performance of the other party's obligation. For example, if A is employed by B for one year, B will ordinarily have an obligation to pay A a portion of his yearly salary on a periodic basis.

If a contract is divisible, then performance of one divisible portion permits the plaintiff to demand performance from the defendant for that divisible portion, even if the plaintiff is in breach with respect to another divisible portion.

For example, if A, the employee on an annual salary with monthly pay periods, works for one month, he is entitled to be paid for that month's work, even if he does not complete the full year's employment.

Contract law acknowledges the fact that parties sometimes embody obligations which are in most respects separable into a single document or agreement. The rules for damages permit the separable components to be treated separately. Though the contract has separable components, for damages purposes, it is still a single contract permitting the damages suffered by each side to be litigated in a single lawsuit.

If the contract requires one party to perform a single task such as building a structure, the fact that the contract requires periodic payments from the owner to the builder does not make it a divisible contract.

Immaterial Breach and Substantial Performance

Under the common law, the plaintiff can sue for breach of contract and collect contract damages if he has substantially performed the contract, even if there is an immaterial (non-willful) breach.

If the plaintiff has not fully performed the contract, the defendant can successfully assert a counterclaim for damages caused by his failure to perform fully.

UCC Rule: The UCC does not recognize the doctrine of substantial performance. Instead, it follows the rule of perfect tender. Except for an installment contract, the seller must tender the correct amount of conforming goods at the time specified in the contract, or the buyer can reject the goods without liability and sue the seller for damages.

Installment Contracts

UCC Rules: An installment contract is one where the seller does not have an obligation to deliver all of the goods to be sold under the contract at one time.

If a contract is determined to be an installment contract, the rule of perfect tender, which permits the buyer to reject non-conforming goods if all of the goods are to be delivered at one time, is inapplicable. The buyer can reject a nonconforming shipment only if it substantially impairs the value of the installment and cannot be cured.

A failure by the seller to deliver the appropriate quantity of conforming goods on time, for one installment of an installment contract, is a breach of the total contract only if the nonconformity substantially impairs the value of the entire contract.

UCC Rule – Implied Warranty of Merchantability

An implied warranty of merchantability is given by all sellers who are merchants.

UCC § 2-314 (2) defines the implied warranty of merchantability:

(1) goods, to be merchantable, must at least pass without objection in the trade under the contract description; and

(2) in the case of fungible goods are of a fair average quality within the description; and

(3) are fit for the ordinary purpose for which goods are used; and

(4) run within the variations permitted by the agreement, or even kind of quality and quantity within each unit and among all units involved; and

(5) are adequately contained, packaged, and labeled as the agreement may require; and

(6) conform to the promises or affirmations of fact made on the container or label, if any.

UCC Rule – Warranty of Fitness for a Particular Purpose

Under UCC § 2- 315 a warranty of fitness for a particular purpose arises whenever the seller has reason to know of any particular purpose for which the goods are required, and that the buyer is relying upon the seller's skill to select suitable goods.

Constructive Condition of Cooperation

A condition of cooperation is implied in every contract. A party who wrongfully hinders the other party's performance breaches the contract. Each party to a contract has an implied duty to cooperate with the other party in achieving the objects of the contract.

Obligations of Good Faith and Fair Dealing

Each party to a contract has an implied duty to act in good faith. Acting in bad faith can constitute a breach of contract and can give the other party a defense to a suit for breach of contract.

Suspension or Excuse of Conditions by Waiver, Election

A waiver occurs when a party to a contract affirmatively represents to the other party that it will not act on or enforce a known right.

A waiver is revocable unless the other party relies on the waiver to its detriment, or the waiver is an agreement supported by consideration.

The conduct of a contracting party in failing to insist on full performance for some time can constitute a course of dealings and a waiver of his right to full performance during the remainder of the contract if relied upon by the other party to his detriment.

If the certification of the performance of a condition is placed in a third party for the benefit of one of the contracting parties, that contracting party can waive the certification.

UCC Rule: A party who had made a waiver affecting an executory portion of the contract may retract the waiver by reasonable notification received by the other party that strict performance will be required of any term waived unless the retraction would be unjust because of a material change of position in reliance on the waiver.

Remedies

Rescission

When a seller induces a buyer's consent to a contract through a material misrepresentation, the resulting contract is voidable at the election of the buyer.

In some cases, a failure to independently inspect property might constitute a defense to a claim of misrepresentation.

However, the buyer is entitled to rely on the truth of material representations made by the seller, and need not conduct independent tests to see whether the seller is lying.

Buyer's and Seller's Obligations Unless Different Terms are Specified

UCC Rule: The seller has an obligation to tender conforming goods at his place of business at the specified time, and the buyer has a concurrent obligation to pay the purchase price at that time.

Cure

UCC Rules: Where any tender or delivery by the seller is rejected because it is non-conforming and the time for performance has not yet expired, the seller may seasonably notify the buyer of his intention to cure and may then within the contract time make a conforming delivery.

Where the buyer rejects a non-conforming tender which the seller had reasonable grounds to believe would be acceptable with or without a money allowance, the seller, may, if he seasonably notifies the buyer, have a further reasonable time to substitute a conforming tender.

Rights of Non-Breaching Party

UCC Rule: If a party to a contract has committed a material breach, the non-breaching party is excused from further performance of the contract.

Demand for Assurances

UCC Rule: A contract for the sale of goods imposes an obligation on each party that the other's expectation of receiving due performance will not be impaired. When reasonable grounds for insecurity arise concerning the performance of either party, the other may in writing demand adequate assurance of the performance and until he receives such assurance may if commercially reasonable, suspend any performance for which he has not already received the agreed return.

Acceptance of any improper delivery or payment does not prejudice the aggrieved party's right to demand adequate assurance of future performance.

After receipt of a justified demand, failure to provide within a reasonable time, not exceeding thirty days, such assurance of due performance, as is adequate under the circumstances of the particular case, is a repudiation of the contract.

Anticipatory Repudiation

Anticipatory repudiation occurs when a party to the contract gives unequivocal notice to the other party that he will not perform his obligations at the time set for performance.

If the non-repudiating party has not relied on anticipatory repudiation by canceling the contract or materially changing his position, the repudiating party may retract the repudiation, providing he gives adequate assurances.

The non-repudiating party then has no right to sue for a breach before the time of scheduled performance.

UCC Rule: When either party repudiates the contract concerning a performance not yet due, the loss of which will substantially impair the value of the contract to the other, the aggrieved party may:

(a) for a commercially reasonable time await performance by the repudiating party; or

(b) resort to any remedy for breach even though he has notified the repudiating party that he would await the latter's performance and has urged retraction; and,

(c) in either case suspend his own performance or proceed in accordance with the provisions of this article on the seller's right to identify goods to the contract notwithstanding the breach or to salvage unfinished goods.

Risk of Loss

UCC Rules: The risk of loss is initially on the seller. It shifts to the buyer when the seller completes his delivery obligation for goods that meet the quantity and quality specifications of the contract.

If nothing is said about the place of delivery or the contract specifies that delivery is at the seller's place of business, the risk of loss shifts to the buyer when the seller places conforming goods on a common carrier with instructions that they be shipped to the buyer.

If the contract requires delivery at the buyer's place of business, the risk of loss does not shift to the buyer until conforming goods arrive at the buyer's place of business.

If the goods shipped are non-conforming, the seller retains the risk of loss until the goods are accepted.

If the buyer initially accepts the goods and then rightfully revokes acceptance, the risk of loss is on the buyer only to the extent that the buyer's insurance covers the goods.

Rights of *Bona Fide* Purchasers

UCC Rule: A *bona fide* purchaser of goods from a person in the business of selling those goods takes superior title to the true owner of those goods.

Seller's Remedies in the Event of Buyer's Breach

UCC Rules: The ordinary measure of damages for non-acceptance or repudiation by the buyer is the difference between the market price at the time and place for tender and the unpaid contract price, together with any incidental damages but less expenses saved in consequence of buyer's breach.

However, if the measure of damages provided in the preceding paragraph is inadequate to put the seller in as good a position as performance would have done, then the measure of damages is the profit (including reasonable overhead) which the seller would have made from the full performance by the buyer, together with any incidental damages provided in this article, due allowances for costs reasonably incurred, and due credit for payments or proceeds of resale.

As a limited alternative remedy, the seller may make the goods available to the buyer and sue for the contract price if the goods cannot be sold in the seller's ordinary course of business.

Buyer's Remedies in the Event of Seller's Breach

UCC Rules: The buyer may seek damages - the difference between the market price and the contract price.

The buyer may fix his damages by purchasing the goods elsewhere and collect the difference between the price he pays and the contract price. This remedy is called "cover."

The buyer may tender the full purchase price and seek an order requiring the seller to deliver the goods if they are unique.

Measure of Damages

Expectancy damages are the usual measure of contract damages, i.e., the amount of money which would put him in the same position he would have been in if the breaching party had performed his obligations under the contract.

The amount of a non-breaching party's expectancy damages on a contract where the non-breaching party has not expended any money towards his obligated performance is the profit which he would have made had the contract been performed.

If the non-breaching party has expended money in the performance of his obligations under the contract, he is entitled to recover those sums plus his profit.

If expectancy damages are too speculative and they cannot be recovered, then the non-breaching party is entitled to reliance damages, the amount expended by him to perform the contract whether or not those expenditures benefited the breaching party.

If payments on a contract are due in installments and there is no acceleration clause, the non-breaching party can only sue for the unpaid installments.

If a party voluntarily incurs additional expenses toward the performance of the contract after he knows that the other party is in breach, he may not recover those additional expenses.

A non-breaching party has a duty to mitigate damages by taking steps to avoid damages which he should have foreseen and could have avoided without undue risk, expense, or humiliation. For example, if the employer breaches an employment contract, the employee must use reasonable efforts to seek substitute employment during the remainder of the contract period.

If he fails to mitigate, the fair value of what he would have received if he had found other employment is deducted from his expectancy damages.

Reasonable expenses, if incurred in seeking to mitigate damage after the breach, are recoverable as incidental damages even if those particular expenses are not connected to a successful mitigation attempt.

The victim of a breach is entitled to recover only those damages which could not reasonably have been avoided.

Failure to take reasonable steps to mitigate damages defeats a claim for consequential damages.

Consequential Damages

Consequential damages are limited to those damages which were reasonably foreseeable by the parties at the time the contract is made.

Liquidated Damages

A provision fixing liquidated damages is unenforceable unless the amount fixed is reasonable when compared to the amount of damages which the parties could anticipate at the time of making the contract, or when compared to the amount of damages incurred.

Specific Performance

Both the buyer and the seller are entitled to sue for specific performance of enforceable land contracts.

Specific performance requiring the defendant to perform is not available as a remedy for a personal services contract.

However, a negative injunction can be granted by the standards for granting injunctions, preventing the defendant from working for a person other than the one to whom he is contractually bound.

Restitution Damages (*quantum meruit*)

If a party is prevented from suing on the contract because the contract is unenforceable due to the Statute of Frauds or otherwise, or because he has committed a material breach of the contract, he is limited to restitution damages.

Restitution damages, also known as *quantum meruit* damages, are the fair value of the benefit conferred on the other party.

An unjust enrichment claim cannot exceed the contract price when all of the work giving rise to the claim has been performed, and the only remaining obligation is the payment of the price.

Restitution damages cannot be greater than the amount of damages which are recoverable if the contract were enforceable.

Impossibility and Frustration

If events after the formation of a contract make the performance by one party illegal or impossible, the doctrine of impossibility is applicable, and the parties are discharged from their contractual obligations.

The doctrine of impossibility applies at common law when the subject matter of the contract is destroyed, or a party to a personal service contract dies.

The destruction of an existing structure renders a contract to repair it impossible, terminating the contract. The contractor has the right to collect for the fair value of the work done in *quantum meruit*, but cannot sue for contract damages because the contract obligations have been discharged.

A party may not rely on the defense of impossibility if he specifically assumes the risk of performing an obligation which is objectively impossible.

UCC Rules: Under the doctrine of impracticability, performance is excused when:

(1) goods identified to the contract are destroyed,

(2) performance becomes illegal, or

(3) performance is prevented by a non-foreseeable event, the nonoccurrence of which was a basic assumption of the contract.

Under § 2-615, when a contract specifies produce which is to be grown on a specific farm and the crop is destroyed by natural forces beyond the control of the farmer, the farmer is excused from performance to the extent of the damage.

Contract Law – Quick Facts

1. A **gratuitous assignee** has rights under a contract that MAY be enforced against **obligor** <u>until or unless</u> the assignment is revoked.

2. Where there is a **delegation of duties**, BOTH the delegator *and* the delegate are LIABLE for the performance of the agreement.

3. Under UCC, a **crop failure** resulting from an unexpected cause excuses a farmer's obligation to deliver the full amount as long as he makes a fair and reasonable allocation among his buyers, which could be allocated *pro rata* between buyers.

   However, the buyer may accept the proposed modification OR terminate the contract.

4. The general rule is that a **contractor** is responsible for the destruction of the premises under construction *prior to completion*; once the residence is complete, the **risk of loss** shifts to the owner.

5. **Performance is excused** where prevented by **operation of law**, despite any stipulations to the contrary; where governmental interference makes the performance of the contract as contemplated illegal, the builder may be excused from performance.

6. A **detriment** exists whenever a promisee gives up the **legal right** to do something, regardless of whether she would have done it otherwise.

7. Under UCC, a **written confirmation** is effective as an acceptance even though it states additional terms UNLESS the acceptance is **expressly made conditional on assent** to the additional terms.

8. An **implied-in-fact** contract is a contract formed by manifestations of assent other than oral or written language (i.e., conduct) – even if there is NO manifestation of mutual assent, the parties will be bound if their conduct objectively appears to manifest contractual intent.

9. **Assignment and delegation** are prohibited where they would substantially alter the obligor's risks, such as an **exoneration clause**, which effectively holds obligor accountable (liable) for obligee's actions.

10. A **novation** substitutes a new party for an original party to the contract—requires the assent of ALL parties, and completely releases the original party.

11. **Despite reliance**, a third-party **donee beneficiary** has NO cause of action against the promise, because the promisee's act is gratuitous and she may NOT be held to it UNLESS she has directly created the reliance by personally informing the beneficiary.

12. Where there is an **oral condition precedent**, evidence of the condition falls outside the parol evidence rule.

Criminal Law

and Procedure

The statements governing Criminal Law and Procedure were compiled by analyzing the criminal law questions released by the multistate examiners and setting forth the principles of law which governed the correct answer to each question.

An analysis of the questions revealed that there are a limited number of legal principles which are tested regularly and repeatedly and that this compilation most likely contains the principles which will govern the majority of the criminal law questions on the examination which you must answer correctly to pass.

You should review these principles before preparing answers to the practice multistate criminal law questions and understand how these principles are applied to obtain the correct answer. Just prior to taking the MBE, you should commit these principles to memory.

Homicide Crimes

To establish criminal homicide liability, the prosecution must show that the defendant's act was the proximate cause of the victim's death.

Murder

When an MBE question or answer choice uses a word like "murder" or "robbery" and provides no further definition of the crime, then it is referring to the common law crime.

You are required to know the elements of common law crimes and how to apply them to specific fact situations.

If the question wants you to apply a definition of a crime different from the common law, they will either define the crime in the question or use a term such as "under modern law."

Definition of Malice for Common Law Murder

The mental state required for common law murder is malice.

Murder has four separate definitions.

  (1) Intent to kill

  (2) Intent to do great bodily harm

  (3) A death occurring in the course of a felony

  (4) Willful and wanton disregard of an unreasonable human risk (i.e., depraved heart killing).

A person under a duty to aid another person because of a contractual or familial relationship is guilty of involuntary manslaughter if death occurs because of unreasonable failure to give that aid.

An intent to kill constitutes malice which is a *mens rea* for common law murder.

A defendant must have the mental state of malice at the time he acts to end the victim's life to be guilty of murder.

Murder – Intentional Killings

Intent to kill has two definitions:

  (1) the desire to accomplish a specific result

(2) engaging in such actions that the result is inevitable even though not specifically desired.

The motive behind that intent is irrelevant in establishing intent. The killing of a terminally ill patient who pleads with a person to end his life is murder at common law because it is an intentional killing.

Consent of the victim is not a defense to an intentional killing.

The doctrine of transferred intent makes a killing of an unintended victim an intentional killing if it occurs as the result of an intent to kill an intended victim.

If a person employs a mechanical device which kills a person when activated, the intention to set up the device is equivalent to the intention to activate it. If there are no mitigating circumstances or defenses to the killing, the person setting up the device is guilty of murder.

An intentional killing by a person who is threatened with death if he does not complete the killing is murder because there is no defense of duress to murder.

Murder – Intent to do Great Bodily Harm

Inflicting serious bodily harm on a victim who was not likely to cause death constitutes murder if the victim dies as the result of the infliction of that serious bodily harm.

A single blow administered by a fist would not ordinarily give rise to an inference that the actor intended serious bodily harm.

However, a serious and prolonged beating or kicking of a victim would indicate such intent.

Likewise, the infliction of any wound with a gun or a knife or other weapon would ordinarily give rise to the inference that intent to do great bodily harm was present.

The victim must die from injuries inflicted with the intent to do serious bodily harm before this form of malice becomes the malice needed for murder.

Felony Murder

Felony murder occurs only when the defendant is in the course of committing or attempting to commit a felony, which qualifies as a felony supporting felony murder.

If the defendant is not guilty of the underlying felony, he is not guilty of felony murder. Often this is the best defense to the charge of felony murder.

A person is not guilty of felony murder if the underlying felony has not commenced or is not completed at the time the death occurs.

Mayhem, Rape, Burglary, Arson, Kidnapping, Escape and Robbery, (acronym MR. BAKER), are the common law felonies which support felony murder.

Manslaughter and assault and battery, even though common law felonies, cannot be the underlying felony for felony murder.

Neither intent to kill, nor intent to commit serious bodily harm, is an element of the malice necessary to support felony murder.

An intentional killing in the course of a felony provides two bases of malice for common law murder.

A death which occurs during the course of a conspiracy to commit a MR. BAKER felony constitutes felony murder, which will be imputed to all persons who are conspirators at the time the killing occurs unless the killing was beyond the scope of the conspiracy.

The killing of a co-felon in the course of a felony by a third person does not sustain a felony murder charge against the surviving felon because, under the Redline rule, the killing is justifiable homicide.

Abandoned or Malignant Heart Murder
(Depraved Heart Murder)

A defendant is guilty of murder if he engages in conduct which involves a wanton and willful disregard of unreasonable human risk and which results in the death of another.

The reckless conduct must involve a substantial or very high degree of risk to human life.

The risk involved is to be assessed in light of what the defendant knows, and the risk taken must be unjustifiable under the circumstances.

Examples of conduct which constitute the malice for malignant heart murder if death occurs as a result of the action are:

- firing bullets in a confined space, through a wall, or into an urban area for confusing police;

- playing Russian roulette;

- deliberately and unjustifiably driving a car onto a crowded sidewalk;

- using deceit to convince an individual to take an action which is likely to get him killed.

Exam Tip

The wording of a question may require you to discard the ordinary pecking order of homicide crimes.

Normally felony murder is considered first-degree murder and more serious than murder under the depraved heart doctrine.

However, a question may suggest that in a certain situation, murder under the depraved heart doctrine is more serious than killing in the course of a common law felony.

To succeed on the MBE, it is crucial to carefully read the question and be prepared to suspend the normal principles of black letter law if the question reads that way.

Degrees of Murder

Since there are no degrees of murder at common law, any question concerning degrees of murder will set forth a statute which controls the way in which degrees of murder are calculated.

Many such statutes will define first-degree murder as killing with deliberate, premeditated malice aforethought, thus limiting first-degree murder to planned, intentional killings.

When the malice for murder is either the intention to do great bodily harm or with the recklessness which constitutes depraved heart murder, the murder is usually classified as second-degree murder.

Voluntary Manslaughter

To reduce a murder crime where the malice was either intent to kill or intent to do great bodily harm, to voluntary manslaughter, there must be:

(a) adequate provocation to inflame a reasonable person into the heat of passion, and

(b) the defendant must have been in such a state, and

(c) the killing must have taken place at a time when the passions of a reasonable person would not have cooled, and those of the defendant did not cool.

Where the malice for murder is felony murder or depraved heart murder, there is no reduction of the murder crime to manslaughter.

A violent battery, witnessing or learning about spousal infidelity, mutual affray, and an illegal arrest all satisfy the adequate provocation element of voluntary manslaughter. Mere words, no matter how insulting, do not.

A second basis for the reduction of murder to voluntary manslaughter occurs when the defendant has the right of self-defense or the right to defend another, but such defense will not result in an acquittal because it was not properly perfected.

For example, a defendant only had a right to use non-deadly force to defend himself but used deadly force, or a defendant failed to retreat in a situation where the retreat doctrine was applicable.

Under the doctrine of transferred intent, the killing will be reduced from murder to manslaughter if the defendant killed the victim mistakenly when he was trying to kill a person whose death would have resulted in manslaughter rather than a murder conviction.

Involuntary Manslaughter

Willful, wanton conduct is behavior slightly less egregious than the conduct which forms the basis of malice in depraved heart murder.

A death caused by the course of willful, wanton, but not the intentional conduct of the defendant is involuntary manslaughter.

If death occurs while the defendant is engaged in a misdemeanor which is also morally wrong (a misdemeanor *malum in se*), he is guilty of involuntary manslaughter.

Generally, there is no affirmative duty to aid a person in peril and no criminal liability on the person in a position to give aid who fails to provide aid.

However, a person is under a duty to aid if he has a contractual obligation to do so, his actions have put the victim in peril, or there is a parent-child or other family relationship between the defendant and the victim. In such circumstances, if the failure to render aid results in death, the refusal to give aid can constitute willful, wanton conduct, causing the defendant to be guilty of involuntary manslaughter.

A defendant must act in a willful, wanton manner in performing the act which ends the victim's life to be guilty of involuntary manslaughter.

An unreasonable belief concerning the threat of harm to the defendant is not a justification to engage in willful, wanton conduct.

Exam Tip

Pay careful attention to the terms of the statute given in the question which separates murder into degrees.

Two of the bases of malice (i.e., intentional killings and felony murder) are classified as first-degree murder. The other two bases of malice, (i.e., intention to do great bodily harm and depraved heart murder) are classified as second-degree murder.

Where you have an intentional killing, you also must determine if the intention was formed as the result of deliberate premeditation and whether there are circumstances which will reduce the crime to voluntary manslaughter, or which will provide a total defense to the murder crime such as self-defense.

Self-Defense

Deadly force is that which is likely to cause death, whether or not death occurs in a particular instance.

Non-deadly force is that which is not likely to cause death, even though death occurred in a particular instance.

A defendant who uses deadly force can successfully raise the defense of self-defense to a homicide charge if he reasonably believes he is in danger of death or great bodily harm even if he is not actually in such danger.

Also, a defendant who uses deadly force can successfully raise a defense if he used that deadly force to apprehend a dangerous felon or to prevent a dangerous felony from being committed

The defense is successful for misdemeanor crimes if the force used is non-deadly.

In a jurisdiction which requires a person to retreat before using deadly force in self-defense, retreat is not required if the person believes that there is no reasonable method of retreat or if he is attacked in his home.

Even though he is in danger of death or serious bodily harm, a defendant does NOT have the right of self-defense if:

- he is in the commission of a felony,

- he is lawfully arrested by a police officer,

- he was the original aggressor, except when he as the original aggressor attacks with non-deadly force and is met with deadly force or unless 1) he completely terminates his status as an aggressor and 2) makes that known to the person he attacked.

Defense of property does not justify deadly force.

If a person has a valid right of self-defense against A and kills B by mistake, he has a defense to a charge that he murdered B because that killing is justified under the doctrine of transferred intent.

Defense of Others

A person who has used deadly force to defend another, in the belief that the person defended has the right to use deadly force in self-defense, has a valid defense in a criminal prosecution, even if the person defended does not, in fact, have the right of self-defense because the person defended was the original aggressor.

A person has the right to use the same force defending others as he does defend himself. The right is not limited to family members.

Other Defenses to Homicide Crimes

Justifiable homicide is a killing commanded by the law, such as the killing by the executioner in a death penalty case, or the killing by soldiers on the battlefield.

Justifiable homicide is not criminal homicide.

Duress occurs when an individual commits an act against his will because of a fear of death or substantial bodily harm threatened by another human being.

Necessity relates to coercion by nonhuman elements, such natural forces which threaten the life of an individual.

Neither duress nor necessity is a defense to a homicide crime.

However, in a felony murder case, duress or necessity can be a defense to the underlying felony, thereby eliminating an essential element of felony murder.

Other Crimes Against the Person

Assault and Battery

A criminal battery is the unlawful application of force, either by direct contact or indirect physical contact, to a person or recognized extension of the person.

The force may be either by direct physical touching or by use of a gun, or other weapon applied either against the body of the victim or something closely associated with the victim.

Intent or conduct amounting to criminal negligence form the *mens rea* for battery.

An individual has the right to use non-deadly force in self-defense if he is attacked with non-deadly force.

A defendant using non-deadly as opposed to deadly force in self-defense against an aggressor does not have to retreat.

The retreat doctrine only applies in limited circumstances to the use of deadly force against the aggressor.

Consent, either actual or implied, is a defense to assault and battery.

Rape

Consent to intercourse would be a defense to rape even if the defendant committed fraud in inducing the victim to have intercourse.

If the defendant commits fraud in the *factum* as opposed to fraud in the inducement, so that the victim does not realize she is having intercourse, then her consent is not a valid defense.

Penetration no matter how slight is the *actus reus* for rape.

At common law, a husband could not be guilty of rape of his spouse.

The underage participant in intercourse cannot be found guilty as a conspirator to commit statutory rape or as an accessory to statutory rape.

In most jurisdictions, mistake of age of the underage participant is not a defense to statutory rape. It is, however, a defense to the crime of attempted statutory rape.

Kidnapping

There are two elements to simple kidnapping:

>   false imprisonment, and

>   asportation (carrying away).

Demand for a ransom is a necessary element of aggravated kidnapping but not an element of simple kidnapping.

For the false imprisonment element of kidnapping to be present, the perpetrator must confine the victim against his will, and the victim must be aware of the confinement.

Any movement of the victim of false imprisonment without his consent from the place where he is imprisoned will satisfy the asportation element of kidnapping.

Property Crimes

Distinguishing the Three Common Law Theft Crimes

The three common law theft crimes are:

> larceny,
>
> embezzlement,
>
> obtaining property by false pretenses.

Since these three crimes are mutually exclusive, many questions require that you distinguish between them.

Larceny requires a tresspassory taking; the defendant cannot have the rightful possession at the time the property is removed from the victim.

Embezzlement occurs when the defendant had rightful possession at the time the conversion occurred.

Obtaining property by false pretenses occurs when the defendant obtains title to the property as well as possession of the property as the result of a fraudulent act.

Larceny

Larceny is the tresspassory taking and asportation (carrying-away) of the personal property of another, with the intent to deprive the possessor of the property permanently.

An intent to destroy the property is equivalent to an intent to deprive the possessor of the property permanently.

Any movement of the property of another, no matter how slight, satisfies the asportation element of larceny.

The specific intent necessary for larceny (i.e., to permanently deprive the person entitled to possession of the property) is missing if the defendant intended to return the property at the time he committed the tresspassory taking.

If the property is unintentionally destroyed while in possession of a defendant who took it with the intention of returning it, the defendant is not guilty of larceny.

If the defendant does not have an intent to steal because he mistakenly thinks, either reasonably or unreasonably, that the property belongs to him, then he is not guilty of larceny.

The tresspassory taking element of larceny is satisfied if an innocent agent of the defendant takes the property at the direction of the defendant.

A person holding title to property can be guilty of larceny if he wrongfully takes that property from a person entitled to possession of it.

If a lower-level employee is in physical possession of his employer's property, he only has custody of it. If he converts that property to his use and has the intent to steal, he is guilty of the crime of larceny, not embezzlement.

If a bailee, who has possession of the totality of the goods entrusted to him by the bailor, breaks into the container holding all of the goods and takes a portion of them, he is deemed only to have custody of the goods taken. Since he does not have a "possession" of the goods, the crime is larceny, not embezzlement.

Embezzlement

Embezzlement is completed when a person in rightful possession of property converts it to his use with the intention of permanently depriving it from the owner of the property. An offer to return the property at a later date does not negate the crime.

Embezzlement only occurs when the defendant in rightful possession of the personal property of another converts it to his use.

Obtaining Property by False Pretenses

To constitute the crime of obtaining property by false pretenses:

(a) There must be a material fact which is false.

(b) The defendant must know that it is false; an honest but unreasonable belief that the statement is true is not enough to constitute guilt.

(c) The victim must rely on the statement of material fact.

(d) The defendant must obtain title to the property. If the property is cash and is deliberately delivered to the defendant, then the defendant's possession would equal title.

(e) The defendant must intend to deprive the victim of the property permanently.

An honest belief in the truth of the representation by the defendant, even if that belief it unreasonable, negates the specific intent necessary for the crime of obtaining property by false pretenses.

Larceny by Trick

Larceny by trick is a form of larceny which occurs when the defendant obtains possession of the property by fraud. Since he does not have rightful possession of the property at the time he forms the intent to steal, there is a tresspassory taking, and the crime is known as larceny by trick. Even though the defendant has physical possession of the property, this is not a conversion from one in possession, so the crime is not embezzlement.

Receiving Stolen Goods

A belief, either reasonable or unreasonable, that the goods possessed by the defendant were not stolen goods is a defense to the crime of receiving stolen goods.

The property must have the characteristic of being "stolen goods" at the time the defendant possesses them for a conviction to occur. If goods once stolen are recovered by the police, restored to their rightful owners, and then offered to a defendant, the defendant cannot be convicted of receiving stolen goods.

Robbery

The underlying crimes of larceny or attempted larceny are essential elements of the crimes of robbery and attempted robbery.

For the crime to be robbery and not larceny, the tresspassory taking must take place from the person through force or intimidation.

The element "from the person" means property within the control of the person.

The force and intimidation must coincide with the larceny.

If all of the elements or robbery are present, the underlying crime of larceny and (if present) the underlying crimes of assault and battery, merge into the crime of robbery.

If the defendant already has stolen some property, the use of force or intimidation to retain possession of it does not constitute the crime of robbery.

The threat to use force in the future and obtaining property through the use of that threat is the crime of extortion, not robbery.

The victim must be intimidated for the crime to be robbery.

Burglary

Common law burglary is defined as breaking and entering the dwelling-house of another (burglary cannot be committed in your own house), in the nighttime, for the purpose of committing a felony therein.

Modern statutes have redefined burglary to eliminate the nighttime requirement and include all buildings.

The breaking and the entering elements of burglary need not occur at the same time.

To be guilty of burglary, the defendant must have the specific intent to commit a felony on the premises at the moment of the entering. There is no requirement for the intended felony to be successful.

If a person enters the property through an open door, the breaking element of burglary is not present.

Burglary is committed if the defendant breaks and enters a part of a dwelling house, even if he does not break and enter when he first enters the dwelling.

Breaking and entering need not occur by force. If the defendant obtains entry to the property through the use of fraud, the breaking and entering elements are present.

Since the common law definition of burglary requires that the property be the dwelling house of another, a person cannot commit burglary by breaking and entering his own home.

There is no breaking when entering through an open window or door or when the premises are open to the public.

However, a defendant who is in a space open to the public can be guilty of burglary if he breaks and enters into adjoining space not open to the public.

There is no breaking and entering if the defendant opens personal property such as a chest while he is in property open to the public.

A defendant is not guilty of burglary if he commits larceny on premises which are open to the public.

If the original entry to the property was not breaking and entering, the defendant could still be guilty of burglary if he breaks into a portion of the real estate once he is on the premises.

A defendant is not guilty of burglary if he enters a commercial establishment while it is open to the public, hides until after closing time, steals and then breaks out of the property.

Arson

Arson at common law is the intentional burning of the dwelling house of another. The definition has statutorily been expanded to the burning of any building, including one's own dwelling house, to defraud an insurer.

Arson has been committed if an act was done under circumstances where there was obviously a strong and plain likelihood that a fire would result even if the defendant did not desire that fire results from his act, or if the fire resulted from reckless conduct by the defendant.

Since the common law definition of arson requires that the property involved be the dwelling house of another, a defendant cannot commit common law arson by burning his own house.

However, most jurisdictions have enacted statutes to include the burning of one's home as arson.

For the defendant to be guilty of arson, there must be some combustion of a portion of the real property.

The burning of personal property alone is insufficient to constitute arson.

Starting a fire accidentally does not constitute the *mens rea* for arson.

However, if the defendant lets an accidental fire continue to burn even though he could have easily put it out, the decision to let it burn is sufficient *mens rea* for arson.

Forgery

Forgery is the fraudulent making of a false writing which has legal significance.

Inchoate Crimes

An inchoate crime (i.e., incomplete crime) is preparing to commit another crime (e.g., attempt).

Attempts

A person cannot be guilty of the crime of attempt to commit any crime unless he intends to commit the crime.

This applies to all crimes, including strict liability offenses where intent to commit the completed crime is not required.

The crime of attempt merges with the substantive crime if the defendant completes the substantive crime.

If the act which the defendant intends to perpetrate is not a crime, he cannot be guilty of an attempt at any stage of his action, even if he thinks his act is a crime and intends to be engaged in criminal conduct.

An attempt requires substantial preparation to commit the substantive crime. Substantial preparation requires proximity to the place and time of the execution of the target crime.

Attempt is likely to be found where all of the acts required for the actual crime have been completed.

Attempt is likely to be found where the defendant has progressed so far that he would be unlikely to stop without outside interference.

Factual impossibility is a defense to an attempted crime if and only if the defendant did not know that the commission of the crime was inherently impossible.

Conspiracy

Conspiracy is defined as a combination for an unlawful purpose.

The agreement among conspirators necessary for that combination can be inferred from the actions of the parties and need not be expressed.

To be a conspirator, a defendant must intend to agree with other conspirators and intend to accomplish the object of the conspiracy.

Conspiracy is a separate crime from the substantive offense which is the object of the conspiracy.

The crime of conspiracy does not merge with that substantive offense if the conspiracy accomplishes its objective.

A conspiracy is a completed crime at common law even if no conspirator has committed an overt act in pursuance of the conspiracy.

The crime is not complete under federal law until an overt act occurs.

At common law, a conspiracy starts at the time of the agreement.

In a jurisdiction in which there must be an overt act to complete the crime of conspiracy, the conspiracy commences when the overt act takes place. It ends when all of the objects of the conspiracy have been accomplished or when it is abandoned.

A person who is a conspirator is guilty not only of the crime of conspiracy but of all substantive crimes committed by co-conspirators according to the conspiracy, so long as they are within the scope of the conspiracy and are committed while the conspiracy is in existence.

For a defendant to be guilty of a conspiracy, he must combine with at least one other human being who is not necessary to the substantive crime to commit an unlawful act or a lawful act by unlawful means.

There must be as many conspirators as there are persons needed to commit the substantive offense plus one. Ordinarily, that means two or more persons to support the crime of conspiracy.

For example, if two persons are needed to commit the substantive crime (e.g., crime of adultery), there must be three conspirators.

A member of a legislatively-protected class, such as a minor involved in statutory rape, cannot be counted as a conspirator.

If all possible conspirators other than the defendant are acquitted of conspiracy, the defendant must be acquitted.

A person who has committed the crime of conspiracy is not guilty of the substantive crimes committed by the other conspirators according to the conspiracy if he withdraws from the conspiracy before the time that the substantive crimes are committed.

To withdraw from the conspiracy, a conspirator must disaffirm the goals of the conspiracy and inform his co-conspirators of the withdrawal.

Withdrawal is not a defense to the conspiracy crime.

If persons combine to perform an act which is lawful, they are not guilty of conspiracy even if they believe that the act they are to perform is illegal.

The impossibility of accomplishing the purpose of the conspiracy is not a defense to the crime of conspiracy.

A person is guilty of conspiracy only if he intends to combine with another to commit a crime.

Solicitation

The act of asking another person to commit a crime with the intent that the person asked should commit that crime is a sufficient *actus reus* and *mens rea* for the crime of solicitation.

Once a person solicited agrees to commit the crime, there is a conspiracy between the solicitor and the person solicited.

The crime of solicitation is merged into the conspiracy so that the solicitor is no longer guilty of conspiracy.

Parties to Crimes

The person who knows that the principal is committing a crime and intends to help the principal is guilty as an accomplice.

A person, even though he intends to help with the commission of an illegal act, is not guilty as an accessory if the act which he is helping the principal commit is, in fact, not a criminal act.

Presence at the scene of the crime without assisting or encouraging the principal does not incur accomplice liability.

However, if a person present at the scene of a crime encourages the principal to commit the criminal act, then he is guilty as an accomplice.

Supplying goods or services which have both criminal and non-criminal uses to a person, with the knowledge that they will be used in a crime, can cause the supplier to be guilty of accomplice liability.

Supplying goods which can only be used for criminal purposes, without precise knowledge of their intended use, can be the basis for accomplice liability if the recipient uses those goods to commit a crime.

An essential element of the crime of accessory after the fact is that the defendant must have aided the felon to hinder the felon's capture or conviction.

General Principles

General Intent Crimes

There must be a coincidence of the intent to accomplish the *actus reus* with the actual accomplishment of the *actus reus* for a defendant to be guilty of a general intent crime.

One definition of intent for purposes of the criminal law is that a person desires a result and that result occurs.

Intent is present even though the person thought the end would be accomplished by different means.

Specific Intent Crimes

To be guilty of a specific intent crime, the defendant must have the required specific intent, which is more than an attempt to accomplish the *actus reus* at the time he is accomplishing the *actus reus*.

For example, in the specific intent crime of larceny, the defendant must have the intent to deprive the possessor of his property at the time he engages in the tresspassory taking.

The mental state of maliciousness is associated with an intentional act, but it can also be present where the defendant acts recklessly.

Strict Liability

In the construction of a statute which does not include language requiring fault, a court may impose liability without fault (i.e., strict liability) after consideration of some factors.

Factors for imposing liability without fault include:

> legislative history,
>
> severity of the punishment for the crime,
>
> seriousness of harm to the public created by the criminal activity,
>
> defendant's opportunities to be informed of the facts which lead to an offense,
>
> difficulty of proving *mens rea*,
>
> number of violations,
>
> likelihood that prosecution is likely to occur.

No mental state is required for the defendant to be guilty of a strict liability offense.

Defendant is guilty of strict liability if he accomplishes the *actus reus*.

A principal can be guilty of a strict liability offense for an act performed by his agent which is within his scope of authority. Specifically forbidding such an agent to perform an illegal act is not a defense.

To be guilty of an attempt to commit a strict liability offense as distinguished from the guilt of the crime itself, the defendant must have the specific intent to commit the offense.

Mistake of Fact and Law

Neither a mistake of law nor a mistake of fact, whether reasonable or unreasonable, is a defense to a strict liability offense.

A reasonable mistake of fact is a defense to a general intent crime.

Neither a mistake of law nor an unreasonable mistake of fact is a defense to a general intent crime.

Both a reasonable and unreasonable mistake of fact and a mistake of law which prevent the specific intent from being formed are valid defenses to a specific intent crime.

If a crime requires the specific intent of "knowing" and the defendant subjectively does not know that his actions are criminal because he has relied on the erroneous advice of a lawyer, he is not guilty of the crime.

Insanity

If the individual knows what he is doing and knows that it is a crime, delusions caused by mental illness will not establish the defense of insanity under the *M'Naghten* test.

The *M'Naghten* test of insanity does not include the irresistible impulse test.

Intoxication

Generally, voluntary intoxication is not a defense to a crime.

However, if voluntary intoxication prevents the specific intent necessary for a specific intent crime from being formed, then the defendant is not guilty of the specific intent crime.

If the crime of first-degree murder requires deliberate premeditation and voluntary intoxication prevents the defendant from premeditating, then the defendant is only guilty of second-degree murder.

Causation

If the defendant sets in motion actions which cause the victim's death, the fact that the victim would have died sooner if he had not set those actions in motion is not a defense to the homicide crime.

A defendant is not guilty of murder, even though he inflicts serious bodily harm which will eventually result in death if the victim dies from an independent cause.

If a defendant inflicts serious bodily harm on the victim, but the harm would not cause death if the victim received proper medical treatment, the defendant is guilty of murder if the victim dies from his wounds because they were not treated properly.

The improper medical treatment is not an independent cause which will relieve the defendant of liability.

Justification

A police officer is not criminally liable if he uses deadly force to apprehend a person when he reasonably believes that the person is either committing or escaping from a dangerous felony.

A police officer is not justified in using deadly force to arrest a person for a non-dangerous felony or a misdemeanor.

A person who assists a police officer in apprehending a criminal has the same right to use force as the police officer whom he is assisting.

Constitutional Protections

Arrest

An arrest warrant is required to validly arrest an individual in his home, except where the arrest occurs when the arresting officer is in hot pursuit.

If the person commits a misdemeanor in the presence of a police officer, the officer has the right to arrest him without a warrant.

A police officer who has a reasonable belief that a person has committed a felony has the right to arrest him without a warrant at any place except in the defendant's home.

The fact that the defendant was unlawfully arrested is not a defense to subsequent criminal prosecution for the offense for which he was arrested.

However, evidence seized as the result of an unlawful arrest is inadmissible in court.

Definition of a Search

Only searches by governmental authorities, persons acting as their agents, or under their direction and control, are governed by the exclusionary rule of the Fourth and Fourteenth Amendments.

The exclusionary rule does not prevent the introduction of evidence obtained by searches by private individuals.

Searches which require warrants or an exception to the warrant requirements to be valid are closely tied to the concept of reasonable expectation of privacy.

While a homeowner has a reasonable expectation of privacy from ground level intrusion in the fenced-in backyard of his home, he has no reasonable expectation of privacy from surveillance from the air. He is protected from searches by advanced devices measuring heat escaping from his home. His person, desk file and file cabinets in a private office at work, a changing room in a clothing store and containers of personal effects are also protected areas.

An individual does not have a reasonable expectation of privacy in open fields which are beyond the curtilage of his home.

Warrantless searches beyond the curtilage of his home are permitted.

The government can obtain financial records in the custody of banks, accountants or other third parties by a subpoena on the third party without obtaining a search warrant.

There is no search and seizure if the object taken is in plain view from a place where the law enforcement agent has a lawful right to be.

Search Procedure – Standing

An individual only has standing to object to searches which violate his reasonable expectation of privacy, not that of third persons.

Ordinarily, he must show a possessory interest in the items seized, and a legitimate expectation of privacy in the areas searched.

The validity of a search cannot be challenged in a grand jury proceeding.

The proper way to raise the validity of a search is by a pre-trial motion to suppress. An objection to the admission of improperly-seized evidence at trial is available only when the facts concerning the search are not known to the defendant beforehand.

A defendant has the right to establish standing without admitting the seized evidence was under his control and without that admission being admissible against him at trial.

A guest in a home has standing to challenge a search of that home.

Search Incident to a Valid Arrest

Objects seized in a warrantless search made pursuant to an invalid arrest are inadmissible.

Objects seized in a search before the time there is a valid ground to make an arrest are inadmissible unless there is another ground than a search incident to an arrest to justify their admissibility.

The police may search the person of a defendant and the area in his immediate control incident to a valid arrest.

To protect their safety, police may, incident to a lawful arrest, search the premises in which the arrest took place to find other persons who may have been present and involved in the crime.

The search must immediately follow or be contemporaneous with the arrest.

Consent Searches

Consent must be by either the owner or the person entrusted with the property.

A person other than the defendant can give valid consent to search areas over which he has access jointly with the defendant.

Consent obtained by fraud or duress is invalid.

The consent given by an individual to search his property must be voluntary, but the suspect need not be warned that he doesn't have to consent.

The superintendent of an apartment house complex or the manager of a hotel does not have the authority to validly consent to the search of an apartment or room in a hotel rented to persons occupying the premises.

Automobile Searches

There is a lesser expectation of privacy in a motor vehicle than in a person's home, and therefore greater latitude to permit warrantless searches.

A non-owner passenger does not have standing to object to the search of an automobile.

If the police engage in the random stopping and searching of motor vehicles, the search is invalid.

The police may conduct a valid search of all vehicles at a fixed checkpoint, at the border, or the functional equivalent of a border.

If the police have probable cause to stop a motor vehicle, including a stop for a traffic violation, they may validly search the entire automobile (including the trunk and containers in the automobile) without a warrant. The search need not take place immediately. If the motor vehicle is impounded, the police may conduct an inventory search.

Regulatory Search

A regulatory search may be made without a warrant even if the search is to obtain evidence of criminal activity.

Regulatory searches are confined to businesses and premises which must be licensed to operate legally (e.g., gambling establishments, businesses serving alcoholic beverages) and businesses selling merchandise where criminal activity is likely (e.g., pawn shops).

Other Warrantless Searches

A "stop and frisk" pat-down search is constitutionally valid even if there are not grounds for a valid arrest, as long as there is reasonable suspicion of criminal behavior. The search is limited to a "pat down" search, but may be extended to a more intrusive search if the pat down uncovers an object which could be a weapon.

A search of school lockers without a warrant is permissible.

Searches Pursuant to a Search Warrant

Police or anther investigatory agencies may not issue a search warrant.

A search warrant may only be issued by a judge or other neutral magistrate based upon probable cause set forth in the application for the warrant.

The application for a search warrant does not require independent evidence on both the basis for the search and the reliability of the informant. The magistrate can issue a valid warrant based upon the totality of the circumstances.

The application for the search warrant must state, with particularity, the place to be searched and the objects of the search.

However, if when executing the warrant, the police find evidence not specifically mentioned in the warrant, they may validly seize it.

If the application for a search warrant is not sufficient to establish probable cause, but the magistrate nevertheless grants a search warrant, and the police execute it believing in good faith that the search warrant is valid, the property seized pursuant to the search is admissible.

If the police are granted a search warrant based upon information which they know is false, evidence obtained according to that warrant is inadmissible because the search is invalid.

Fruits of an Illegal Search

If a search is illegal, and information obtained as a result of that illegal search is used to conduct further searches which would otherwise be proper, or to obtain admissions from a defendant which they would otherwise not have obtained, the information or the evidence so obtained will be excluded from evidence as the fruits of an illegal search.

Coerced Confessions

If either the police or a private individual obtains a confession or admission by coercion (either physical or psychological), the statement made is inadmissible for any purpose.

This rule against admission by coercion applies even if the defendant has been given his Miranda warning and waived it.

If a coerced confession is improperly admitted, the conviction will not be overturned on appeal if the admission of the confession constitutes harmless error.

Miranda

The Miranda warning is applicable only when there is interrogation by the police while the defendant is in custody.

An individual is in custody if his freedom to leave the presence of the police is restricted.

A statement made to a private individual not working in concert with the police is not subject to the limitations of Miranda rights.

Volunteered statements are not the products of interrogation.

However, if the police engage in conduct other than questioning the defendant which is designed to elicit a statement from the defendant, that statement is considered the product of interrogation.

Statements made by a defendant in custody as the result of interrogation are inadmissible in evidence at a subsequent trial unless the defendant is warned of his Miranda rights and waives them.

If the defendant exercises his Miranda rights by demanding a lawyer, all statements made in response to questioning after that demand and before a lawyer is present are inadmissible. Further questioning can take place only after the defendant consults with his lawyer and agrees to further questioning.

A statement given in violation of the defendant's Miranda rights is admissible to impeach his credibility if he takes the stand in his trial and testifies in a manner inconsistent with the statement he previously gave.

If the defendant exercises his Miranda right to remain silent while in custody, that silence in the face of accusations made to him that he committed the crime cannot be used in the trial as an adoptive admission.

The police need not inform the defendant of the charge they are investigating to obtain a valid waiver of Miranda rights.

If a defendant waives his Miranda rights and agrees to submit to interrogation, he can be questioned about more subjects than the crime which is the primary object of the police interrogation.

Once a defendant is indicted or otherwise formally charged with a crime, the right to counsel accrues, and the defendant cannot be interrogated by police except in the presence of counsel, even if he has been given his Miranda warnings and has waived his Miranda rights.

Lineups and Other Forms of Identification

There is a right to counsel at a lineup only after the criminal process, such an indictment, has occurred.

The fact of a lineup identification without counsel present after an indictment is not admissible at trial, but the victim can still make an in-court identification.

Both testimonies about the lineup identification and a subsequent in-court identification are inadmissible if the pre-trial identification offends due process standards.

Due process is violated when the likelihood of proper identification is so remote because the victim could not observe the criminal or because the lineup, whether pre-indictment or post-indictment, is very prejudicial.

Right to Counsel

A conviction is invalid if the defendant has not had the opportunity of the assistance of counsel in the trial of all felonies and all misdemeanors for which the defendant is incarcerated.

A defendant has the right to refuse to have counsel appointed for him and to act as his lawyer.

If he acts as his own lawyer, he cannot later complain about the inadequacy of his representation or that he was denied his right to counsel.

A defendant has the right to have counsel provided for him to prosecute only one appeal.

A defendant's conviction will be reversed even if he had a lawyer if the representation is ruled inadequate.

An attorney representing a defendant who also represents a co-defendant may have a conflict of interest which is so serious that he cannot render effective assistance of counsel.

Public Trial

That public's right to a public trial can be enforced by the news media even if both prosecutor and defendant object.

The court has the discretion to ban or limit the public at a trial if there is either a substantial likelihood of prejudice to the defendant or a need to limit access to ensure an orderly proceeding.

Fair Conduct by the Prosecutor

A prosecutor has an affirmative obligation to disclose to the defendant all material known to him or in possession of the prosecutor's office which is exculpatory.

Speedy Trial

The beginning point to measure a defendant's right to a speedy trial is the time criminal proceedings commence, not the time that the crime is committed.

The prosecution can wait until the day before the statute of limitations expires to indict and thus start the clock on the right to a speedy trial.

The passage of time alone does not give the defendant the right to dismissal for lack of a speedy trial.

The defendant must also show prejudice from the delay.

Jury Trial

In a criminal case, the defendant is entitled to a jury trial if the greatest possible sentence can exceed six months in jail.

The defendant is entitled to be tried by a jury chosen from a venire in which there is no systematic racial, ethnic or gender exclusion.

There is a right to challenge the racial makeup of a jury even if the defendant is not a member of the race excluded from the jury.

When selecting a petit jury, neither the defendant nor the prosecutor may use peremptory challenges to systematically exclude individuals of one race or gender from the jury.

The state may constitutionally try a defendant before a petit jury which contains no members of the defendant's minority group as long as the procedure for selecting the jury venire was proper, and there was no systematic exclusion of jurors through the exercise of peremptory challenges.

To constitutionally satisfy the right to trial by jury, the jury need consist of only six persons.

A six-person jury may constitutionally convict only by a unanimous verdict.

If the defendant is tried before a twelve-person jury, he can constitutionally be convicted by the affirmative vote of nine jurors.

There are some procedural steps which a judge must take before she accepts a guilty plea. Otherwise, the plea will not satisfy the process standard that the plea is voluntary and intelligent.

The judge must inform the defendant that he:

> need not plead guilty,
>
> has a right to a jury trial.

The judge must also explain 1) the elements of the crime with which the defendant is charged and 2) the maximum possible legal penalty.

Confrontation

The prosecution has satisfied the defendant's right to confront the witness against him if the witness appeared at a preliminary hearing where the defendant had the right to cross-examine, and there is a valid excuse for the witness's failure to appear at trial.

The evidence given at the preliminary hearing is admissible under the prior testimony exception to the hearsay rule.

A criminal defendant does not have the Sixth Amendment constitutional right to confront his accuser at a preliminary hearing.

If the accuser is a child who might suffer substantial emotional damage by appearing in the same room as his accuser, the right of the accused to confront the witness is satisfied if the defendant can watch the testimony on closed-circuit television.

Severance

When two individuals are charged with the same crime and one of them has given a confession which implicates the other, the non-confessing defendant has the right to have his trial severed from that of the confessing defendant unless the statements in the confession which implicate the non-confessing defendant can be excised.

When a confession is admissible against the confessing defendant but is inadmissible against the non-confessing defendant, severance is not required under *Nelson v. O'Neil* (1971) if the confessing defendant testifies at the trial, because the non-confessing defendant has the right to cross-examine him about the truthfulness of that confession.

Standard of Proof

To satisfy its burden of proof in a criminal case, the prosecution must prove all elements of the offense beyond a reasonable doubt.

In a murder case, the burden of proof includes showing that the elements which would reduce murder to manslaughter are not present.

If state law so provides, the defendant can be given the obligation to plead affirmative defenses and prove them by a preponderance of the evidence.

Unless the state has shifted the burden of proof on insanity to the defendant, once a criminal defendant has raised the defense of insanity, the prosecution has an obligation to prove that he is sane beyond a reasonable doubt.

In a voluntary manslaughter prosecution, lack of justification is an element of the crime and must be proven by the prosecution beyond a reasonable doubt.

Imposition of the Death Penalty

A court can only order the death penalty when the defendant has committed a murder crime.

When there is a felony murder where several conspirators participated in the felony, the death penalty can only be administered to the individual who caused the death.

A statute which mandates the death penalty for a specific crime is unconstitutional because a jury must have the opportunity to impose the death penalty only after considering mitigating factors.

A death penalty can only be imposed by a jury.

A judge can not impose the death penalty after the jury has convicted the defendant of the substantive crime.

Fair Trial – Post-Trial Stage

The appellate court may constitutionally vacate a sentence and order a new trial if it determines that the verdict is against the weight of the evidence.

While the prosecution cannot, except in rebuttal, introduce a defendant's criminal record in a criminal trial, the judge can review the record for purposes of deciding the appropriate sentence.

Double Jeopardy

Jeopardy attaches so that the double jeopardy clause is operational in a criminal jury trial when the jury is sworn.

In a jury-waived trial, the double jeopardy clause becomes operational when the first witness begins to testify.

The defendant does not have the defense of double jeopardy when the judge declares a mistrial to benefit the defendant, or the appellate court orders a new trial as the result of the defendant's appeal.

The prosecution has the right to appeal a criminal judgment of not guilty only if a judgment of the appeals court will have the right to reinstitute a guilty verdict and there will be no new trial.

If a defendant is tried and convicted of a criminal offense of assault and battery and the victim later dies, the defense of double jeopardy does not apply to a subsequent homicide prosecution for the death arising out of the acts which constituted the assault and battery.

The statute of limitations on criminal activity starts to run at the time that the last act which is an element of the crime occurs.

Double jeopardy prevents prosecution in a subsequent case for any crime which is an essential element of the crime prosecuted in the first case.

However, double jeopardy does not prevent prosecution for a crime which occurred simultaneously with but was not an essential element of, the crime which was first prosecuted.

Collateral Estoppel

Under the collateral estoppel branch of the double jeopardy clause, the prosecution may not constitutionally litigate issues which have been litigated and decided in favor of the defendant in a previous criminal case.

Guilty Pleas and Plea Bargaining

Plea Taking Colloquy

A conversation between a judge and a criminal defendant (4 requirements):

> nature of charge,

> maximum authorized sentence and mandatory minimum,

> defendant's right to plead not guilty and go to trial, and

> by pleading guilty, a defendant is waiving trial and case proceeds to sentencing.

The court must ask the defendant if he understands each of these points, and must receive a voluntary affirmative response.

Failure by the court to advise the defendant of any of the above points supplies the grounds for a collateral attack on the plea.

If such an attack is successful, the guilty plea will be withdrawn, and the defendant will be given the opportunity to enter a new plea.

A defendant may withdraw a guilty plea after sentencing if:

> problem with colloquy,

> jurisdictional defect,

> defendant prevails if deprived of effective assistance of counsel, and

> prosecutor fails to fulfill his part of the bargain.

5th Amendment Privilege Against Compelled Testimony

Anyone can assert in *any* proceeding where individual testifies under oath.

Must be asserted *at first opportunity* or else it is lost.

Application:

> protected from compelled testimony only,

> doesn't apply to state's use of a person's bodies, and

> prosecutors cannot comment on its assertion.

Ways to eliminate privilege (3 methods):

I.   Prosecutorial grant of use and derivative use immunity.

The prosecution cannot the defendant's testimony or anything derived from it to convict.

However, a defendant can be convicted based on evidence obtained prior to a grant of immunity.

II. Defendant takes the stand.

Defendant waives the 5th as to anything properly within the scope of cross-examination.

III. Statute of limitations.

If Statute of Limitations (SOL) has run on underlying crime (because of no criminal prosecution).

Punishment

8th Amendment prohibits

1) Criminal penalties that are *grossly* disproportionate to the seriousness of the offense committed.

2) Death penalty statute that creates an automatic category for imposition.

3) Juries must be allowed to hear *all potentially mitigating evidence.*

4) Death penalty *prohibited* for: mentally disabled person,

presently insane,

under 18 at time of the offense.

Criminal Law and Procedure – Quick Facts

1. **Attempting**, even *with* criminal intent, to do an act which is NOT itself a crime is NOT a conviction that is likely to be upheld.

2. **Larceny** – the **taking** and **asportation** (i.e., carrying away) of personal property of another by *trespass* and with **intent to permanently deprive** the person of his interest in the property.

   For example: the moving of a refrigerator (by sales clerk) to the loading dock constitutes a taking and carrying away; since clerk did NOT have permission to move merchandise in this way, it was trespassory. Since the clerk intended to permanently deprive the store of an interest in the refrigerator when he moved it, his subsequent *change of heart* was **too late**.

3. The element of **carrying away** (i.e., **asportation**) is satisfied when there is some **movement** of the property as **a step** in carrying it away.

4. The **continuing trespass doctrine** renders continued possession of the property to be trespassory.

   So, if the trespasser later develops the intent to steal, the actions are considered **larceny**.

5. **Attempted murder** is a *specific intent* crime; though a defendant can be found guilty of murder when his actions demonstrate a very high degree of recklessness.

   If the charge is **attempted murder**, it MUST be shown that the defendant committed an act with the **intention** of killing someone.

6. The Fourth Amendment is NOT violated by a statute authorizing warrantless searches of a **probationer's home** where there are reasonable grounds to believe contraband is present.

7. If a statute is intended to **protect members of a limited class from exploitation**, members of that class are presumed to have been intended to be immune from liability, even if they participate in the crime in a manner that would otherwise make them liable.

8. The defendant has a legitimate defense where the **statute** under which he was charged was **NOT published or made reasonably available** before the conduct.

9. For an **affirmative defense** (e.g., insanity) it is permissible to impose the **burden of proof on the defendant**.

10. **Larceny by trick** occurs when **possession** of the property is obtained by the defendant's **misrepresentations.**

    Pretenses are the appropriate offense when the misrepresentations have prompted the victim to **convey title** of the property to the defendant.

Evidence

The statements of governing evidence law were compiled by analyzing the evidence questions released by the multistate examiners and setting forth the principles of law which governed the correct answer to each question.

An analysis of the questions revealed that there are a limited number of legal principles which are tested regularly and repeatedly since the correct answer to evidence questions is governed by the Federal Rules of Evidence (FRE). This compilation most likely contains the principles which will govern the majority of the evidence questions on the examination which you must answer correctly to pass.

You should review these principles before preparing answers to the practice multistate evidence questions and understand how these principles are applied to obtain the correct answer. Just prior to taking the MBE, you should commit these principles to memory.

Presentation of Evidence

Personal Knowledge

A witness must testify from his first-hand knowledge, except when testifying to statements which are defined out of hearsay or come within exceptions to the hearsay rule. Expert witnesses are an exception to this rule.

Under Federal Rule of Evidence 612, if a witness uses a writing to refresh memory for testifying, either while testifying or before testifying, if the court in its discretion determines it is necessary for the interests of justice, an adverse party is entitled to have the writing produced at the hearing to inspect it, cross-examine on it, and introduce into evidence those portions which relate to the testimony of the witness.

Leading Questions

Leading questions are permitted on direct examination when a trial judge declares the witness hostile.

Leading questions are permissible on cross-examination and direct examination concerning preliminary matters, for young children, and when the witness's memory is exhausted.

A lawyer for a party called by the opponent is not entitled to examine on cross-examination on new matters with leading questions

Argumentative Questions

A question in which the examiner argues with the witness is not permitted on direct or cross-examination.

Refreshing Recollection

If the memory of a witness is exhausted, the examiner is permitted to show him documents or make suggestions in an attempt to revive his memory so that he once again can testify from personal knowledge.

When a witness testifies from present memory, even if it is refreshed by reference to a document, testimony which he gives from that present memory based upon his knowledge is not hearsay. Since the evidence offered is the witness's present knowledge, the document itself need not be admissible.

If it is not possible to refresh the memory of a witness, but, at a time when his memory was fresh, the witness recorded that memory, the record of that past recollection is admissible as an exception to the hearsay rule, as long as it satisfies the requirements for the admissibility of a writing. Under Federal Rule of Evidence 803 (5), the document itself is not admissible, but the contents may be read to the jury.

If a witness refers to a document immediately before testifying or brings it with him to the witness stand, opposing counsel can examine it in the course of cross-examination.

Offers of Proof

If on direct examination, the judge sustains an objection to a question, the party conducting the examination must state for the record what the answer to the question would be (i.e., make an offer of proof), if he intends to appeal on the basis that the trial judge erroneously excluded the question from evidence.

An offer of proof is not required if a question is excluded from cross-examination.

Preservation of Issues for Appeal

Counsel must object to evidence at the time it is offered if he desires to claim on appeal that it was improperly admitted.

If counsel only files a general objection to the admissibility of evidence, which is overruled and the evidence is admitted, an appeal of that ruling will fail if that evidence is admissible for any purpose.

Preliminary Questions

The court shall determine preliminary questions concerning the qualifications of a person to be a witness, the existence of a privilege, or the admissibility of evidence. In making its determination, the judge is not bound by the rules of evidence, except those concerning privileges.

Thus, hearsay evidence which would be inadmissible at trial is admissible before a judge hearing evidence on a preliminary question of fact (Federal Rule of Evidence 104 (a)).

Hearing on preliminary questions of fact must be held by the trial judge out of the hearing of the jury when the interests of justice require it.

When the relevance of evidence depends upon the fulfillment of a condition of fact, the court shall admit it upon or subject to the introduction of evidence sufficient to support a finding of the fulfillment of the condition.

For example, if the issue in a case is whether the person making a contract was an authorized agent of a principal, the court will admit the evidence of the purported agent's conduct with respect to the contract, on the condition that proper evidence of agency is introduced.

Federal Rule of Evidence 104 (d) provides that the accused, by taking the stand on a preliminary matter, does not become subject to cross-examination as to other issues in the case, and thus any waiver of the right of self-incrimination is limited to the subject matter of direct examination, not a general waiver.

Lay Opinions

A witness who is not qualified as an expert can give an opinion on matters in which laypersons are competent to form opinions, provided that the opinion is based upon the witness's knowledge and is helpful to the trier of fact.

A lay witness who forms an immediate opinion based upon observations to which he testifies can testify to the opinion based upon his recent perception.

Expert Witnesses

An expert in a subject may be qualified and testify as an expert if scientific, technical, or other specialized knowledge will assist the trier of fact.

Even if he has been qualified as an expert by the trial judge, an expert witness can be cross-examined about specific matters in his background which bear on his qualification as an expert, because such testimony affects the weight which a jury should give to his opinion.

An expert witness is not required to testify from personal knowledge. He may draw inferences from out-of-court facts presented to him and may rely on the opinions of other experts if it is customary to do so in the field of expertise.

Federal Rule of Evidence 703 does allow an expert to rely on hearsay in reaching a conclusion, so long as other experts in the field would reasonably rely on such information.

However, Rule 703 distinguishes between expert *reliance* on the hearsay and *admitting* the hearsay at trial for the jury to consider.

Generally, hearsay will not be admissible when offered only because the expert relied upon it.

An expert witness may testify in response to a hypothetical question and is permitted to give his opinion with the use of hypothetical questions. If a hypothetical question is used, the assumptions contained in that question must contain all relevant facts.

Facts (or data) that are otherwise inadmissible shall not be disclosed to the jury by the proponent of the opinion or inference unless the court determines that their probative value in assisting the jury in evaluating the expert's opinion substantially outweighs their prejudicial effect.

An expert witness can give an opinion on the ultimate issue in a case, except for an opinion on the mental state of a criminal defendant.

The expert may testify in the form of an opinion and give reasons without prior disclosure of the underlying facts or data unless the court requires otherwise.

The expert may, in any event, be required to disclose the underlying facts or data in support of that opinion on cross-examination.

Qualifications and Competence of Witnesses

Under the Federal Rules of Evidence, witnesses who understand the obligation to testify truthfully are competent witnesses.

As a general rule, the Federal Rules of Evidence apply to matters of competency of witnesses and privilege in cases tried in federal courts.

An exception occurs where jurisdiction is based upon diversity of citizenship, or where state law provides the basis for decision in the federal court.

In those cases, the law of the state whose substantive law is applicable would determine the evidentiary rules to be applied for competency and privilege.

A juror may testify at a hearing on post-trial motions that the jury considered material from outside sources not properly introduced into evidence.

Judicial Notice

In civil cases, a jury is bound to take as true those matters which have been judicially noticed.

Under Federal Rule of Evidence 201 (g), a judge may not instruct a jury to find a fact in a criminal case, even if it is a fact that is subject to judicial notice.

Such an instruction to the jury to find a fact in a criminal case would violate the accused's Sixth Amendment right to a trial by jury on all elements of the crime.

A judicially-noticed fact in a criminal case allows the court to instruct on a permissible inference, but nothing more.

A court can take judicial notice on its authority, even if not requested by any party.

A party is entitled, upon timely request, to an opportunity to be heard as to the propriety of taking judicial notice and the tenor of the matter noticed.

In the absence of prior notification, the request may be made after judicial notice has been taken.

Judicial notice may be taken at any stage of the proceeding.

A jury in a criminal case is not bound to take as true matters which have been judicially noticed.

Cross-Examination

The testimony of a witness on direct examination will be stricken if effective cross-examination is denied, either because the witness does not appear for cross-examination, or refuses to answer questions relevant to the direct examination.

The striking of the testimony on direct examination is applicable even if a claim of privilege justifies that refusal.

If one party succeeds in admitting a portion of a document, the other party is entitled to introduce the remainder of the document even though there is no independent basis for admitting it, if in fairness it ought to be considered in conjunction with the portion of the document already admitted.

An out-of-court declarant whose testimony is received through admissible hearsay may be impeached by the same methods used to impeach a witness who testifies on the witness stand.

Exculpatory evidence elicited during its case-in-chief does not bind the government.

Who May Impeach

The credibility of a witness may be attacked by *any* party including the party calling him.

The character of a witness for truthfulness cannot be introduced until that character trait has been attacked.

The defense in a criminal case can offer either opinion evidence or reputation evidence of character traits of the criminal defendant which are inconsistent with the alleged criminal activity.

Prior Inconsistent Statements

Unless a prior inconsistent statement qualifies as an admission, a hearsay exception, or was given under oath; it is admissible only to impeach the credibility of the witness who made it and not for the truth of the matters contained in it.

Under Federal Rule of Evidence 613 (b) extrinsic evidence of a prior inconsistent statement is inadmissible to impeach credibility unless the attention of the witness is called to the statement on cross-examination or unless the witness is subject to recall.

This provision does not apply to the admissions of a party opponent as defined in Federal Rule of Evidence 801 (d) (2).

Bias

Evidence which suggests a reason why the witness might be testifying in a manner which is either favorable or hostile to the position of either party is admissible to impeach a witness.

Evidence of bias is considered important and, generally speaking, it is liberally admitted.

Extrinsic evidence can be introduced to prove bias.

If relevant on the issue of bias, evidence of insurance coverage and prior criminal convictions of the defendant are admissible.

Impeachment - Convictions

Evidence of prior convictions of a criminal defendant is only admissible to impeach his credibility and therefore is not admissible unless he has testified.

A party calling a witness who has a criminal record can anticipate the use of criminal convictions to impeach by introducing evidence of those convictions during direct examination.

The court must admit evidence of any conviction less than ten years old for misdemeanors or felonies involving dishonesty or false statement against any witness, including the defendant.

The court must admit evidence of a conviction less than ten years old for a non-fraud crime punishable by death or at least one-year imprisonment, of any witness other than the defendant unless the objecting party shows that the prejudicial effect of the impeachment substantially outweighs the probative value of the evidence.

The standard is reversed for the criminal defendant. Evidence of such crimes is admissible against the accused only if the impeaching party shows that the probative value outweighs its prejudicial effect.

The court *may* admit evidence of a conviction more than ten years old for any witness only if the impeaching party first shows that the probative value of the conviction substantially outweighs its prejudicial effect.

Federal Rules of Evidence 609 (c) permits the introduction of a juvenile conviction of a witness other than the accused in a criminal case if the conviction would be admissible to attack the credibility of an adult and the trial judge determines that admission of the evidence of the conviction is necessary for a fair determination of guilt or innocence.

Evidence of convictions for misdemeanors not involving dishonesty or false statement is always *inadmissible* to impeach credibility.

Impeachment - Prior Bad Acts

Under Federal Rule of Evidence 608, to impeach credibility, a witness can be cross-examined about specific instances of conduct which show fraudulent conduct.

If the bad acts bear on other character traits, the probative value of the acts as to credibility is substantially outweighed by the risks of prejudice, confusion, and delay, and would be excluded under Federal Rule of Evidence 403.

The examiner must take the answer given on cross-examination and cannot introduce extrinsic evidence of that conduct to rebut the answer given.

Impeachment - Reputation for Veracity

The character of a witness for veracity can be impeached by the introduction of extrinsic evidence, either in the form of opinion by a person who knows him to be a liar or by evidence of a person who knows of his reputation for veracity in the community and that his reputation is poor.

The character of a witness for veracity can be established in the same way it can be attacked, but such evidence is only admissible for a witness whose character for veracity has been attacked.

The reputation of a person's character among associates or in the community is admissible as an exception to the hearsay rule when it is admissible to prove character.

A criminal defendant's reputation for veracity cannot be attacked unless he has testified.

Expert testimony on credibility is usually found inadmissible because credibility issues are for the jury, not for the imprimatur of an expert.

Impeachment by Contradiction

Extrinsic evidence can be used to impeach a witness by contradicting him on a material issue in the case.

However, it cannot be introduced to contradict a witness on a collateral matter.

Impeachment of the Hearsay Declarant

When a hearsay statement or an admission has been admitted in evidence, the credibility of the declarant may be attacked and, if attacked, may be supported by any evidence which would be admissible for those purposes if the declarant had testified as a witness.

Evidence of a statement or conduct by the declarant at any time inconsistent with the declarant's hearsay statement is not subject to any requirement that the declarant may have been afforded an opportunity to deny or explain.

Rehabilitation and Redirect Examination

A judge is required to admit a question asked on redirect examination only if it relates to matters first raised on cross-examination or is designed to rehabilitate the credibility of a witness in the manner which that credibility was attacked on cross-examination.

For example, evidence of his good character concerning credibility is admissible only if evidence was introduced showing his bad character for credibility.

Evidence of lack of bias is admissible only if the credibility of a witness for bias was introduced.

A judge, at her discretion, can permit other evidence on redirect examination or in rebuttal, such as evidence which should have been present in direct examination or the case in chief.

Presumptions

A party seeking the benefit of a presumption does so by introducing evidence on the basic fact.

For example, to use the presumption concerning the regularity of the mail, a party introduces evidence that a letter is properly mailed.

Once a party activates a presumption by introducing credible evidence on the basic fact, and the opposing party produces no evidence on the presumed fact, the jury is obligated to find the presumed fact if they find the basic fact.

For example, the jury must find that a letter is received if they find that it was mailed unless the opposing party introduces evidence of non-receipt.

Once the party against whom the presumption operates introduces evidence on the presumed fact, the artificial procedural effect of the presumption disappears.

However, the jury can draw appropriate inferences from the basic fact to find the existence of the presumed fact.

For example, if one party proves that a letter was mailed, and the other party denies that it was received, a presumption is not operative, but the jury can draw an inference from the fact that the letter was mailed that it was received and that the evidence of non-receipt is not credible.

Application of Federal Law

The Federal Rules of Evidence apply in cases in the Federal Court except in diversity cases, where the evidentiary issue is:

1) the application of rules of privilege,

2) the competency of witnesses, or

3) the effect of a presumption.

In these three limited instances, the court will apply the governing state evidentiary rule.

Privileges and Exclusions

Husband-Wife Communications

Under the witness-spouse rule, a witness-spouse can refuse to take the witness stand and testify in any manner in a case where the criminal defendant is her/his spouse at the time of the trial.

The defendant spouse cannot prevent the witness-spouse from testifying if she/he voluntarily waives the right to refuse to testify.

Confidential communications between individuals who are at the time of the communication married to each other are privileged, even if the spouses are no longer married at the time of trial.

Each spouse is the holder of the privilege and can prevent the other spouse from testifying to the confidential communication.

The confidentiality necessary for the privilege is destroyed if the conversation takes place in the presence of third parties capable of understanding the conversation unless that third party is an eavesdropper whose presence is unknown to the spouses.

Attorney-Client Privilege

The claim of the attorney-client privilege applies only to confidential communications between a "client" and an "attorney" for the purpose of obtaining legal advice.

Both the terms client and attorney have expanded meanings for purposes of defining the privilege.

If a person consults a person whom he reasonably believes to be an attorney, for the purpose of obtaining legal advice, the privilege is applicable even though the person consulted is not, in fact, an attorney.

The privilege applies to conversations between a person seeking to hire an attorney and the attorney even if the prospective client does not in fact hire the attorney.

The attorney-client privilege belongs to the client who has the right to waive it.

However, the attorney has an affirmative obligation to assert the privilege in the absence of a waiver by the client.

Communications made to an attorney in the presence of third parties such as secretaries or investigators, who are reasonably necessary for either the attorney or the client to perform their duties, do not destroy the confidentiality required for the privilege to be applicable.

The attorney-client privilege protects communications between a client and a person working for the lawyer to provide the legal services requested by the client.

Disclosure made in the presence of persons not necessary, for either the attorney or client to perform their duties, destroys confidentiality and therefore the applicability of the privilege.

If two clients consult an attorney jointly concerning a common legal problem, communications in the presence of both clients and the attorney are privileged in any suit with a third party concerning the common legal problem.

Communications between the common clients and the attorney in the presence of each other are not privileged in litigation between the two clients.

An admission of a past criminal act by a client to an attorney is privileged, but the privilege is inapplicable if the client's purpose of the communication was to commit fraud or engage in criminal conduct in the future.

If the client knows that the purpose of the communication was to assist in the commission of fraud or future criminal conduct, there is no privilege even if the lawyer was not aware of the purpose of the communication.

The privilege is inapplicable if the client or a disciplinary body calls the attorney's conduct into question and the attorney must reveal the confidential communication to defend himself.

Documents in existence before the commencement of an attorney-client relationship do not become privileged merely because they are delivered to an attorney.

Written communication to an attorney seeking legal advice and written communications from the attorney to the client containing legal advice are privileged.

The attorney-client privilege protects communications from counsel to a corporation, including in-house counsel to an employee of the corporation concerning advice on legal matters relevant to the corporation's business.

Physician-Patient Privilege

The Federal Rules of Evidence do not recognize the physician-patient privilege.

In states where it is applicable, the physician-patient privilege applies to confidential communications made to a physician, and observations made by the physician when they are made for purposes of diagnosis or treatment.

The confidential nature of the communications or observations required for the physician-patient privilege to be applicable is not destroyed by the presence of third persons necessary to the performance of the physician's duties.

A patient is the holder of the physician-patient privilege.

The patient waives the privilege if he introduces evidence on his physical condition, or sues the physician.

Self-Incriminating Statements

The privilege against self-incrimination only gives a person the right not to incriminate himself through testimony.

The privilege against self-incrimination does not give an individual a right to refuse to exhibit physical characteristics, to give samples of bodily fluids, or to try on clothing.

The privilege against self-incrimination does not give an individual the power to suppress a statement which he has already made, except when there is a coerced confession or a statement is made in violation of his Miranda rights.

A defendant who testifies on a preliminary matter in a criminal case retains his right to refuse to testify in the trial on the merits.

In a preliminary hearing in a criminal case, a defendant who testifies cannot be asked on cross-examination questions beyond the scope of the issues at the preliminary hearing.

A defendant's admission of ownership of property to establish standing in a preliminary motion to suppress evidence does not carry over as an admission of ownership for purposes of trial on the merits.

When a defendant testifies after being granted immunity, neither his testimony nor evidence derived from his testimony can be used in a criminal prosecution against him.

If a witness at a hearing claims the privilege against self-incrimination, the judge must sustain the claim of the privilege if the witness reasonably believes that he might incriminate himself.

Other Privileges

By statute, some jurisdictions recognize:

> priest-penitent privilege,
>
> social worker-client privilege,
>
> privilege not to disclose one's vote,
>
> newsperson's sources privilege, and
>
> government secrets privilege.

The Federal Rules of Evidence do not recognize such privileges.

Relevancy and Its Counterweights

Probative Value

Evidence is not admissible unless it is relevant to a material issue in the lawsuit or is relevant to the impeachment of a witness.

Under Federal Rule of Evidence 403, the trial judge may exclude otherwise relevant evidence if its probative value is substantially outweighed by:

1) the danger of unfair prejudice,

2) confusion of the issues,

3) misleading the jury,

4) considerations of undue delay,

5) waste of time or

6) needless presentation of cumulative evidence.

The admissibility of a rape victim's sexual conduct is limited to two circumstances, providing the judge determines that the probative value of the evidence outweighs its prejudicial effect:

(1) if it involves other sexual conduct between the alleged perpetrator and the alleged victim, or;

(2) it involves sexual conduct with a person other than the defendant at the time of the alleged rape.

Use of Character to Prove Actions

In cases in which the character or a trait of character of a person is an essential element of a charge, claim, or defense, character is "an issue."

That character trait can be proved by evidence of reputation, opinion, or specific acts.

In defamation cases, character concerning the alleged defamation evidence is relevant both to whether the plaintiff has a certain character and to the extent of damages.

In a civil case, evidence of a character trait to show a propensity to act in accordance with that trait is always inadmissible.

The defense in a criminal case can offer either opinion evidence or reputation evidence of character traits of the criminal defendant which are inconsistent with the alleged criminal activity.

If the defense offers such evidence, the prosecution can rebut with similar reputation or opinion evidence consistent with the alleged criminal activity.

If the alleged crime does not involve fraud or deceit, character evidence concerning the defendant's honesty is admissible only if he takes the stand. In that circumstance, the prosecution can introduce character evidence concerning dishonesty and the defendant can rebut that evidence with character evidence showing honesty.

If the defendant has raised the defense of self-defense in a homicide case, the prosecution can introduce character evidence of the peaceful nature of the victim and the defense can then introduce character evidence of his quarrelsome nature.

Otherwise, the prosecution cannot initiate the proof of character in a criminal case.

Federal Rule of Evidence 405 prohibits evidence of specific acts indicative of a person's character when that character evidence is offered to prove that a person acted in accordance with the character trait on occasion in question at trial.

On cross-examination of a character witness for a criminal defendant, the examiner may inquire into the witness's knowledge of specific instances of the defendant's conduct to show that the witness's assessment of the defendant's character is not credible.

Courts require that the cross-examiner must have a good faith belief that the event occurred before inquiring into the act on cross-examination.

Evidence of the past sexual history of a rape victim is inadmissible except for prior sexual conduct with the defendant on the issue of consent or evidence that the defendant was not the person who engaged in the sexual conduct which constituted the rape.

Evidence of past sexual crimes by the accused is admissible in sexual assault cases and child molestation cases.

Evidence of Other Crimes

Under Federal Rule of Evidence 404 (a), evidence of other crimes, wrongs, or acts is not admissible to prove the character of a person to show actions in conformity therewith.

Under Federal Rule of Evidence 404 (b), prior bad acts can be admitted to prove the defendant's conduct if offered for some purpose other than to show that the defendant is a bad person, that is, that the defendant has a tendency to engage in particularized activity that sets him apart from others.

Evidence of prior bad acts is admissible to prove motive, opportunity, intent, preparation, plan knowledge, identity or absence of mistake, or accident.

There must be something unique about the method of committing the other crime for it to be probative on the identity of the defendant.

Proof of other crimes or acts is permitted by the introduction of substantial evidence that the defendant committed them. Convictions need not have occurred or be proven.

If the defendant raises the defense of entrapment, evidence that the defendant has committed other crimes is admissible to negate the inference that the police initiated the commission of the crime.

Under Federal Rule of Evidence 414, in a criminal case where the defendant is accused of child molestation, the defendant's commission of another offense or offenses of child molestation is admissible and may be considered for its bearing on any matter for which it may be relevant.

Habit, Custom and Routine Practice

Under Federal Rule of Evidence 406, evidence of habit of a person or of the routine practice of an organization, whether corroborated or not, and regardless of the presence of eyewitnesses, is relevant to prove that the conduct of the person or organization on a particular occasion was in conformity with their habit or routine practice.

Subsequent Safety Measures

Evidence of subsequent remedial measures (e.g., making repairs after the accident or posting warning signs), is not admissible to prove negligence or culpable conduct.

Evidence of subsequent remedial measures is admissible to prove ownership or control of the premises where the accident occurred, if the defendant has raised the issue.

Evidence of a change in the design of a product after an accident has occurred is not admissible to show that the change could have been made earlier.

Offers of Settlement

An offer made to settle a disputed claim and all statements made in such a context of the settlement negotiations, even if they are admissions of liability, is not admissible to prove liability.

An offer in compromise before the opposing party has made a claim is not made inadmissible by this rule because, until such time as the other party has made a claim, no disputed claim exists.

Evidence of an offer in compromise which has been accepted is admissible in a suit in contract to enforce it.

Federal Rule of Evidence 408 does not require the exclusion of any evidence otherwise discoverable merely because it is present in the course of compromise negotiations.

Federal Rule of Evidence 408 does not require exclusion when the evidence is offered for another purpose, such as proving bias or prejudice of a witness, negating a contention of undue delay, or proving an effort to obstruct a criminal investigation or prosecution.

Payment of Medical Expenses

Under Federal Rule of Evidence 409, an offer to pay or the payment of medical expenses, even one made before a dispute exists, is not admissible to show liability.

However, a statement made in connection with an offer to pay medical expenses is admissible as an admission.

Criminal Proceedings

If a criminal action has not commenced, an offer made to avoid criminal proceedings, and a statement made in connection therewith is admissible in a subsequent trial.

Once the criminal process has begun, evidence of an attempt to compromise in the form of an offer to plead guilty to a lesser offense or to plead guilty in exchange for a lighter sentence which was rejected, and statements made in connection therewith, are not admissible in a subsequent criminal trial.

Liability Insurance

Evidence that a person was or was not insured against liability is not admissible upon the issue whether the person acted negligently or otherwise wrongfully.

Federal Rule of Evidence 411 does not require the exclusion of evidence of insurance against liability when offered for another purpose such as proof of agency, ownership, control, bias, or prejudice of a witness.

Similar Happenings and Transactions

Evidence of events or circumstances which are similar to the material events in the lawsuit is not admissible to prove the relevant event unless the probative value is compelling.

For example, proof that a large number of people eating the same food at the same restaurant became sick with the same symptoms would be admissible on the issue of the cause of food poisoning.

However, proof that a driver had many accidents similar to the one involved in the litigation would not be admissible

Experimental and Scientific Evidence

Evidence of a scientific test which is carefully designed to represent a relevant event fairly is admissible even if the opposing party had no notice of the test and did not participate in conducting the test.

Demonstrative Evidence

The judge has the discretion to exclude relevant demonstrative evidence which is highly inflammatory when the less inflammatory material is available to prove the same point.

Writings as Evidence

Authentication: Chain of Custody, Voice & Proof of Signatures

Objects which do not have any identifying characteristics (e.g., cocaine or heroin), must be authenticated by proving a chain of custody from the point at which the object became relevant to the time of trial.

If the objects are sealed in some form of identifying container, such chain of custody proof is not necessary.

If someone is familiar with the image shown on a photograph and testifies from personal knowledge that it fairly and accurately depicts a relevant event, the photograph is admissible even though the person authenticating the photograph is not the photographer.

A witness may authenticate a voice, whether heard first-hand, through mechanical or electronic transmission or recording, by giving a lay opinion based upon hearing the voice at any time under the circumstances connecting it with the alleged speaker.

Telephone conversations can be authenticated by evidence that a call was made to a number assigned at the time by the telephone company to a particular person or business, if

> A) in the case of a person, circumstances, including self-identification, show the person answering to be the one called, or;

> B) in case of a business, the call was made to a place of business and the conversation related to business reasonably transacted over the phone.

A person who receives a telephone call cannot authenticate the voice on the other end of the conversation if he is not familiar with that voice even though the voice on the other end of the conversation identifies himself.

If a lay witness testifies that she is familiar with a signature, even though that familiarity was the product of a brief encounter in the distant past, the testimony of that lay witness is all that is required to authenticate the signature.

A handwriting expert can authenticate a signature by giving an opinion based upon a comparison of the disputed signature with an admittedly genuine signature.

A lay witness cannot can authenticate a signature by comparison.

If there is an admittedly genuine signature available, a jury can compare that signature with a disputed signature and make a finding on the genuineness of the disputed signature without any expert testimony to guide it.

An item can be authenticated by the circumstantial evidence of the manner in which the police obtained possession of it.

Certified copies of official records are self-authenticating and their contents, if required to be kept, are admissible as a hearsay exception.

Best Evidence Rule

To prove the content of a writing or recording, which consists of letters, words, numbers or their equivalent, set down by handwriting, electronic recording, other form of data compilation (e.g., photograph, X-ray films, videotapes), the original is not required.

Other evidence of the contents of a writing or recording is admissible if:

> a) All originals are lost or have been destroyed (unless the proponent lost or destroyed them in bad faith), or no original can be obtained by any available judicial process, and

> b) at a time when an original was under the control of the party against whom offered, that party was put on notice by pleading or otherwise that the contents would be a subject of proof at the hearing and that party does not produce the original at the hearing.

Secondary evidence used to prove a collateral matter is admissible despite the best evidence rule.

If a witness has first-hand knowledge of an event and has also made a record of his actions at the time he obtained that first-hand knowledge, he can testify about the event without producing the record. The best evidence rule does apply in this situation.

For example, a doctor who performs an autopsy can testify about it without producing the autopsy report.

The best evidence rule only applies when a party wants to introduce the content of a writing or recording.

Hearsay

Definition of Hearsay

Hearsay is a statement that is an oral assertion, written assertion, or the nonverbal conduct of a person intended by the person as an assertion, offered in evidence to prove the truth of the matter asserted.

Assertive statements made by the declarant while testifying at the trial or at a hearing are not hearsay.

Nonverbal conduct would be hearsay only if the person intended to make an assertive statement by the conduct.

For example, if a witness at a lineup points to the person he believes is the perpetrator of the crime, the act of pointing is assertive nonverbal conduct and hearsay.

A triage officer who separates the living from the dead at the scene of an accident is not making an assertive statement that a particular individual is dead or alive.

If the words of the out-of-court declarant must be believed for his testimony to be relevant, then that testimony is hearsay and must either be:

>   1) defined as non-hearsay by the rules, or

>   2) come within an exception to hearsay to be admissible in court.

If an out-of-court statement is hearsay and contains within it another out-of-court statement which is also hearsay, there must be a hearsay exception permitting the admissibility of each level of this totem pole of hearsay (see below) before the statement within the statement is admissible.

Evidence Used Circumstantially as Non-hearsay

Out-of-court statements which are relevant, even if you need not believe that the words contained in them are true, are only used circumstantially and are not hearsay.

Examples of non-hearsay statements include statements which show the knowledge or state of mind of either the declarant or the recipient of the statement, or the meaning to the parties of the words involved in a statement.

Non-hearsay – Prior Inconsistent Statement Given Under Oath

Under Federal Rule of Evidence 801(d) (1) (A), the prior inconsistent statement given under oath of a witness who testifies is defined as non-hearsay and is admissible for the truth of the matters contained in that prior inconsistent statement.

Unless a prior inconsistent statement of a witness on the stand:

  1) qualifies as an admission,

  2) qualifies under a hearsay exception, or

  3) was given under oath,

it is admissible only to impeach the credibility of the witness who made it and not for the truth of the matters contained in it.

Prior Consistent Statement

If a person testifying on the witness stand has made an out-of-court statement consistent with his testimony, that statement ordinarily is inadmissible as hearsay.

However, it is admissible for the truth of the matters stated in it if the purpose of offering the prior consistent statement is to show that the testimony given on the witness stand is not a recent contrivance after the opposing party has impeached credibility of the witness by use of a prior inconsistent statement, or when it is used to rebut an inference of bias, as long as the prior consistent statement occurred before the time that the bias arose.

In all other circumstances, a prior consistent statement is inadmissible hearsay.

Non-hearsay – Prior Out-of-Court Identification by Witness at Trial

Testimony of a prior, out-of-court identification of the criminal defendant by a witness is admissible if the witness is on the stand and testifying subject to cross-examination.

Non-hearsay – Admissions by Party

An out-of-court statement of a party to the lawsuit can be introduced by the opposing party as an admission, even though the statement was in the party's interest at the time he made it, and even though the party had no personal knowledge of the facts contained in the statement.

Evidence of his actions which are inconsistent with the position a party is taking in a case is admissible against him as an admission by conduct.

Non-hearsay – Adoptive Admissions

If a party through his actions adopts a statement of another, they are admissible as admissions.

Adoptive admissions usually occur when a party remains silent when a statement is made in his presence by another which he would deny if it were false.

Statements are not admissible as adoptive admissions when they are made in the defendant's presence at a time when he is entitled to remain silent because he is in custody and has Miranda rights.

A party may adopt a statement of another without knowing the precise nature of the statement if he indicates that its author is a reliable person concerning the subject matter of the statement.

Non-hearsay – Vicarious Admissions

Statements made by an authorized agent within the scope of his agency, a partner for partnership matters or a predecessor in the title for issues of the title are admissible as vicarious admissions.

The contents of a statement by a purported authorized agent are admissible to prove that an agency existed, but independent evidence is needed before the agency relationship is established.

Non-hearsay – Statement by Employee

Even though it is not admissible as a vicarious admission because the employee is not authorized to speak on behalf of his employer, the statement of an employee made at a time when he is employed, concerning matters within the scope of his employment, is admissible as an admission against the employer.

Non-hearsay – Statement Made by a Conspirator

During the time a conspiracy is in existence, statements made by one co-conspirator are admissible against another co-conspirator if they are made within the scope of the conspiracy and in furtherance of it.

A conspiracy terminates at the time the conspirators are arrested.

The contents of a statement by a purported conspirator are admissible to prove the existence of the conspiracy, but by themselves are insufficient to establish it.

Inadmissible Hearsay

Evidence which is hearsay and does not come within any hearsay exception is inadmissible except when offered on a preliminary question of fact.

Totem Pole Hearsay

If an assertive out-of-court statement contains within it another out-of-court assertive statement made to the first out-of-court declarant, the evidence contains totem pole hearsay.

Each out-of-court statement must come within an exception to the hearsay rule for the evidence to be admissible.

Hearsay Exceptions Requiring Declarant Be Unavailable

Definition of Unavailability

Federal Rule of Evidence 804 exceptions, those statements made in contemplation of impending death, declarations against interest, former testimony and statements of personal and family history are admissible only if the out-of-court declarant is unavailable.

The other exceptions, Rule 803 exceptions, do not require unavailability.

"Unavailability of a Witness" includes situations in which the declarant

> 1) is exempted by ruling of the court on the ground of privilege from testifying concerning the subject matter of the declarant's statements, or

> 2) persists in refusing to testify concerning the subject matter of the declarant's statement despite an order of the court to do so, or

> 3) testifies to lack of memory of the subject matter of the declarant's statement, or

> 4) is unable to be present or to testify at the hearing because of death or then existing physical or mental illness or infirmity, or

> 5) is absent from the hearing and the proponent of a statement has been unable to procure the declarant's attendance by process or other reasonable means.

A declarant is not unavailable as a witness if exemption, refusal, claim of lack of memory, inability or absence is due to the procurement or wrongdoing of the proponent of a statement to prevent the witness from attending or testifying.

Hearsay Exception – Prior Testimony

If the parties in a civil case where former testimony is offered are not identical to the parties who gave the testimony, the prior testimony is admissible only if the opposing attorney in the first trial had an opportunity and the same motive for cross-examination as the party against whom the statement is offered in the second trial.

Testimony given at a deposition is admissible as former testimony if the deponent is unavailable, or the rule of civil procedure authorizing the deposition does not require that the deponent be unavailable.

For former testimony to be admissible in a criminal trial, the testimony must have been given in a case where the defendant was a party.

Testimony given at a preliminary hearing in a criminal case where the defendant had a right to cross-examine qualifies as former testimony.

Hearsay Exception – Declaration Against Interest

A statement made by an unavailable out-of-court declarant is admissible as an exception to the hearsay rule if at the time it was made:

(1) was contrary to the declarant's pecuniary or proprietary interest, or

(2) would likely subject him to criminal or tort liability, or

(3) would likely render invalid a claim which he might possess.

If a declaration against interest is offered to exonerate a criminal defendant by showing that the out-of-court declarant committed the crime, the evidence must be corroborated before it is admissible.

The declaration against interest exception is not applicable to a statement or confession offered against the accused, made by a codefendant or other person implicating both himself and the accused.

Exception – Statement Made with Impending Death

A statement made with knowledge of impending death concerning the circumstances of the impending death is admissible only in civil cases and criminal homicide prosecutions.

There is no requirement that the declarant dies for the statement to be admissible in a civil case.

The out-of-court declarant must know that death was imminent at the time the statement is made.

Forfeiture Exception

Under Federal Rule of Evidence 804 (b) (6), a statement is admissible as a forfeiture for wrongdoing when it is offered against a party that has engaged in wrongdoing that was intended to and did procure the unavailability of the declarant as a witness.

Limitation on Hearsay Exceptions in Criminal Cases

Even though evidence may be admissible under a hearsay exception recognized by the Federal Rules of Evidence, the out-of-court statement will be inadmissible in criminal cases because of the confrontation clause, unless the out-of-court statement would have been admissible as a hearsay exception which was recognized at the time the Sixth Amendment became part of the constitution.

Catchall Exception

Evidence is admissible under the catchall exception if prior notice is given, it is offered on a material fact which is more probative on the issue than other evidence, and its admission will serve the purpose of these rules.

Hearsay Exceptions Not Requiring Unavailability

Hearsay Exception – Present Sense Impressions

If an out-of-court declarant makes a statement describing or explaining an event while it is happening or immediately after that, the statement is admissible as a present sense impression.

A person on the witness stand may testify to a declarant's present sense impression even though that witness was not able to observe the facts related by the declarant.

Hearsay Exception -- Excited Utterance

An excited utterance is a statement relating to a startling event or condition made while the declarant was under the stress of excitement caused by the event or condition.

A present sense impression must be more contemporaneous with the prompting event than an excited utterance but does not require an *exciting* event.

Hearsay Exceptions -- Statements of Mental or Physical Condition

A statement of present mental intention is admissible as an exception to the hearsay rule.

An inference that the person who possessed a present mental intention carried out that intention can be used to prove actions in accordance with that mental state.

A statement of present physical condition is admissible as an exception to the hearsay rule. Anyone hearing such a statement can testify to it.

A statement of past physical condition is admissible as an exception to the hearsay rule only if made to a doctor or other health care professional to obtain a medical diagnosis or treatment.

Hearsay Exception – Past Recollection Recorded

A statement is admissible as past recollection recorded only if the person whose recorded recollection is offered is on the witness stand and testifies that he has no present memory of the matter which is recorded.

When a document is admissible as past recollection recorded because the witness on the stand had testified that he had a present memory of the contents of the document when it was made, but does not have a memory presently, the contents of the document may be read to the jury, but the document itself is not admissible.

Hearsay Exception – Business Records

A memorandum or record of acts, events, opinions or diagnoses is admissible as a business record (provided it was kept in the custody of the regular custodian of those records) if it:

1) made at or near the time of the matter;

2) made by, or from information transmitted by, a person with knowledge;

3) kept in the course of a regularly conducted business activity, and;

4) was the regular practice of that business activity to make this memorandum report, record or data compilation.

A statement in a document does not come within the business records exception to the hearsay rule if the statement was outside of the scope for records about the business and kept by the business.

Statements contained in business records which are prepared for litigation are not admissible under the business records exception to the hearsay rule.

A record is admissible under the business records exception to the hearsay rule if it is made by a person who transcribed the record in the ordinary course of business and received the information transcribed from a person who obtained that information in the ordinary course of business.

Hearsay Exception -- Absence of Business Records

Under Federal Rule of Evidence 803 (7), a certification offered to prove the absence of a business record in reports which qualify as business records are admissible to prove the nonoccurrence or nonexistence of the matter if the matter was of a kind which the business record would ordinarily contain.

Hearsay Exception -- Public Records

Under Federal Rule of Evidence 803 (8), records, reports, statements or data compilations in any form of public offices or agencies

A) setting forth the activities of the office or agency, or

B) matters observed pursuant to duty imposed by law as to

which matters there was a duty to report, excluding reports of matters observed by police officers in criminal cases, qualify as exceptions to the hearsay rule.

Hearsay Exception -- Absence of Public Records

Under Federal Rule of Evidence 803 (10), a certification offered to prove the absence of a public record qualifies as an exception to the hearsay rule.

To be admissible, the certification must be prepared by a public official and must on its face indicate that a diligent search of the records was conducted.

Hearsay Exception – Learned Treatise

A learned treatise is a writing which has been established by an expert as authoritative on a particular subject on which expert testimony is offered.

The authoritative nature of the treatise can be established by cross-examination of an expert whose credibility is sought to be impeached by the treatise or can be established by another expert.

Under Federal Rule of Evidence 803 (18), the learned treatise exception applies only after an expert relies on the treatise upon direct examination or the treatise is called to the attention of the witness on cross-examination and the authoritative nature of the treatise is established.

The learned treatise exception allows statements from a treatise to be read into evidence when the treatise is "established as a reliable authority by the testimony or admission of the witness or by other expert testimony or by judicial notice."

The learned treatise exception allows statements from a treatise to be read into evidence where the treatise is "called to the attention of an expert witness" and is found to be reliable by the court. The rule does not require that an expert *relies* on the treatise.

When a learned treatise is admitted as an exception to the hearsay rule, the passage in the learned treatise is admitted not only to impeach the credibility of an expert but is also admitted substantively.

The treatise itself is not admitted as an exhibit, but relevant passages can be read to the jury.

Hearsay Exception -- Family History

Family records and reputation concerning family history, contained in documents such as family Bibles, are admissible to prove family relationships without proving the unavailability of the author of that history.

If the declarant is unavailable, his statement concerning his personal history is admissible as an exception to the hearsay rule.

Hearsay Exception -- Ancient Documents

As long as they are held in custody in a place where such documents are customarily kept, statements contained in documents more than 20 years old are admissible under the ancient documents exception to the hearsay rule.

Evidence – Quick Facts

1. The record on appeal MUST show that a **timely, specific objection** was made during the trial and that the challenged evidence was inadmissible on that ground, before the trial court's action can be considered an **error**.

2. The court is NEVER required to state the **reason for overruling an objection**.

3. The Federal Rules of Evidence have abolished the Common Law requirement that a witness is given an opportunity to explain **prior inconsistent statements** BEFORE extrinsic evidence of the statement can be admitted. The witness' opportunity to explain prior inconsistent statements may be provided AFTER the introduction of the statement.

Real Property

The statements governing Real Property were compiled by analyzing the property questions released by the multistate examiners and setting forth the principles of law which governed the correct answer to each question.

An analysis of the questions revealed that there are a limited number of legal principles which are tested regularly and repeatedly and that this compilation most likely contains the principles which will govern the majority of the property law questions on the examination which you must answer correctly to pass.

You should review these principles before preparing answers to the practice multistate property questions and understand how these principles are applied to obtain the correct answer. Just prior to taking the MBE, you should commit these principles to memory.

Real Property Law – Overview

Personal Property: goods or chattels that are not real property

Tangible property: physically defined property, such as goods, animals, and minerals

Intangible property: represents rights that cannot be reduced to physical forms, like stock certificates and bonds.

Choice of Categories

At common law, all found property is categorized in one of five ways:

Abandoned property – the owner has discarded or voluntarily forsaken with the intention of terminating his ownership, but without vesting ownership in any other person.

Lost property – the owner has involuntarily and unintentionally parted with through neglect, carelessness, or inadvertence and does not know the whereabouts.

Mislaid property – the owner has intentionally set down in a place where he can again resort to it and then forgets where he put it.

Treasure trove – a category exclusively for gold or silver in coin, plate, bullion, and sometimes its paper money equivalents, found concealed in the earth or a house or other private place. Treasure trove carries with it the thought of antiquity, i.e., that the treasure has been concealed for so long as to indicate that the owner is probably dead or unknown.

Embedded property – personal property which has become a part of the natural earth, such as pottery, the sunken wreck of a steamship, or a rotted-away sack of gold-bearing quartz rock buried or partially buried in the ground.

Under these doctrines, the finder of lost property, abandoned property and treasure trove acquires a right to possess the property against the entire world, but the rightful owner, regardless of the place of finding.

The finder of the mislaid property is required to turn it over to the owner of the premises who has the duty to safeguard the property for the true owner.

Possession of embedded property goes to the owner of the land on which the property was found.

Law of Finders for Personal Property

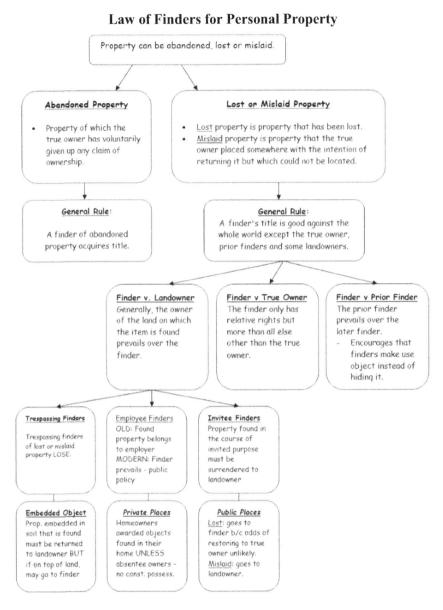

One of the major distinctions between these various categories is that only lost property necessarily involves an element of involuntariness.

The four remaining categories involve voluntary and intentional acts by the true owner in placing the property where another eventually finds it.

However, treasure trove, despite not being lost or abandoned property, is treated that the right to possession is recognized to be in the finder rather than the premises owner.

The Estate System

Fee Simple

A conveyance from owner to "A" or to "A and his heirs" creates a fee simple interest in A and no interest in the heirs of A.

Fee Simple Determinable

A fee simple determinable is a created by a conveyance which limits the fee by the words of the grant with words such as "so long as."

The interest in the grantor following a fee simple determinable is a possibility of reverter, a reversionary interest not subject to the rule against perpetuities.

In the case of a fee simple determinable, when and if the event which is a limitation on the fee occurs, the interest of the present interest holder is automatically terminated and the title goes to the grantor as the holder of the future interest.

A right given to a third person after the termination of a fee simple determinable (to A, so long as the premises are used for church premises and if they are not so used, then to B) creates an executory interest in B which is subject to the rule against perpetuities. That executory interest is invalid unless any right in the third party must occur within the period of the rule (lives in being plus 21 years) if it will ever occur.

Where an invalid executory interest fails, the grantor then takes because he still retains the possibility of reverter.

Fee Simple Subject to Condition Subsequent

A fee simple subject to condition subsequent is created by a conveyance which grants a fee simple interest and then terminates it if a contingency occurs, usually with the words "but if."

The reversionary type interest in the grantor is called a "right of entry for condition broken," and is not subject to the rule against perpetuities.

If the right of entry is given to a person other than the grantor, that right is an executory interest subject to the rule against perpetuities.

If the executory interest is invalid after a right of entry for a condition broken, the grantor takes nothing, and the grantee holds in fee simple.

A fee simple determinable or a fee simple subject to a condition subsequent are the only devices which will allow a seller who retains no land in the vicinity of the property conveyed to control the use of the property.

While the possibility of reverter becomes possessory automatically upon the breach of the condition, a person holding a right of entry for condition broken must bring a court proceeding to enforce that right before obtaining ownership.

Future Interests

A reversion is a future interest in the grantor which consists of any interest that he does not convey. A reversion is considered vested and is not subject to the rule against perpetuities.

A remainder is a future interest which is created in a party other than the grantor in the same instrument as the prior possessory interest and which is capable of taking effect at the termination of the prior interest.

A remainder is vested if it is ready to take in possession whenever and however the previous possessory interest terminates. For example, in the conveyance "to A for life and then to B," the remainder is vested because either B or B's heirs or devisees will own the property upon the termination of the life estate in A.

A remainder is contingent if there is a condition precedent which must be satisfied before the interest becomes possessory.

For example, in the conveyance to "A for life and then to B if B survives A," neither the remainderman, B, nor his heirs will take if B predeceases A.

A remainder is also contingent if the holders of the interest, such as heirs of a living person or unborn children, are unascertained.

A contingent remainder becomes vested once the condition precedent is satisfied or the indefinite beneficiaries, such as heirs of a living person, become identified when that person dies.

If a fee simple interest is conveyed subject to a condition precedent, title and possession remain in the grantor. The grantee does not take until the condition precedent has been satisfied.

While a remainder interest to the "children of A, a living person" is contingent if A has no children, that interest is classified as vested subject to open if A already has one or more children.

The interests of the existing children are reduced as the class expands to include afterborn children of A.

If there is a class gift, one to individuals bearing a family relationship to a named individual, such as the "grandchildren of A," afterborn members of the class can join the class until the class closes. If the grantor does not indicate otherwise, the class closes at the time any member of the class is capable of taking possession of the gift.

For example, if the gift is "to my grandchildren at the time they reach age 21," the class closes at the time the first grandchild is eligible to take the interest by reaching age 21.

A future interest, whether vested or contingent, can be alienated prior to its becoming possessory. However, the grantee of a contingent remainder takes nothing if the condition precedent is never satisfied.

An executory interest is an interest in land to a third person after a fee simple subject to divestment.

If an interest in land is a contingent remainder and cannot become possessory immediately upon termination of the prior estate because the condition precedent has not been satisfied, then the interest is transformed into an executory interest, which will take in possession at the time that the condition precedent to its taking is satisfied.

In the meantime, there is a reversion in the grantor.

Life Estates

At the termination of the measuring life of a life estate, the property reverts to the grantor unless the grantor has also deeded a remainder interest after the life estate, in which case title then vests in the remainderman.

A life estate which is also limited by an event such as remarriage is a determinable life estate and will terminate either on the death of the holder or upon the happening of the event, whichever occurs sooner.

Waste is an action of the life tenant which reduces the value of the future interest in the property.

However, if the life tenant takes an action which increases the value of the remainder, that action is ameliorating waste, and the life tenant is not liable for any destruction which occurs in the process of increasing value.

Both vested and contingent remaindermen have standing to enjoin a life tenant from committing waste.

The holder of a possibility of reverter, a right of entry for condition subsequent, or an executory interest after a fee simple subject to a condition subsequent does not.

When a mineral extraction activity had commenced before the property was divided between a life tenancy and a remainder interest, the life tenant can continue that extraction activity without being liable for waste and without having to account to the remainderman.

If a person holds a life estate *per autre vie*, the measuring life is a person other than the holder of the possessory interest, the estate terminates at the death of the person who is the measuring life, and not upon the death of the person in possession.

When a grantor conveys property subject to a mortgage to a life tenant and remainderman, the life tenant has an obligation to pay the interest on the mortgage and current real estate taxes so long as the property generates income sufficient to make such payments and the remainderman must make principal payments.

Neither life tenant nor remainderman is personally liable on the mortgage note.

If there is no income generated by the property, the life tenant is not personally liable to the remainderman for interest and taxes paid by him.

If the grantor deeds a life estate to a grantee, the grantee's life is the measuring life.

If the grantee sells his life estate, the grantee's life, not the purchaser's life, remains as the measuring life.

The Rule Against Perpetuities

The common law rule against perpetuities provides that no interest in land is valid unless it must vest, if it ever vests, within 21 years of lives in being at the creation of the interest.

The rule against perpetuities does not apply to reversions retained by the grantor and reversionary type interests such possibilities of reverter and rights of entry for conditions subsequent, or to the grantee who holds such a reversionary interest because of a conveyance from the grantor.

The rule against perpetuities does apply to future interests created in persons other than the grantor. Those interests are remainder interests, executory interests, and rights of first refusal.

The validity of the interest to which the rule against perpetuities applies depends on whether the interest must vest, or in some circumstances must become possessory, within the statutory period set by the rule.

The first issue in determining the validity of interest is when the period established by the rule starts to run.

If a will creates the interest in land, the period starts to run at the death of the testator. Individuals alive at that time are eligible to be measuring lives.

If an *inter vivos* conveyance creates the interest in land, the period starts to run at the time of the conveyance. Individuals alive at that time are eligible to be measuring lives.

If an *inter vivos* conveyance creates the interest in land to a trust, and if the trust is irrevocable, the period starts to run at the time of the conveyance.

If the trust is initially a revocable trust, the period starts to run at the time the power to amend or revoke the trust is terminated through the death of the person with the power to amend or terminate it or the relinquishment of the power thereof.

A child conceived, but not born, at the time of the commencement of the rule will be considered a life in being.

Thus, if a father dies before his child is born, that child will be considered a life in being at his death.

The period during which an interest must vest under the rule is a minimum of 21 years from the time when the period begins to run.

That period is extended by the lives in being at the time of the creation of the interest so that the maximum period for vesting is extended to 21 years after the death of a life in being at the creation of the interest, otherwise known as a measuring life.

An interest vests when all persons taking the interest have been ascertained, and there is no condition precedent which prevents their interest from becoming possessory whenever and however the preceding interest terminates.

If an interest must vest within 21 years of the time when the period of the rule starts to run, it is valid without considering any measuring lives which might extend the period during which the rule runs.

However, the 21-year period does not make it so that persons born within 21 years of the time that the running of the rule commences constitute measuring lives.

Remainders which may remain contingent beyond the period of the rule, executory interests which may not become possessory during the period of the rule, and rights of first refusal which may not become operative during the period of the rule, are invalid because of the rule against perpetuities.

Under the common law rule against perpetuities, any person is irrebuttably presumed capable of having children until death.

If the presence of that possibility prevents an interest from becoming vested during the period of the rule, then that interest is invalid.

Under the common law rule against perpetuities as it is applied to class gifts, the entire disposition is invalid if the interest of any member of the class is invalid.

When an interest is invalid because of the rule against perpetuities, the following rules determine the construction of the conveyance:

If the conveyance has multiple alternative dispositions and only one is invalid, the disposition is construed with the invalid gift deleted.

If the invalid interest is the residuary clause of a will, then the testator's heirs take. Those heirs under the modern law are determined as if the testator died at the time that the last valid interest terminated, not at the time of the testator's death.

If a conveyance creates the invalid interest, then the grantor or the grantor's heirs take by way of a reversion.

Powers of Appointment

A power of appointment permits the holder of the power either during that holder's lifetime or in the holder's will to direct the disposition of assets set up in trust by the grantor of that trust containing the power.

A power of appointment is special if the potential beneficiaries of the exercise of that power are limited, and it is general if the holder of the power can direct the assets to anyone.

Jurisdictions are split on the issue of whether the residuary clause of a will which does not specifically refer to a general power of appointment, in fact, exercises that power in favor of the residuary beneficiary.

The period of the rule against perpetuities does not start to run until the power of appointment of the holder is either exercised or expires.

The period for the rule against perpetuities for a special power of appointment starts to run when the trust becomes irrevocable.

Restraints on Alienation

A right reserved by the seller to repurchase the property at the same price which the owner could obtain it from a third party, a right of first refusal, is not an invalid restraint on alienation.

However, if such a right can possibly be exercised in a time which extends beyond the operative time for the rule against perpetuities, it is invalid, even during the fixed 21-year period of the rule.

A prohibition in a conveyance by the grantor of a grantee's right to alienate property or a provision forfeiting an interest if the grantee attempts to alienate property is invalid.

If an owner of property enters into a contract which restricts his right to alienate property that contract is valid.

Restraints on alienation are invalid only when they are imposed on the grantee of property by the grantor.

Characteristics of Co-tenancies

There is no right of survivorship when parties own property as tenants in common.

A joint tenancy is not devisable or inheritable, and cannot be severed by a will.

A co-tenant who makes improvements to property cannot charge his co-tenants for contribution to the cost of the improvements, but those improvements can be considered in a partition proceeding.

When property is partitioned, it is accompanied by an accounting between co-tenants concerning payments of expenses and collection of rents.

A co-tenant who occupies the property which he owns as a co-tenant does not owe rent to his fellow co-tenants.

Co-tenants who hold as joint tenants or tenants in common have an inalienable right to partition. The only ways in which a tenancy by the entirety can be partitioned is by joint deeds of the two co-owners, or when the tenancy by the entirety is converted to a tenancy in common by divorce.

The preferred method of partition is a physical division of the property. When a physical division is not feasible or cannot be accomplished so that each party is fairly treated, the partition is accomplished by a sale at auction and a division of the proceeds among the co-tenants.

When parties hold property in either a joint tenancy or in a tenancy by the entirety, at the death of one of the tenants complete title vests in the surviving tenant.

Furthermore, an involuntary lien placed against the interest of the dead co-tenant does not burden the surviving co-tenant.

If one joint owner mortgages his interest in the property and later dies, his interest passes to the other joint tenant free of the mortgage.

One tenant in common owes a fiduciary duty to permit the other co-tenant to maintain his proportionate ownership of the property by paying his proportionate share of the debt if one co-tenant acquires the property at a foreclosure sale.

Co-tenancy between Husband and Wife

A tenancy by the entirety can only be created between husband and wife who are married to each other.

Neither party can terminate the tenancy by the entirety by a unilateral act during the marriage.

If one spouse attempts to convey his or her interest, the conveyance is void, and the husband and wife still hold the title as tenants by the entirety.

If two persons who are not married to each other take title as tenants by the entirety, they hold title as joint tenants.

Conversion of Joint Tenancies into Tenancies in Common

The conveyance by one joint tenant of his interest to a third party converts the title to tenancy in common rights between the other original joint tenant and the third party grantee.

The joint tenancy is terminated even if the third party then reconveys to the original joint tenant.

If a mortgage on the property only creates a lien under state law, the granting of a mortgage by one joint tenant does not terminate the joint tenancy.

If the granting of a mortgage under state law vests title in the mortgagee subject to a right of redemption, then the granting of a mortgage by one joint tenant terminates the joint tenancy and transforms it into a tenancy in common between the original joint tenants.

The simultaneous death of two joint tenants creates an undivided one-half interest as a tenant in common in the estates of each joint tenant.

If A and B, who hold the entire fee in a parcel of land, jointly convey an undivided one-third interest in the property to C, A and B still hold an undivided two-thirds interest as joint tenants and not as tenants in common.

However, C holds his interest as a tenant in common with A and B.

Rights and Liabilities of Adjoining Landowners

The owner of land which is in its natural state can successfully sue an adjoining landowner who disturbs the support which the adjoining land provides on a strict liability theory without showing negligence.

The owner of improved land can successfully sue an adjoining landowner who disturbs that support only if he proves that the adjoining landowner is negligent.

Rights In Land

Express Easements

An express easement, or easement by grant, must be in writing and signed by the grantor of the burdened land to be valid.

If permission is given orally by the owner of land for the use of that land a license, not an easement, is created.

The license is terminable at the will of the owner of the land.

Express easements are interests in land subject to the recording system.

An easement by grant must be recorded to burden *bona fide* purchasers of the burdened land.

An express easement is subject to superior rights which exist on the servient estate at the time it is recorded.

If a mortgage which exists on the property at that time is foreclosed, the purchaser at the foreclosure sale is not burdened by the easement.

An easement is appurtenant if it burdens one parcel of land, the servient estate, for the specific benefit on another parcel, the dominant estate.

A conveyance of a parcel of land, which has the benefit of an appurtenant easement, automatically transfers to the grantee the rights in that appurtenant easement even if it is not mentioned in the conveyance.

If the benefits of an easement are appurtenant to one parcel of land, the owner of that land cannot use the easement to benefit an adjacent parcel which he owns. The easement is deemed to be "overburdened."

A holder of an appurtenant easement can only transfer the benefits of that easement by transferring the ownership interest in the benefited estate.

An attempted alienation of the easement rights to a person who does not own the benefited estate destroys the easement.

The holder of an easement has the right to make repairs to property within the easement which he has a right to use, such as stairs, pipes or roads, but does not have an obligation to repair unless he agrees to do so.

A person cannot have an easement on land which he owns in fee simple.

Therefore, if the holder of the benefited estate acquires the servient estate in fee simple, the easement is destroyed by merger.

If the two estates are separated at a later date, the deed to the dominant estate creates an easement over the servient estate only if the easement right is specifically granted in the deed.

However, this principle is not applicable unless the holder has identical interests in both the dominant and servient estates.

Even though an oral agreement will not create an easement, if a landowner induces a neighboring landowner to substantially rely on the fact that the owner will not assert his property right, the owner will be estopped from asserting property rights which he said he would waive.

Overuse of an easement can be prohibited by an injunction but does not destroy the easement itself.

When the exact location of an easement is not specified, the owner of the servient estate has the right to reasonably locate the precise right-of-way.

Once the location of that right-of-way is established, the easement's location becomes fixed and cannot be moved without the consent of the owners of the servient and dominant estates.

An express easement can be terminated by adverse possession if the owner of the land affirmatively bars the easement holder from using the easement for the statutory period.

However, failure to use an easement right, by itself, is insufficient to terminate an easement.

An express easement is valid for an indefinite time unless its duration is limited in the grant itself, or subsequently limited in time by the holder of the dominant estate.

The end of the reason for creating an express easement does not terminate an express easement.

Profit-a-Prendre

A *profit-a-prendre* is the combination of an easement right to enter the land of another and the right to sever interests such as timber or minerals from the land and take them off of the land.

Because a profit-a-prendre incorporates an easement right, it is an interest in property which must be created and recorded with the same formalities as an express easement and is unlimited in time unless a time limit is specified.

A profit-a-prendre can give the holder an exclusive right to sever property from the land so that the fee simple owner of the land no longer has that right.

If the holder has an exclusive right, he also has the right to divide that right and assign portions to other individuals.

If the profit-a-prendre is not exclusive, the holder cannot apportion it.

Easements by Necessity and Implication

Easements by necessity and implication arise out of the presumed intent of the parties to a conveyance.

If the document specifically states there is no intention to create implied easement rights, then neither an easement by necessity nor implication will arise.

An easement by necessity arises only where the parcel which is being severed by a conveyance of part of a larger parcel is landlocked and has no legal access of any kind.

The easement is an easement by reservation if the grantor is the party retaining the landlocked parcel of land.

An easement by implication (a situation where a *quasi*-easement exists at the time of the separation of the dominant and servient estates) will be created as long as the easement is reasonably necessary to serve the dominant estate.

An easement by necessity or implication arises only when there is no express easement.

An easement by necessity or implication can only be created at the time of the division of a commonly owned parcel.

If a parcel later becomes landlocked because of an eminent domain taking or otherwise, there is no easement over the larger parcel of land from which the landlocked parcel came.

An easement created by necessity ends when the necessity ends.

For example, if the government provided access to a formerly landlocked parcel, the easement by necessity which it once held over adjoining land would terminate.

An easement for light and air or for a view can only be created by an express easement. Such an easement does not arise by necessity or implication.

An easement by necessity or implication need not be recorded to be effective against *bona fide* purchasers.

Adverse Possession

Title by adverse possession is obtained if the possessor is in continuous, open and notorious adverse possession, and has exclusive possession for the statutory period.

The method of calculating the statutory period is:

> The period for adverse possession does not start to run while the true owner is a minor or is adjudicated mentally incompetent.

> If the adverse possessor initially goes into possession while a competent adult owns the property, the subsequent transfer of ownership to a minor or a person with a disability does not interrupt running of the statutory period.

> If the true owner transfers title to the property while the adverse possessor is in possession, the running of the statutory period is not interrupted.

> The adverse possessor is entitled to aggregate his time in possession against each successive owner to achieve adverse possession for the required statutory period.

> The consensual transfer of possessory rights from one adverse possessor to a subsequent adverse possessor permits the subsequent adverse possessor to include the time which his predecessor was in possession to achieve adverse possession for the required statutory period.

The requirement of continuous and exclusive possession states that:

> If the true owner possesses the property in common with the adverse possessor at any time during the required statutory period, the adverse possessor is no longer maintaining continuous, exclusive possession and must start the statutory period all over again once the true owner leaves.

> The actions necessary to satisfy the exclusive and continuous requirements depend upon the type of property involved.

The requirements are less strict for an uninhabited rural or seasonal property than for urban property.

Fencing in property adjacent to property owned or placing all or part of a building on property adjacent to property owned will satisfy the continuous and exclusive requirements.

The requirement that possession be adverse states that:

Because a co-tenant has a right to occupy all of the property which he holds as a co-tenant, open, notorious, and exclusive possession by one co-tenant for the statutory period will not establish adverse possession unless explicit notice was given to the other co-tenant at the beginning of that period.

Such notice is usually in the form of one co-tenant barring another from the use of the property.

Unless it is established that the possession was permissive, possession by an individual where nothing concerning permission is established is considered adverse.

An adverse possessor need not know that he possesses the property of another to obtain property by adverse possession.

Fencing in property belonging to a neighbor in the mistaken belief that the adverse possessor is fencing in his property is sufficient to establish adverse possession.

Title by adverse possession can be obtained to airspace by projections from a structure which overhang the abutting property.

After the actions of an adverse possessor have enabled him to obtain title by adverse possession, the interruption of his exclusive possession by anyone, including the true owner, will not defeat his title.

Neither title by adverse possession, nor an easement by prescription, need be recorded to be valid against the record title holder or purchasers from him.

If two persons act together to obtain title by adverse possession, the adverse possessors hold as tenants in common, not joint tenants.

If one of two adverse possessors dies, his interest in the property goes to his heirs or devisees, not to the surviving joint adverse possessor.

Easements by Prescription

The difference between the conduct necessary to achieve an easement by prescription and that needed to obtain title by adverse possession is that possession need not be exclusive to obtain an easement by prescription.

The manner in which the property is used during the period necessary to acquire an easement by prescription will define the scope of the easement at the conclusion of the prescriptive period.

Once the conduct necessary to obtain an easement by prescription continues for the time necessary to achieve the easement, continuous use of the easement after that is not necessary to maintain it.

An easement by prescription can be obtained even if the person acquiring an easement by prescription uses the property of another without communicating to him that the use is adverse.

If the use of property commenced as a permissive use, then notice to the owner that its character had changed and was adverse would be required to obtain an easement by prescription.

The holder of an easement by prescription has no obligation to keep it in repair.

Fixtures

Upon default, the holder of a properly recorded purchase money security interest can remove a fixture over the objection of a mortgagee of the real estate if the property subject to the interest is removable, even if the date of the mortgage preceded the date of the security interest.

A tenant for a fixed term has the right to remove personal property commonly known as trade fixtures, which are attached to the real estate by him, at the end of his lease term, even though the attachment of the property might cause it to be characterized as real property,

A person having an estate of uncertain duration (such as a life estate) who plants crops on that land can enter the land and remove the crops at the end of the growing season even if the possessory property right has terminated.

A person having an estate of uncertain duration who attaches fixtures to the real estate, which can easily be removed without damage to the real estate, can remove them within a reasonable time after the estate terminates.

In the case of a life estate, the fixtures can be removed by the personal representative.

The mortgagee cannot prevent the mortgagor from removing portions of the real estate secured by his mortgage if removing the structure would leave adequate security for the mortgagee and the removal is reasonable and proper in the proper management of the business.

Covenants

Covenants run with the land and bind successor owners if:

- they are in writing and formed a contract between the original parties;
- they touch and concern the land;
- the burdened party has notice of the covenant, either actual notice or constructive notice, through recording;
- privity exists between the party originally imposing the restriction and the party enforcing it;
- privity exists between the party originally burdened by the restriction and the party against whom it is being enforced.

The person who imposes a covenant which runs with the land cannot enforce that covenant against a subsequent purchaser of the burdened land unless at that time he is the owner of the land which was intended to be benefited by the covenant.

Zoning ordinances do not automatically override a private restrictive covenant. Whichever is stricter (i.e., zoning ordinance or covenant) will prevail.

To be binding, a restrictive covenant must be placed on the property at the time when it is conveyed.

The burden cannot be attached to a parcel of land at a later time by someone who has no interest in that parcel of land.

Although the Statute of Frauds applies to covenants, the recording of a deed containing a covenant running with the land, by a grantee of land burdened by the covenant, is a satisfactory substitute for a memorandum signed by the grantee.

Covenants running with the land can be enforced with injunctive relief.

Common Schemes

If the grantor consistently imposes similar covenants on a group of lots in a subdivision, he has created a common scheme.

There are two effects of the creation of a common scheme which are not true of covenants in general:

(1) The owner of any lots burdened by the restrictions of the covenant can sue the owner of any other lot burdened by the covenant to enforce the restrictions.

(2) The grantor can be required to impose similar restrictions on all remaining lots in the subdivision, even if he has not promised in writing that he will do so.

If there is no common scheme, persons owning lots not owned by the person imposing the restriction at the time it was imposed cannot enforce the restriction.

Mortgages

Once a mortgage is validly given by the owner or owners of the property, it remains a lien on the property until the obligation securing it is paid in full and the mortgage is discharged, or the holder of the mortgage voluntarily gives a discharge before being required to do so.

If the mortgagor agrees not to transfer the property subject to the mortgage without the consent of the mortgagee, the transfer without the mortgagee's consent constitutes a breach of the mortgage, permitting the mortgagee to declare the full amount of the mortgage note immediately or to foreclose.

The following rules apply when a mortgage is foreclosed:

If a mortgage foreclosure sale brings more than enough to satisfy the outstanding encumbrance, the balance is first paid to satisfy holders of junior encumbrances, and then any remaining balance is paid to the mortgagor.

A judgment lien is a junior lien to existing mortgages on property held by the debtor when the mortgage lien is filed.

If the mortgage foreclosure sale brings less than the amount necessary to satisfy the mortgage note and foreclosure expenses, the holder of the mortgage note may be able to collect the remaining balance on the note from the mortgagor or from purchasers from the mortgagor depending upon the terms of the mortgage note and the terms of the subsequent transfer of the property.

The title of a mortgage foreclosure purchaser is not subject to encumbrances placed on the land after the mortgage. For example, if O gives a mortgage to A and subsequently gives a mortgage to B, then P may take the property free of the mortgage to B if he purchases at the foreclosure of the mortgage to A.

However, a junior encumbrance is not eliminated by the foreclosure of a prior mortgage unless notice of the mortgage foreclosure is given to the holder of the junior encumbrance.

The holder of the junior encumbrance still may redeem the property from the foreclosing prior mortgagee, or he may still foreclose his mortgage.

A mortgagee has the right to take possession of the property to preserve it if the mortgagor is in default by failing to make the required payments or by breaching other mortgage covenants.

When a mortgagee takes possession, he assumes the tort liabilities of the equitable owner.

When a second mortgage is foreclosed, the purchaser at the foreclosure sale must continue to pay the first mortgage which remains as a valid prior encumbrance on the property.

If the mortgagor has given the mortgagee a mortgage on several parcels of land and has after that transferred some of the parcels without discharge of the mortgage and the mortgage is in default, the mortgagee must first foreclose on the remaining parcel owned by the mortgagor.

Furthermore, if he is not satisfied in full by that foreclosure, he may foreclose on the remaining parcels in the inverse order in which the mortgagor alienated them.

The following rules apply when the owner of the property who has given a mortgage transfers property without discharging the mortgage:

If the buyer agrees to assume and pay the mortgage, the buyer is primarily liable on the mortgage note, and the original mortgagor is only secondarily liable on the mortgage note.

If the mortgagor is required to pay the mortgage note, he can collect the amount paid from the buyer who purchased the property.

If the buyer takes subject to the mortgage (i.e., without agreeing to pay the debt), the buyer is not liable for any deficiency judgment on the mortgage note in the event of foreclosure but can lose the property through foreclosure if he does not pay the mortgage.

The original mortgagor is still primarily liable for any deficiency judgment on the mortgage notes.

If the mortgagor, buyer, and mortgagee enter into a novation at the time of transfer of the property, the buyer is liable to the mortgagee on the mortgage note, and the mortgagor has no liability on the mortgage note.

The following priorities apply when there are multiple security interests on the property:

A mortgage given by the purchaser to the former owner as part of the purchase price of the property, which is recorded immediately after the deed, takes precedence over any other liens placed on the property at the time of the conveyance.

The holder of a valid personal property security interest has the right to remove that property on default over the objections of a mortgagee who held a valid lien on the real estate at the time the personal property was affixed to the land.

The following rules apply to equitable mortgages, which occur when the owner of the property gives a deed rather than a mortgage to secure a debt, with the understanding that the creditor will deed the property back to the debtor when the debt is paid:

Neither the *parol evidence rule* nor the *Statute of Frauds* prevents the debtor from proving by oral evidence that a mortgage transaction rather than a sale of the property was intended when the debtor gave a deed to the creditor.

When the debt has been repaid, the debtor can require a reconveyance of the property if the title is held by the creditor or by someone who knew that the deed constituted an equitable mortgage.

If the creditor has transferred title to a *bona fide* purchaser, the debtor cannot obtain reconveyance of the property but can obtain damages from the creditor.

If the debtor defaults on the payment of the debt secured by an equitable mortgage, the creditor is not the automatic owner of the property but must foreclose the mortgage under state law.

The mortgagor of property may do such acts on the mortgaged property including removing part of the building which is part of the mortgaged premises in the course of good husbandry.

When there is an outstanding mortgage on real estate at the time the testator dies and devises it, the devisees take the property subject to the mortgage, unless the testator requires the executor to discharge the mortgage with other assets of the estate.

Other Security Devices

Other security devices, such as installment sales contracts, where the purchaser is given possession of property but does not receive a deed until all installments are paid, will be treated as a mortgage by a court.

Appropriate procedures required for foreclosure and redemption to protect the equity of the owner are required if the possessor of the property defaults on his obligation.

Choice of Property Devices

Covenants which run with the land are the most useful property devices to control the use of land without harming the marketability of title. It is subject to the limitation that the person enforcing the covenant must own the benefited land.

Easements are useful when a limited use of a parcel is desired for an indefinite period.

A conditional fee simple which takes the title away from the party in possession in the event he breaches his obligations is useful only where the marketability of the possessor's property interest is not an issue.

The holder of the residuary interest who will take if the condition is broken need not be the owner of any benefited land.

Zoning and other forms of governmental control are limited because they are subject to change by the political process.

Water Rights

Under the common law, each landowner through whose land a watercourse flows have the right to make reasonable use of the water.

In determining reasonable use, domestic uses such as drinking water, and water for toilets and washing are superior to artificial uses such as irrigation.

In states where riparian rights are governed by the doctrine of prior appropriation, the first riparian user to appropriate water for use on his property has the right to continue to use that quantity of water even to the detriment of other riparian owners.

Water from melting snows and rain is diffuse surface water.

A landowner may impound diffuse surface waters as long as he does not do so maliciously.

Vendor and Purchaser

Statute of Frauds

An action for specific performance of a land contract must ordinarily satisfy the Statute of Frauds.

The Statute of Frauds is satisfied if a memorandum signed by the party to be charged contains the essential terms of the agreement, namely, the price and an adequate description of the property.

The requirement of a memorandum signed by the party to be charged is not applicable if there are actions which constitute part performance.

A deposit is not necessary to make a written purchase and sale agreement enforceable, which satisfies the Statute of Frauds.

The Statute of Frauds applies to an agreement among co-owners to change the form in which they own the property, such as a change from a tenancy in common to a joint tenancy.

An oral agreement to waive the application of the Statute of Frauds is not effective.

The Statute of Frauds is not satisfied by a memorandum creating a brokerage contract.

Payment of the purchase price by the buyer and acceptance by the seller is in itself not sufficient part performance to take an oral agreement out of the Statute of Frauds.

Part Performance

If there is no written agreement, a court of equity can specifically enforce an oral agreement to convey if the part performance doctrine is satisfied.

In all cases, there must be an oral agreement to purchase the land which is relied upon by the purchaser to his detriment.

Part performance is satisfied in many jurisdictions if the seller has engaged in equitable fraud.

In other jurisdictions, the court will order a conveyance only if the conduct of the parties unequivocally proves that an oral agreement to convey existed.

This test is ordinarily satisfied when the purchaser pays the purchase price, has possession of the land with the permission of the seller, and makes improvements on the land. This test is known as unequivocal referability.

Enforceability of Purchase and Sale Agreements by Specific Performance

Both buyer and seller have the right to specifically enforce purchase and sale agreements for land as well as the right to a damage remedy.

Rights under a purchase and sale agreement survive the deaths of either the seller or the buyer and may be enforced by the executors of their respective estates.

Equitable Conversion

Because both buyer and seller have the right to specific performance of a contract to sell land, the doctrine of equitable conversion fixes the time of transformation of property from personalty to realty at the time a binding purchase and sale agreement is executed between buyer and seller.

Where the doctrine is applicable, upon the execution of a binding purchase and sale agreement, the buyer's interest is immediate interest in realty, and the seller's interest is immediately interest in personalty.

The risk of loss is on the buyer from the time that a binding purchase and sale agreement is executed.

A binding purchase and sale agreement which is recorded serves as notice to any subsequent purchaser from the seller, preventing them from becoming a *bona fide* purchaser.

Time of Closing

If a purchase and sale agreement contains a provision that "time is of the essence," then the seller and the buyer are in default if they do not close or tender performance on the date specified in the agreement.

If a purchase and sale agreement does not contain a provision that "time is of the essence," then each party must close within a reasonable time, and neither is in default if they fail to close on the date specified in the agreement.

Marketable Title

A seller need not own the property nor have marketable title to it at the time he enters into a purchase and sale agreement for the agreement to be valid.

If a purchase and sale agreement is silent with respect to the title to be conveyed, the seller is required to deliver marketable title.

The title of the holder of a fee simple determinable or a fee simple subject to a condition subsequent is not marketable.

The title is not marketable if there is an undivided interest which is not being conveyed or an encumbrance on the property which is not to be discharged.

The limitation placed by a zoning ordinance on the future use of the property does not render the title unmarketable.

However, if the property violates a zoning ordinance at the time set for the closing, the title is unmarketable.

If the state of the title would expose a potential buyer to litigation which is not frivolous, the seller's title is unmarketable.

A person who has obtained title to the property by adverse possession does not have a marketable title unless his title has been confirmed in a judicial proceeding.

A seller's obligation to deliver marketable title occurs at the time of the closing. He can use portions of the purchase price to pay off encumbrances which would otherwise destroy marketable title.

Survival of Covenants in the Purchase and Sale Agreement

If the buyer accepts a deed in fulfillment of the seller's obligations under a purchase and sale agreement, covenants contained in the purchase and sale agreement are no longer enforceable unless the agreement specifically states that they survive the closing.

The buyer nevertheless has the right to sue for a breach of warranty of the covenants contained in the deed.

Failure to Disclose Hidden Defects

Failure by the seller to disclose a latent material defect which could not be discovered by inspection will give the buyer a right to sue for damages or to rescind the transaction.

Title

Delivery and Validity of a Deed

To be valid, a deed must be signed by the grantor, adequately describe the property to be conveyed, and adequately describe the grantee.

Consideration is not needed for a deed to be valid.

However, consideration is necessary to enforce a promise to convey property.

A fraudulently altered release, a forged deed or an undelivered deed which is stolen, is a nullity, conveying no title.

Even if the instrument is recorded, a *bona fide* purchaser who relies on it in good faith is not protected.

If a deed is placed into escrow as part of as a commercial real estate transaction and the transaction is completed, the time of the transfer of title dates back to the time when the deed was delivered into escrow.

The recording does not deprive a grantor of a cause of action to rescind a conveyance against his immediate grantee.

The recording system protects only an innocent purchaser from the immediate grantee.

Title to real estate is transferred from the grantor to the grantee when the grantor delivers to the grantee a validly executed deed, even if the deed is not recorded.

Handing the deed to the grantee or his agent raises a rebuttable presumption of delivery.

The fact that a deed has been recorded raises a presumption that it has been delivered.

The subsequent redelivery of the original deed which has not been recorded from the grantee to the grantor does not retransfer title to the grantor.

A new deed signed by the grantee to the grantor is required to revest title in the grantor.

The requirements of a valid transfer of title are the delivery of a valid deed which has been accepted by the grantee.

Acceptance is presumed if the gift is beneficial.

However, the title has not been transferred if the grantee has affirmatively indicated that he has not accepted the deed.

The existence of a grantee who is identifiable with certainty is a requirement of a valid deed.

However, a deed which is delivered with the grantee intentionally left blank is valid and authorizes the person receiving the deed to fill in the name of the grantee.

A deed to a grantee who is dead at the time of the conveyance does not convey title to the grantee or his estate.

Unless a deed specifies a lesser interest such as a life estate, a deed conveys a fee simple interest.

A gift *causa mortis* may only be made of the personal property.

A gift may be made of real estate.

A deed is required as an element for a gift.

Description of Property

A property must be described with reasonable certainty to satisfy the condition that the property conveyed be reasonably identified in a deed.

A reference in a deed to a survey or plan in a deed is sufficient to identify the property, even if the survey or plan is not recorded.

If the deed description can not determine the exact location of the property conveyed, parol evidence is admissible to clarify the parties' intent.

If it is not possible to describe the property conveyed from the contents of the deed itself or with the aid of ancillary procedures, the deed is invalid.

Where there is a metes and bounds description of the property, and there is a conflict between distances set forth in the deed and monuments on the ground, the monuments prevail over distance.

If a boundary of the property is described as a private way, the owner owns to the midpoint of the way.

If the deed to property understates the acreage that the parties intended to convey, the grantee is entitled to have an equity court reform the deed to reflect the correct amount of acreage conveyed.

If abutters, uncertain of their exact boundary, fix a line by agreement, either oral or written, and after that abide by the boundary line, the agreement is valid and enforceable in fixing the boundary even though the boundary fixed by their respective deeds may be different.

Covenants of Title

A quitclaim deed contains no covenants so that the grantee has no claim under the deed against the grantor if the title is defective.

A warranty deed contains present covenants, such as a covenant that there are no encumbrances on the property, which run only to the grantee and do not run to his successors.

Present covenants are breached, if at all, at the time of conveyance, and thus are limited by a statute of limitations which starts at the time of the conveyance.

A warranty deed also contains future covenants which run to the grantee and successors.

The future covenant of quiet enjoyment is breached only at the time that the grantee or his successor in title is ousted from possession from all or part of the land by one having superior title.

The covenants of title in a warranty deed do not carry with it the obligation to pay for the defense of that title.

There is no requirement that a grantee who receives a deed with covenants need be a *bona fide* purchaser to sue his grantor for breach of warranty if the covenants are not true.

Estoppel by Deed

Estoppel by deed applies to validate a deed (in particular a warranty deed) that was executed and delivered by a grantor who had no title to the land at that time, but who represented that he or she had such title and who after that acquired such title.

For example, if A gives a warranty deed of Blackacre to B at a time when A does not own it, and A later acquires title from O, the true owner, then B is the owner of the property without the delivery of a new deed, at the moment A acquires title from O.

Operation of the Recording System

A deed or other instrument which has been delivered need not be recorded to be effective with respect to the original parties to the transaction.

A *bona fide* purchaser who is a subsequent grantee will prevail over a prior grantee who fails to record his deed.

A *bona fide* purchaser takes free of any encumbrance on the property given by his grantor which has not been recorded.

A mortgage lien does not automatically have priority over a judgment lien.

A mortgagee who loans money after a judgment lien is recorded is considered to have constructive notice of the judgment lien, and thus cannot be a *bona fide* purchaser and does not have priority over the judgment lien.

If O, the owner of property, delivers a deed to a grantee A and A records immediately, but O then subsequently delivers a deed of the same property to another grantee B, B loses in an action against A because he cannot be a *bona fide* purchaser with respect to a deed that has been properly recorded.

The issue of which grantee prevails does not turn on whether the first grantee is a *bona fide* purchaser.

That inquiry is relevant only for the second grantee.

If A receives and promptly records a deed to property as a gift and is thus not a purchaser, he will prevail in an action by B, a subsequent grantee, even if B paid O for an interest in the property.

The act of recording a valid purchase and sale agreement establishes the purchaser's order of priority in determining his rights against subsequent grantees or subsequent lien holders.

Bona fide purchasers who acquire from a person who appears to have good record title, but who obtained that title by a forged deed, are not protected by the recording system.

Bona fide purchasers who acquire from a person who has good record title, but who has lost title by adverse possession, are not protected by the recording system and will lose to the person acquiring title by adverse possession.

The following scenario demonstrates a deed that is recorded out of order in the chain of title in the recording system:

    (1) A deeds to B with a warranty deed but A does not own the property.

    (2) B records.

    (3) O, the true owner, deeds to A.

Under the doctrine of estoppel by deed, the deed passes immediately to B.

The deed from A to B is valid even though it is recorded before A had title.

In this case, someone searching title would not find the deed from A to B which made B the owner of the property if he were searching O's name in the grantor index. Instead, he would find the deed from O to A.

The same problem occurs, in the following scenario, when the grantee records late:

    (1) O deeds to A.

    (2) A fails to record promptly.

    (3) O deeds to B as a gift. B records.

    (4) A records.

In this case, B also prevails as the owner over A. Someone searching title would not find the deed from O to A in the grantor index if he were to search A's name until the time O alienated the property by deeding to B.

In each case, a subsequent purchaser can be a *bona fide* purchaser and prevail over the true owner because the deed recorded out of order is not constructive notice to a subsequent *bona fide* purchaser.

If a subsequent *bona fide* purchaser obtains title, the prior grantee has no further interest in the property.

For example, if O deeds to A who does not record and then deeds to B, a subsequent *bona fide* purchaser, and B then deeds to C, who knows of the deed from O to A, C will prevail over A because B prevails over A.

Characteristics of a *Bona Fide* Purchaser

Not all persons who might have an interest in property are "purchasers" who have the protection of the recording system.

Judgment lien holders, in particular, are frequently denied protection.

A statute frequently used in multistate questions provides:

"Any judgment properly filed shall, for ten years from filing, be a lien on the real property then owned or subsequently acquired by any person against whom the judgment is rendered."

If such a statute is in effect, the judgment lien, even though recorded, does not prevail against an owner who took from the person against whom the judgment was rendered but did not record his deed before the judgment was recorded.

A person who takes a conveyance in satisfaction of a prior debt is considered a purchaser in most jurisdictions.

A person need not search title and rely on the registry records to qualify as a *bona fide* purchaser, although he would be charged with the notice that such a search would provide.

If the subsequent grantee has actual knowledge of the deed to the prior grantee, he cannot prevail even if the prior grantee's deed is not properly recorded.

Any fact which would be discovered by an inspection of the property and lead to further inquiry can destroy a buyer's status as a *bona fide* purchaser.

Even though a donee is not a purchaser and will not prevail over a prior grantee who has not recorded, a *bona fide* purchaser from the donee will prevail over a prior grantee if the prior grantee has not properly recorded at the time that the purchaser from the donee accepts the deed and records.

Types of Recording Systems

There are two principal types of recording systems:

(1) The standard notice type recording statute provides:

"No conveyance or mortgage of real property shall be good against subsequent purchasers for value and without notice unless the same be recorded according to law."

(2) The standard race-notice recording system provides:

"No unrecorded conveyance or mortgage of real property shall be good against subsequent purchasers for value without notice, who shall first record."

The following transactions illustrates the difference between the two systems:

(1) O, the owner of Blackacre conveys to A.

(2) O, then conveys to B a purchaser for value who has no notice of the deed to A.

(3) A records.

(4) B records.

In a notice jurisdiction, B prevails because A had not recorded at the time B paid consideration and received a deed.

In a race-notice jurisdiction, A prevails even though B is a *bona fide* purchaser because A recorded before B.

Landlord-Tenant Relationship

A landlord-tenant relationship arises when the owner, or possessor of property, grants a party the exclusive use of the property for some time.

A lessor who knows of a hidden defect in the premises has an obligation to warn the tenant about that defect.

If a landlord denies a tenant the beneficial use of the property and the tenant moves out; he is not liable to pay the rent because the denial of that beneficial use is a constructive eviction.

Under the doctrine of retaliatory eviction, a landlord cannot lawfully terminate a month-to-month tenancy or bring eviction proceedings at the termination of a lease, if he is taking that action in retaliation for the tenant's exercise of his legal rights, such as reporting building code violations.

The landlord, not the tenant, is the beneficiary of a covenant not to assign a lease and has a right to waive the covenant.

Types of Tenancies

A periodic tenancy arises when there is no written lease, and the tenant occupies the property and pays rent on a periodic basis.

A periodic tenancy also occurs when the tenant continues to occupy at the end of the term of a lease.

The duration of a periodic tenancy is determined by the length of the period between rent payments.

A periodic tenancy is terminated by notice from one party to the other, given before the commencement of a rental period.

A term for years is a tenancy of any fixed duration. Except for short-term leases of less than one year, the Statute of Frauds applies to a term for years.

A term for years is terminated at the end of the term without notice by either party.

If the tenant holds over, a periodic tenancy is created as soon as the landlord accepts rent after the end of the term.

A tenant at sufferance occurs when a tenant has entered the property under either a term for years or a periodic tenancy, and that tenancy has been terminated.

A landlord may bring immediate eviction proceedings against a tenant at sufferance.

Assignment and Subletting of Tenancies

The tenant is obligated to pay rent during the entire term because of his lease contract unless the landlord, tenant, and assignee enter into a novation, in which case the assignee has the contractual obligation to pay rent and the tenant is no longer liable for the rent.

If the lease is silent on the subject, the tenant may assign his lease and sublet the property.

A covenant against assignment does not prevent a tenant from subletting the property and vice versa.

An assignee is a person who has received from a tenant an assignment of his entire remaining leasehold interest.

A person can become an assignee and entitled to possession even if he has not contractually assumed the obligations of the lease.

Even if he is not contractually obligated on the lease, an assignee is obligated to pay rent to the landlord during the time that he possesses the leasehold property because he is in privity of estate with the landlord.

If an assignee is no longer in privity of estate because he has further assigned the lease, he is not obligated to pay rent unless he has contractually assumed the obligations of the lease.

When a tenant validly assigns a lease, and the assignee assumes the lease, the assignee and the landlord (or the landlord's successors) are bound by all of the covenants in the lease which run with the land, such as a covenant to pay taxes or a covenant giving the tenant a right to purchase the property.

If the tenant enters into a subtenancy, leasing the property for a term less than the remaining term, there is a new leasehold between the tenant, who is in effect a landlord, and the subtenant.

Where a subtenancy is created, there is no privity of estate between the subtenant and the landlord, and the subtenant is not obligated to pay rent to the landlord unless he specifically agrees to do so.

License

A license is permission to use the land of another. It may be oral, written, or implied. It is revocable and is not subject to the Statute of Frauds.

Licenses are created when the occupier of land does not have an exclusive right of possession.

In contrast to a lease, a license permits the holder of a license to occupy the property but creates no property interest in the occupier.

If he holds the license according to a contract, he cannot specifically enforce the contract.

For a license to be irrevocable because of estoppel, the holder of the license must have justifiably incurred a detriment such as the expenditure of funds to upgrade the property subject to a license in reliance upon an agreement not to revoke it.

Real Property – Quick Facts

1. A proposed use (or improvement) of an **express easement** must NOT exceed the scope of the express burden.

2. A **plat** is ONLY intended to be a representation of the actual survey as made upon the land itself.

    The plat is like a certified copy of an instrument that will be controlled by the original.

    Where a survey as made and marked upon the ground conflicts with the plat, the survey prevails.

3. In a **partial condemnation case**, the landlord-tenant relationship continues, as does the tenant's obligation to pay rent for the remaining lease term.

4. The law of **landlord-tenant** traditionally refuses to recognize <u>frustration of purpose</u> as grounds for termination of a lease.

5. Where **joint tenant** A informs joint tenant B that he can do something with a portion of the land, and joint tenant B reasonably relies on those statements to his detriment, joint **tenant A will probably be estopped** to its effect.

6. The Statute of Frauds prevents the enforcement of an **oral agreement** concerning an interest in land.

7. **Reasonable Use Doctrine**— concerning the use of underground water—extends use to just about any use on the land that is NOT merely malicious or a waste of water.

8. **Special Exception to Rule Against Perpetuities** for *options to purchase attached to leaseholds*—when the one who holds the option is the current lessee, RAP does NOT apply.

9. If at the time a lease is entered into, the **landlord knows of a dangerous condition** that the tenant could NOT discover upon reasonable inspection, the landlord has a **duty to disclose** the dangerous condition; failure to disclose results in liability for any injury resulting from the condition.

10. When a **tenant continues in possession AFTER the termination** of her right to possession, the landlord has TWO choices of action:
    (a) he may treat the holdover tenant as a trespasser and evict her under an unlawful detainer statute; or

(b) he may, in his sole discretion, bind the tenant to a new **periodic tenancy**, in which case the **terms and conditions** of the expired tenancy apply to the new tenancy.

11. **Marketable title** is title **reasonably free from doubt**, which generally means free from encumbrances and with good record title.

    Easements are generally considered encumbrances that render title unmarketable.

    However, a majority of courts have held that a **beneficial easement** that was **visible/known** to the buyer does NOT constitute an encumbrance.

12. **Reformation** may be available where there is a **mutual mistake**.

13. In general, courts presume that **time is NOT of the essence** in land contracts.

14. The **doctrine of equitable conversion** holds that once an enforceable contract of sale is signed, the purchaser's interest is real property, and the seller's interest (right to proceeds) is personal property.

Torts

The statements governing Torts were compiled by analyzing the tort law questions released by the multistate examiners and setting forth the principles of law which governed the correct answer to each question.

An analysis of the questions revealed that there are a limited number of legal principles which are tested regularly and repeatedly and that this compilation most likely contains the principles which will govern the majority of the tort law questions on the examination which you must answer correctly to pass.

You should review these principles before preparing answers to the practice multistate tort law questions and understand how these principles are applied to obtain the correct answer. Just prior to taking the MBE, you should commit these principles to memory.

Tort Law - Overview

Definitions

Tort: a non-contractual civil wrong

Workers' compensation: laws that apply to those who are injured at work

Tortfeasor: one who commits a tort

Punitive damages: money awards meant to punish and discourage such behavior

Cause of action: the basis upon which a lawsuit may be brought to court

Personal injury practice deals with lawsuits or claims for money damages for injuries.

The most common type of personal injury case involves automobile accidents.

Intentional Torts

An intentional tort is one in which the party committing the tort intends to do the *act* (*knowing* – or with a substantial certainty that – it will cause an injury).

In situations where the same act is both a tort and a crime, the cases will be handled separately (civil and criminal court proceedings) within the legal system.

Intentional Torts against Persons

- Assault – apprehension of imminent harm

- Battery – unlawful contact with another

- False Imprisonment

- Defamation of Character

- Misappropriation of the Right to Publicity

- Invasion of the Right to Privacy

- Intentional Infliction of Emotional Distress

Intentional Torts against Property

- Trespass to Land

- Trespass to and Conversion of Personal Property

Unintentional Torts (Negligence)

Elements of Negligence

- Duty – defendant owed a duty of care to the plaintiff.

- Breach – defendant breached the duty of care.

- Causation – defendant's negligent act caused the plaintiff's injury.

- Damages – plaintiff suffered an injury.

Special Negligence Doctrine

- Negligent Infliction of Emotional Distress

- Negligence *per se* (i.e., violates a statute or regulation)

- *res ipsa loquitur* ("*the thing speaks for itself*")

Strict Liability – liability without fault

- Defective Products (e.g., product liability)

- Ultra-hazardous Activities (e.g., blasting activities)

- Dangerous Animals (e.g., wild animals)

Intentional Torts

Children under the age of 7, while not liable for negligence as a matter of law, can be liable for intentional torts if they possess the requisite intent.

Assault

To render a defendant liable for assault, the plaintiff must prove:

(1) that the defendant intended at the time of the act either to commit a harmful or offensive bodily contact, or to instill apprehension of such contact, and

(2) that the plaintiff was placed in apprehension of such imminent or immediate bodily harm.

No actual damages must be proven to complete the tort of assault.

Intent to cause apprehension of the offensive bodily contact is the state of mind required for assault.

Intent to make actual contact is not required.

The apprehension must be that the contact will be immediate.

A conditional threat of harm in the future does not constitute an assault but could constitute intentional infliction of emotional distress.

The tort of assault cannot be accomplished by words which create the required apprehension unless there is also an actual or apparent ability to cause an offensive contact.

Where the defendant intends to commit an assault, but not a battery, and the conduct which causes the assault results in a battery, the intention to commit the assault fulfills the intent requirement for a battery.

There is a privilege to commit an assault in self-defense, in defense of others, and to eject trespassers.

These privileges exist as long as the actor reasonably believed that the circumstances called for the conduct necessary to use an assault in one of these privileged circumstances, even if the actor was mistaken.

Battery

There are four elements for the tort of battery:

 (1) there must be an intention to cause a touching,

 (2) there must be a touching,

 (3) there must not be "consent" to the touching, and

 (4) the touching must be harmful or offensive.

Proof of actual damages is not required.

The Intent Element

If the defendant lacks the mental capacity to know that he is engaged in a touching, then he is not liable for battery.

If a party intended only to assault the plaintiff (placing in fear of imminent danger) and instead caused a touching, the intent to commit the assault is the intent necessary for the tort of battery.

Reckless or even willful conduct does not supply the mental intent for battery.

The Consent Element

Even if consent to physical contact is given in the course of an athletic contest, an intentional force which is beyond the scope of that consent will result in an actionable battery.

The Touching Element

Ordinarily, the defendant commits a battery by touching the actual person of the plaintiff.

However, the touching of an object close to the plaintiff, such as an item of clothing or a horse on which the plaintiff is riding, will satisfy this element of the tort.

Placing in motion events which will cause an offensive contact constitutes the offensive contact necessary for battery.

The Defense of Privilege

There is a privilege to use reasonable force to commit a battery in self-defense, in defense of others, and to eject trespassers.

These privileges exist as long as the actor reasonably believed that he was acting in circumstances which gave rise to the privilege and that the force was reasonable, even if there was a mistake.

An unreasonable belief will not sustain the privilege.

If a party is privileged to commit a battery on a third party, the fact that he unintentionally caused a touching of the plaintiff will not give the plaintiff a cause of action in the battery.

However, the plaintiff may have a cause of action in negligence.

An individual has a privilege to commit a battery if the battery will prevent an actual injury to the plaintiff and the actor reasonably believes that the plaintiff is in danger of receiving an actual injury.

False Imprisonment

The tort of false imprisonment contains the following elements:

(1) confinement (generally, knowledge by the confined)

(2) intention to confine

(3) lack of consent to the confinement

Since false imprisonment is an intentional tort, no actual damage must be proved as an element of the tort.

Confinement

Confinement occurs when the plaintiff's ability to move from his present location is restricted.

Physical force to restrict that movement is unnecessary.

Confinement requires that the plaintiff be aware of the limitation on his movement.

If the plaintiff knows he has a reasonable and existing alternate route to avoid the limitation of his movement, he is not confined.

Intention

The defendant's intentional action must be the cause of the plaintiff's confinement.

Privilege

A shopkeeper has a privilege to use reasonable force to detain someone reasonably suspected of shoplifting for a limited time, only to determine if that person has engaged in shoplifting.

A citizen has the right to arrest, which constitutes confinement if he reasonably believes a felony has been committed and he reasonably believes that the person detained was the felon.

A police officer has the right to arrest if he is executing an arrest warrant or is arresting for a felony or misdemeanor committed in his presence.

Therefore, a person who has the right to arrest is privileged to confine and has a defense against false imprisonment.

A wrongful arrest constitutes false imprisonment.

The fact that the person arrested was not guilty of the crime for which he was arrested does not automatically give rise to a cause of action for false imprisonment.

Trespass to Land

If the defendant intends to occupy the space he physically occupies, then a mistaken belief that the land which he occupies is not the land of the plaintiff will not be a defense to trespass.

Actual damages are not necessary to be successful in an action for trespass to land.

Nominal damages can be recovered.

If the defendant is unintentionally placed upon the plaintiff's land, there is no trespass, but there could be an action in negligence.

The negligence action requires damage to the plaintiff's land.

Nominal damages are not sufficient in a negligence action.

Consent of the landowner, whether express or implied, to the defendant's presence on his property, is a defense to trespass.

A person may be privileged under emergency circumstances to enter upon the property of another to protect his person or property.

An entry under such circumstances will not constitute a trespass, although the person using the property is required to pay the owner or possessor for any damage done to the property.

A property owner has a right to use reasonable means to bar people from his land (through the use of fences or other obstructions) and has a privilege to use reasonable force to eject a trespasser, but does not have the right to commit a battery on the trespasser which is not connected with the ejection.

A landowner is not liable to a trespasser for ordinary negligence but is liable if he could have prevented the injury after having become aware of it.

Conversion

Conversion requires a substantial interference with the plaintiff's personal property.

If the defendant has wrongfully appropriated the plaintiff's personal property and substantially damaged or lost it, or if the defendant refuses to return it after demand, plaintiff has an action in conversion for the full value of the property at the time when the defendant first appropriated it.

Trespass to Chattels

The tort of trespass to chattels (i.e., personal property), unlike the tort of trespass to land, requires proof of actual damage or actual interference with the plaintiff's possessory rights to the personal property.

Trespass to chattels occurs when there is an interference with chattels which is not substantial enough to constitute conversion.

The damages which are recoverable for trespass to chattels are limited to the diminution in the value of the chattels and compensation for the plaintiff's lost use of the chattels.

Intentional Infliction of Emotional Distress

The tort of intentional infliction of emotional distress is composed of the following elements:

(1) extreme and outrageous conduct by the defendant,

(2) intention of the defendant to cause severe emotional distress.

The plaintiff must suffer emotional distress but need not suffer physical harm and can collect damages for embarrassment and mental anguish.

The defendant's conduct must ordinarily be so extreme or outrageous that it would likely cause emotional distress in a person of normal sensibilities, but conduct can also be extreme or outrageous if the defendant knows of the plaintiff's unusual sensibilities and tailors his conduct to cause the plaintiff's emotional distress.

The defendant who commits an intentional tort might be liable for intentional infliction of emotional distress to a family member of the victim if the defendant knew that a family member was a witness to that intentional tort.

Negligent Infliction of Emotional Distress

If the defendant's negligence causes damage to an individual, a person who does not suffer physical injury as a direct result of the negligent conduct can recover for negligent infliction of emotional distress only if:

> (a) he experiences some actual physical harm as opposed to embarrassment or mental anguish, from the defendant's negligence, and;
>
> (b) he is either within the zone of danger or,
>
> (c) he witnesses harm to a family member.

The plaintiff could recover for negligent infliction of emotional distress only if the defendant's conduct was sufficient to cause emotional distress in a person of normal sensitivities.

Once this objective test is met, the plaintiff can recover for any emotional harm he suffers, even if the harm is unusual.

Negligent infliction of emotional distress caused by negligence in the handling of the remains of a loved one is compensable without proof of physical harm.

If the plaintiff only suffers property damage, as opposed to a physical personal injury caused by the defendant's negligence, damages for emotional distress cannot be recovered.

Once a plaintiff suffers physical injury caused by the negligence of the defendant, mental distress is an element of his damages, and the distinct elements of the tort of negligent infliction of emotional distress need not be met for the plaintiff to recover.

Nuisance

Private Nuisance

Nuisance is a theory of tort liability which is independent of intentional torts and negligent torts.

A plaintiff has a cause of action in nuisance when the defendant's use of neighboring land unreasonably interferes with the use and enjoyment of his land.

If there is an actual physical invasion of the plaintiff's land by the defendant's use of neighboring land, the cause of action is for trespass, rather than a nuisance.

Nuisance is applicable when there is detrimental use but not a physical invasion of the plaintiff's land.

A nuisance is a private nuisance if it unreasonably interferes with only a limited number of neighbors' use and enjoyment of their land.

Those neighbors have a cause of action for private nuisance.

Unreasonable Interference

Use of one's land in a particular manner before a neighbor arrived is a factor, but not a dispositive factor, when considering whether a use unreasonably interferes with a neighbor's land.

If the neighbor claiming unreasonable interference is using his land in a manner which requires freedom from normal neighborhood activity, he is unlikely to prevail in a suit with a landowner who has been conducting such normal activity before the time the plaintiff moved into the neighborhood.

However, the more objectionable the use of the defendant's land, the more likely that an adjoining landowner, even a newcomer, will prevail in nuisance.

The fact that a particular use is permitted on the offending land by local land use regulations does not *per se* establish that the use is not a nuisance, but it is evidence of the reasonableness of the use.

Courts can impose either injunctive or damage remedies in nuisance cases.

The social utility of the use of land which affects neighboring land, such as an operation which recycles material, will influence the court's choice of remedy and can lead to the denial of injunctive relief.

Public Nuisance

A nuisance is a public nuisance if it interferes with the use and enjoyment of a large area of neighboring land.

In general, only public agencies have standing to pursue the public nuisance cause of action.

However, a private plaintiff has standing to sue for public nuisance if the harm affects the plaintiff's land more directly and intensely than it does to the larger area affected.

Strict Liability

Product Liability - Strict Liability of Manufacturers

To prevail on a strict liability theory, a plaintiff must prove that the product:

(1) was defective when it left the defendant's hands,

(2) was rendered unreasonably dangerous by that defect, and

(3) caused the injury.

The exercise of utmost care by the defendant in manufacturing or handling the product will not defeat the plaintiff's strict liability claim if the product was defective, dangerous and caused injury.

A product could be defective because it is unreasonably dangerous, even if the manufacturer did not know of the danger and even if a regulatory authority approved its distribution.

The plaintiff must prove that the defective product was causally related to the plaintiff's injuries.

Suits against users of a product which causes injury must be based upon negligence, not strict liability.

Defenses to Strict Liability of Manufacturers

If the product was not defective when it left the manufacturer's or vendor's possession, alteration of the product after it left their possession is a defense to the plaintiff's strict liability action.

Plaintiffs can sue on a strict liability theory for harm from unavoidably unsafe drugs (including blood) only if the supplier does not notify the physician of the potential dangers.

Assumption of the risk is a defense in strict products liability actions.

In jurisdictions which recognize comparative negligence in product liability cases, the defense of assumption of the risk is merged into that defense.

In those jurisdictions , the plaintiff's damages can be reduced but not eliminated when he has assumed the risk or is negligent.

Misuse by the plaintiff is not a complete defense unless that misuse was unforeseeable, but it can be the basis of negligence in a comparative negligence jurisdiction so that damages will be reduced.

The following are NOT defenses to a strict liability action:

(1) Privity between the plaintiff and the manufacturer is not a condition which must be satisfied in a strict liability case against the manufacturer or seller of a product.

Liability extends to all foreseeable users and even bystanders injured by the product.

(2) Negligence in the use of a product by the owner of the product which harms a third party is not a defense in product liability cases brought by the third party but might be the basis for contribution among joint tortfeasors.

(3) Jurisdictions which retain contributory negligence as a defense in negligence actions do not recognize it as a defense in strict liability actions.

Strict Liability - Failure to Warn

Failure of the labeling on a product to warn of dangers of a specific use can cause the product to be defective for product liability purposes when used in a way which the manufacturer should have warned against, even though the product is not dangerous if used in other ways.

If the basis of product liability is a failure to warn about a dangerous product, the dangerous or defective nature of the product is not the relevant issue.

If the defect consisted of a failure to warn, the plaintiff must show that the injury would not have occurred if the warning had been made.

Product Liability - Strict Liability of Subcontractors

An assembler of a product which is dangerous is liable on a product liability theory if the dangerous nature of the product was caused by the defective parts supplied by a third party which was included in its finished product.

If a product is dangerous because of a defect in a component part, the manufacturer of the finished part and the manufacturer of the defective component are jointly liable to the plaintiff in strict products liability.

The manufacturer of the component would also be required to indemnify the manufacturer of the finished product if the finished-product manufacturer is required to pay the judgment.

Strict Liability Vendors

Strict liability in tort applies to a seller who is not the manufacturer when:

(1) the seller is engaged in the business of selling the type of product involved,

(2) the product is expected to and does reach the consumer or user without substantial change in the condition in which it was sold, and

(3) such a seller would have a claim for indemnification from the manufacturer if the manufacturer caused the defect.

Products Liability - Claims in Negligence

Plaintiffs have the right to sue manufacturers and retailers for negligently manufacturing or selling products which cause harm to them.

In such suits, evidence of due care by the defendant in manufacturing the product or the retailer in inspecting the product is relevant.

In jurisdictions which retain contributory negligence, it is a defense in a product liability action based on negligence.

A manufacturer is not liable for negligence if it used reasonable care to inspect the component parts assembled into a finished product.

Abnormally Dangerous or Ultra-hazardous Activities

Ultra-hazardous activity is that which:

(1) is not common in the area and

(2) involves a risk of serious harm to others which cannot be eliminated by the exercise of utmost care.

Blasting is an ultra-hazardous activity.

Defendants are liable in strict liability for abnormally dangerous operations.

A person hiring an independent contractor to engage in an ultra-hazardous activity is vicariously liable for his torts.

Plaintiff can recover in strict liability for damage caused by the defendant permitting substances (most commonly liquids) to escape from his land onto his neighbor's land.

If the person engaging in the ultra-hazardous activity warns of the danger, and the victim ignores the warnings and deliberately stays in the danger zone, then the victim has assumed the risk and cannot recover.

Animals

Owners of wild animals (e.g., reptiles, insects, and birds), are strictly liable for the harm caused by them.

Owners of domesticated animals (e.g., dogs, cats, and farm animals), are only liable for their negligence regarding the care and control of the animals.

Negligence

In all negligence actions, the plaintiff must prove actual, as opposed to nominal, damages caused by the defendant's negligence to prevail.

Risk and Duty

To be liable in negligence, the defendant must be under a duty to the plaintiff to avoid the risk of harm which occurred.

Generally, one has a duty to act reasonably, but one usually does not have a duty to act affirmatively to come to the aid of someone from a danger that he or she did not create.

Only the creator of the peril, someone under a contractual duty to protect those using a facility, or a close family member, such as a parent, has a duty to come to the aid of a person in danger.

Even though a person does not have an affirmative duty to come to the aid of a person in peril, once one undertakes to rescue, he has a duty to act with reasonable care.

Statutes in many jurisdictions called Good Samaritan statutes either exempt such individuals from liability or limit liability to situations where the defendant is grossly negligent.

A defendant who endangers only himself is also liable for his negligence to anyone who tries to rescue him from his own misconduct.

However, if the defendant is not negligent in placing himself in danger, he is not liable to an injured rescuer.

A police officer has a duty to intervene to protect citizens from criminal activity and does not have a cause of action.

The citizen whose negligent conduct gave rise to the need for intervention.

General Standard of Conduct

Except in special cases prescribing a different standard of care (e.g., the standard for a minor or a skilled professional), the standard of care applicable in negligence actions is that the person must act like a reasonable adult in the circumstances.

Evidence that the defendant complied with the customs established for the reasonable care of a customer is admissible but does not warrant a directed verdict in the defendant's favor.

Statutory Standard of Conduct

Violation of a statute is negligence *per se* or evidence of negligence, depending on the rule in the jurisdiction, if it can be shown that:

(1) the plaintiff was a member of the class of persons whom the statute was intended to protect,

(2) the harm which occurred was the type of hazard the statute was designed to protect against, and

(3) the violation contributed to the harm.

While violation of a statute may be negligence *per se* or evidence of negligence, compliance with an appropriate statute is not conclusive proof of the absence of negligence.

The fact that the defendant did not possess a license required to legally perform the act he was performing is irrelevant to the proof of negligence.

Even if the defendant has violated a statute and is negligent *per se*, the defense of contributory or comparative negligence is available.

Some jurisdictions impose a standard of gross negligence when a gratuitous guest sues his driver.

Standard of Conduct of Classes of Persons

Children under the age of seven as a matter of law cannot be found to be negligent.

Parents can be held liable for the torts of their child when they fail to exercise due care in raising or supervising the child.

Persons acting in the role of parents can be liable for the negligent supervision of the children.

An owner of a domestic animal is liable in negligence for harm caused by his failure to restrain an animal which he knew had a propensity to cause harm.

Method of Proving Fault

In tort actions based upon negligence, the trier of fact must find that the defendant is negligent by a preponderance of the evidence.

That standard of negligent by a preponderance of the evidence can be met if the plaintiff shows a probability that the defendant was negligent but is not met when the evidence only shows the possibility that the defendant was negligent.

Negligence can be proven by other means than by direct evidence.

Enough evidence concerning negligence can be proven by inference or circumstantial evidence to warrant sending the issue to the jury.

If the plaintiff died because of the conduct of the defendant, and there are no living witnesses to the accident other than the defendant, the plaintiff has met his burden of producing evidence of negligence by showing that the defendant might have been negligent in causing the plaintiff's death.

To satisfy his burden of producing evidence on negligence, a plaintiff must produce expert testimony only if the jury cannot determine, based on their everyday knowledge and experience, whether the defendant was negligent, or whether the defendant's negligence was the cause of the plaintiff's harm.

Res ipsa loquitur

Res ipsa loquitur (i.e., Latin for "the thing speaks for itself") is a doctrine which permits a plaintiff to offer proof that the defendant was negligent by circumstantial evidence.

If the plaintiff can offer evidence on all of the elements necessary to establish *res ipsa loquitur*, then he has satisfied his burden of producing evidence on negligence and will avoid a directed verdict.

The elements which must be proven to establish *res ipsa loquitur* are:

(1) that the injury to the plaintiff would not ordinarily take place in the absence of negligence and

(2) the defendant was in control of the instrumentality which caused the injury.

The plaintiff can prevail without direct proof of the defendant's negligence if he can prove (or the circumstances alone indicate) that he would not have been harmed if the defendant had not been negligent.

The plaintiff need only show that it is more likely than not that the defendant was negligent and that there is a causal connection to the plaintiff's harm.

The defendant can negate the inference which comes from the doctrine of *res ipsa loquitur* from arising by showing that it is just as likely that someone else's negligence caused the plaintiff's harm.

If the plaintiff attempts to prove negligence by *res ipsa loquitur*, the defendant can introduce direct evidence that he was not negligent.

Res ipsa loquitur is inapplicable in product liability cases.

Causation

The plaintiff cannot recover in tort unless the defendant's conduct is the proximate (i.e., sufficiently related) cause of the injury suffered.

The first issue in causation is "but for" causation.

Except in rare instances, for the plaintiff to prevail, he must prove that the harm he incurred would not have occurred if the defendant had not acted in a tortious manner.

Even if the plaintiff proves "but for" causation, he must also prove proximate cause.

The determination of proximate cause is usually a factual question for the jury to be determined by some broad guidelines.

If there is "but for" causation, but it is determined that a separate "but for" cause is a superseding cause, the defendant's tortious conduct is not the proximate cause of the plaintiff's harm, and he cannot recover.

If the separate "but for" cause were foreseeable by the defendant, it would not be considered a superseding cause, and the plaintiff will recover.

For example, an injured plaintiff will require medical treatment. It is foreseeable that the plaintiff will suffer additional injury from negligent medical treatment.

The defendant is liable for the additional harm caused by that treatment.

The original defendant is not liable for the harm caused by a superseding intervening cause.

However, the original defendant is liable for any harm which would have occurred if not for the superseding cause.

If the defendant has tortiously injured a plaintiff in a manner which includes a permanent disability, the plaintiff is entitled to be compensated for all of those injuries but is not entitled to be compensated for subsequent injuries which would not have occurred if the plaintiff did not have that permanent disability.

A subsequent tortfeasor is not liable for the injuries which occurred prior to the time he committed his tort.

In tort actions involving damages caused to children because of drugs taken by their mothers while they were pregnant, or in other cases involving a long period of time between the ingestion of the dangerous substance and the injury, the ordinary tort rule that the plaintiff must prove that the defendant's product caused the harm is relaxed. Each defendant drug manufacturer will be liable for damages in proportion to the market share of the drug which the defendant has at the time the drug was taken.

Allocation of Liability among Joint Tortfeasors

Defendants are joint tortfeasors when their concurrent tortious actions combine to injure the plaintiff, and it is not possible to reasonably allocate portions of the plaintiff's injury to separate defendants.

In any question where there are a plaintiff and defendants who are alleged to be joint tortfeasors, you should follow the following process.

(1) Determine how the negligence of the plaintiff affects the total amount of the award due him.

(2) Determine how much in damages the plaintiff can collect from each of the defendants.

(3) Determine the rights of a defendant who pays damages to collect from the remaining defendants.

Effect of the Plaintiff's Negligence on His Damages

If the jurisdiction retains contributory negligence, the plaintiff loses if he is negligent in any degree.

If the jurisdiction uses pure comparative negligence, the plaintiff prevails if the defendant is negligent no matter how negligent the plaintiff is, but his percentage of his negligence reduces the award. A plaintiff can be 99% negligent and the defendant 1%, and the plaintiff will recover.

If the jurisdiction uses modified comparative negligence, the plaintiff prevails only if the negligence of all of the defendants is greater than the negligence of the plaintiff.

Again, the plaintiff's recovery is reduced by the percentage of his negligence.

Comparative negligence does not change the rule of joint and several liability between joint tortfeasors.

Amount Collected from the Defendant

Under common law, joint tortfeasors are jointly and severally liable for the entire judgment of the plaintiff.

If the common law has been modified so that the joint tortfeasors are severally liable but not jointly liable, the plaintiff can collect from each joint tortfeasor the amount of the judgment for which he is ultimately liable.

Relations Between Joint Tortfeasors

Under common law, a joint tortfeasor who pays more than his equal share of a judgment is entitled to seek contribution from the other joint tortfeasors in the amount of any excess he paid.

If the jurisdiction provides that joint tortfeasors are only liable in proportion to their percentage of negligence, then a joint tortfeasor who pays more than his allocated share of a judgment is entitled to seek contribution from the other joint tortfeasors in the amount of any excess he paid.

If a person is liable on a vicarious basis, then he can seek indemnification from the party who is ultimately liable and collect from him the entire amount he paid.

A negligent defendant is only entitled to contribution (not complete indemnification) from a negligent joint tortfeasor.

However, a negligent tortfeasor is entitled to indemnification if his joint tortfeasor has committed an intentional tort.

Liability of Owners and Occupiers of Land

A landowner owes a business invitee a duty to use reasonable care to prevent him from suffering injuries while on the premises.

An individual is a business invitee if he enters the premises with the intention of conducting business on the premises, whether or not he conducts it.

A landowner owes a business invitee a duty to use reasonable care to prevent him from suffering from criminal activity of third parties when on the premises.

The status of a person on the premises can depend on the area where the injury occurs and whether the public has been invited to that area.

If the issue is the negligence of the defendant because of the condition of the premises, evidence of occurrences similar to the accident in issue due to the same condition is admissible, if relevant to prove that the defendant had notice of the dangerous condition.

Without incurring tort liability, a landowner can construct a legally permitted building on his land to deprive the adjoining land of light and air and can remove a building on his land which exposes his neighbor's land to sunlight.

At common law, a licensee (social guest) is only owed a duty to warn of dangers known to the owner or occupant but not obvious to the licensee.

This rule has been changed in many jurisdictions to permit a licensee to successfully pursue a tort claim if the landowner is negligent.

A landowner is not liable to a trespasser for ordinary negligence but is liable if he could have prevented the injury after having become aware of the danger to the trespasser.

Attractive Nuisance

At common law, a trespasser is only owed a duty to avoid gross negligence or wanton, willful misconduct.

A possessor of land is subject to liability for physical harm to children trespassing thereon caused by an artificial condition upon the land if:

(1) the possessor knows or has reason to know that children are likely to trespass in the location of the danger (attractive nuisance),

(2) the possessor knows or has reason to know that the condition will involve an unreasonable risk of death or serious bodily harm to such children,

(3) the children, because of their youth, do not discover the condition or realize the risk involved,

(4) the utility to the possessor of maintaining the condition and the burden of eliminating the danger are slight as compared with the risk to the children involved, and

(5) the possessor fails to exercise reasonable care to eliminate the danger or otherwise protect the children.

If attractive nuisance applies, then the landowner owes a duty of reasonable care to the infant trespasser(s).

It is not necessary that the children be attracted onto the land by the nuisance.

The doctrine is not applicable if the nuisance would only be attractive to those old enough to be able to recognize its hazards.

Vicarious Liability

Employers are vicariously liable for the torts of their employees committed within the scope of their employment.

An employer-employee relationship exists where the person contracting for services controls the manner in which the job is accomplished.

Indicia of an employer-employee relationship are periodic payments to the worker rather than payment by the job and ownership of the tools by the contractor rather than by the worker.

The intentional tort of an employee would be within the scope of his employment if it were committed to further the master's (i.e., employer's) business even though the employer specifically forbade the conduct.

In addition to being held vicariously liable on a *respondeat superior* theory, an employer can be held liable for his negligence in hiring or supervising his employee.

A plaintiff who is injured by a servant may sue the servant and/or the employer.

A defendant, who has not been personally negligent and who has been held vicariously liable, has a right to recover the entire amount of the judgment by way of indemnification from the party whose negligence caused the vicarious liability.

Parents are not vicariously liable for the torts of their children but can be held liable for their negligence in raising or supervising them.

Joint Enterprise Liability

When two persons join together to accomplish a task which is labeled a joint enterprise, such as participating in an automobile race, each person is liable for torts committed by the other within the scope of the joint enterprise.

Liability for Independent Contractors

The person hiring an independent contractor is not liable for the torts of the independent contractor with the following exceptions:

The person hiring a contractor is liable for ultra-hazardous activity (e.g., blasting) undertaken by him.

If a person has a non-delegable duty to see that such activity is performed safely, he cannot relieve himself of tort liability by hiring an independent contractor to perform it.

An additional theory of liability is that a person who hires an independent contractor can be held liable for his negligence in hiring an unfit contractor.

Assumption of Risk

The assumption of the risk would be a valid defense only if the plaintiff had actual, subjective knowledge of the risk which caused the harm and voluntarily assumed it.

The defense of assumption of the risk will not be applicable if a defendant is in a difficult situation which he has not caused and he takes a reasonable chance to extricate himself.

The assumption of the risk is not available in product liability cases where the jurisdiction has adopted a comparative negligence doctrine which is applicable in product liability cases.

The assumption of the risk is combined with comparative negligence as a means of reducing the total amount of the plaintiff's recovery.

Last Clear Chance

While contributory negligence will bar the plaintiff's recovery, that doctrine is not applicable if the defendant had the last clear chance after the plaintiff's negligence occurred to avoid the accident.

Attribution of a Related Party's Negligence

The negligence of one party will not ordinarily be attributed to another party, even if the parties are related.

Thus, the negligence of a minor child is not attributed to the parent, but the parent can be liable for negligent supervision of his child.

However, the negligence of a decedent will be attributed to his executor in a wrongful death case.

Elements of Tort Damage

The plaintiff cannot recover in negligence without proving damage.

If an element of tort damage is future medical expenses, the plaintiff must produce expert testimony to prove the amount of expenses which are expected to be incurred.

If a court determines that the defendant's tortious conduct proximately caused damages, the fact that the particular damages suffered by the

plaintiff were not foreseeable by the defendant will not be a valid defense.

If a tort victim is especially prone to injury, the tortfeasor must pay all damages incurred because a tortfeasor takes his victim as he finds him.

Economic loss to third parties caused by injuries to the defendant is not compensable as an element of tort damage.

If a tort committed on a mother before conception causes damage to a later-born child, the child could recover damages, but there is a doubt that the damages to the child are an element of the mother's damages.

Even though an employee's recovery against his employer is limited to worker's compensation, he may still pursue tort claims against third parties who contributed to his injuries.

Defamation

The plaintiff must prove fault of the defendant in publishing an untrue defamatory statement about the plaintiff.

If the plaintiff is a public figure, a public official or a person very well known in the field in which the defamation occurs, the plaintiff must prove that the defendant acted with "malice," that is, that the defendant either knew the statement was untrue or published it with a reckless disregard of the truth.

If the plaintiff is not a public figure, he must prove that the defendant was negligent in publishing the untrue defamatory statement.

A statement is defamatory when it might lower the esteem, in the eyes of a reputable segment of the community, of the person who is the subject of the statement.

Publication of the defamatory statement is an essential element of a defamation action.

The plaintiff must prove that the defendant intended or acted in a way that it is reasonably certain that at least one person other than the plaintiff heard and understood the statement.

The element of publication has been satisfied even if the person who received the defamatory statement did not believe that it was true.

If a statement by the defendant is directed only to the plaintiff but is overheard by a third person, the issue of publication is determined by whether the defendant should have reasonably foreseen that the statement would be overheard.

A defendant can be liable in defamation by republishing a defamatory statement made by a third party.

Libel

If the defamation is in the form of a writing or other permanent form of communication such as a recording, the plaintiff may prevail without proving special damages in the form of a monetary loss because of the defamation.

Humiliation, shame, or emotional distress are sufficient.

Libel *per se* is a statement which is defamatory to anyone receiving the communication who had no other information concerning the plaintiff.

Libel *per quod* is a statement which is defamatory only when taken in conjunction with facts known by those to whom the libel is published.

Slander

Defamation in the form of oral communication is slander.

An essential element of the cause of action for slander is the requirement that the plaintiff proves special damages in the form of a monetary loss caused by the defendant's defamatory statement.

The requirement of special damages is not applicable if the slander states that the plaintiff has committed a crime, has a loathsome disease, has engaged in sexual misconduct or is incompetent in business.

Defenses

Truth

If the words of the communication are true as those words are reasonably construed, the defendant has a complete defense to a defamation action even if the words are not true.

Privilege

Relevant statements made in a judicial proceeding are absolutely privileged, but those given in an administrative proceeding only enjoy a qualified privilege.

Statements made by a former employer to a prospective employer concerning an employee enjoy a qualified privilege.

The defendant is liable even though he has a qualified privilege if he makes a statement which he knows is false or makes a statement with reckless disregard of the truth.

Privacy

The tort of invasion of privacy consists of four separate torts involving interference with a person's right to be left alone. Those torts are:

(1) Unreasonable intrusion on the plaintiff's seclusion.

Publication is not an element of this form of invasion of privacy.

(2) Appropriation of the plaintiff's name or likeness for commercial purposes.

Consent by the plaintiff to having his picture taken does not constitute consent to use the photo for commercial purposes.

(3) Unreasonable publication of the plaintiff's private life.

The material published must be highly offensive to a reasonable person.

Truth is not a defense to this form of invasion of privacy, but newsworthiness of the event in the plaintiff's private life is a defense.

Publishing information in the public record cannot generally be considered an unreasonable invasion of the plaintiff's private life.

(4) Publicity which unreasonably places another in a false light.

The information published need not be defamatory to give rise to this form of invasion of privacy, as long as it is untrue.

Deceit

For the plaintiff to recover in common law deceit, there must be a misrepresentation of material fact by the plaintiff who was relied upon by the defendant to his detriment.

A statement of opinion is not a misrepresentation of a material fact.

Actual damages are an essential element of a cause of action in deceit.

Failing to make a disclosure is the basis for a cause of action in deceit when there is a legal or fiduciary duty to make a disclosure.

The plaintiff must sustain more than nominal damages to have a cause of action for misrepresentation.

Third parties could not sue for negligent misrepresentation unless the purpose of supplying the information were to permit third parties to rely on it.

Torts – Quick Facts

Negligence:

1) Duty – the defendant owed a legal duty to the plaintiff

2) Breach of duty – defendant breached his legal duty by acting (or failing to act) in a certain way.

3) Causation – it was the defendant's action (or failure to act) that caused the plaintiff's harm.

4) Damages – the plaintiff was harmed or injured as a result of the defendant's actions (or inactions).

   A cause of action for negligence requires measurable harm to the plaintiff.

1. The swearing out of a complaint that was **proper** at the time may NOT serve as a basis for a **false imprisonment action** despite the failure to cancel the complaint.

2. A landowner generally owes NO duty to an undiscovered trespasser.

   However, if a landowner discovers OR should anticipate the presence of a trespasser, then landowner MUST exercise **ordinary care** to warn the trespasser of OR to make safe concealed, unsafe, artificial conditions *known to the landowner*, that involve a risk of death or serious bodily harm.

3. A **private nuisance** action requires a showing that the defendant's interference with the use and enjoyment of the plaintiff's property was <u>unreasonable.</u>

   A characterization of unreasonable requires that the severity of the inflicted injury outweigh the utility of the defendant's conduct.

4. Commercial invitees are owed the duty to be warned of non-obvious dangerous conditions AND for the defendant to make reasonable inspections to discover dangerous conditions and make them safe.

5. The tort of conversion does NOT require that the defendant damage or permanently deprive the owner of the chattel – all that is required is that the defendant's volitional conduct result in a serious invasion of the chattel interest of another in some manner.

6. A bailee is liable to the owner for conversion IF the bailee uses the chattel in such a manner as to constitute a material breach of the bailment agreement.

7. A plaintiff can recover for defamation where there was **negligent communication** of the defamatory statements to third persons.

8. A defendant will NOT be liable to a child's parents if he can show that the child *appreciated the risk* of the activity giving rise to the injury.

9. One of the **duties** that doctors, dentists and other healthcare professionals owe their patients is the duty to provide a patient with enough information about the risks of a proposed course of treatment or surgical procedure to enable the patient to make an informed consent to the treatment.
   However, even if there is a **breach of duty**, there MUST ALSO be **damages.**

Civil Procedure

(Federal Rules of Civil Procedure)

Under Article III of the United States Constitution, the judicial power of the United States is vested in the United States Supreme Court and such lower federal courts as Congress may create. Congress, under that power, has established a trial court, the United States District Courts in each state and an intermediate appellate court, the Circuit Courts of Appeal.

The United States Supreme Court has original jurisdiction, as provided in the Constitution. Legislation has also established the appellate jurisdiction of the Supreme Court.

The NCBE added Civil Procedure to the MBE for examinees beginning in February 2015. This topic requires the application of 1) the Federal Rules of Civil Procedure and 2) the sections of Title 28 of the U.S. Code on trial, appellate jurisdiction, venue and transfer.

The NCBE reports that approximately two-thirds of the procedure questions cover the topics of jurisdiction and venue, pretrial procedures and motions.

Federal Jurisdiction

Original and Appellate Jurisdiction of The United States Supreme Court

Article III, Section 2 of the Constitution provides that "In all cases affecting ambassadors, other public ministers and consuls, and those in which a state shall be a party, the Supreme Court shall have original jurisdiction."

In all other cases within the judicial power of the United States, "the Supreme Court shall have appellate jurisdiction, both as to law and fact, with such exceptions, and under such regulations as the Congress shall make."

Cases and Controversies

The judicial power extends to "cases" and "controversies."

Factors considered in determining when a case or controversy exists include mootness, standing, ripeness, whether the case involves a political or administrative question, whether a case is collusive and whether the parties are seeking a merely advisory opinion.

Article III – Judicial Branch

Article III of the U.S. Constitution establishes the judicial branch of the federal government.

Under Article III, the judicial branch consists of The Supreme Court of the United States, as well as lower courts created by Congress.

Article III defines the judicial power as "cases and controversies."

Article III prohibits advisory opinions.

The text of the Constitution does not articulate the power of the judicial courts.

The authority for judicial review was established in *Marbury v. Madison* (1803) where the court created the authority for federal judicial review of federal legislative and executive actions.

Marbury declared "that it's the province of the judicial department to say what the law is."

The court sets limits on the federal judicial power.

Whether the plaintiff is the proper party to bring a matter to the court for adjudication (i.e., justiciability doctrine) has four requirements:

> standing,
>
> ripeness,
>
> political question, and
>
> mootness.

These doctrines will render a controversy "nonjusticiable" if a court decides that any one of the four essential elements is absent.

1) Standing: the ability of a party to demonstrate to the court sufficient connection to and harm from the action challenged to support that party's participation in the case.

Injury: the plaintiff must allege and prove that she has been, or imminently will be, injured

The plaintiff may assert only personally suffered injuries:

Sierra Club v. Morton (1971): Disney wanted to build a ski resor. The Sierra Club sued to stop construction, and the Supreme Court ruled the Sierra Club lacked standing.

2) Causation and redressability: the plaintiff must allege and prove that the defendant caused the injury so that a favorable court decision is likely to remedy the injury.

3) No third party standing: plaintiff cannot represent the claims of others not before the court (i.e., must be a personal injury).

There is an important exception where third-party standing is allowed.

A plaintiff who meets the other standing requirements and one of these exceptions may bring a suit with proper standing:

> A close relationship between the plaintiff and the injured third party,
>
> Plaintiff can be trusted to represent the third party adequately,
>
> Doctor/patient relationship: laws limiting abortion inflicted injuries on the doctors (loss of business), so doctors chose to represent the rights of their patients.

Supreme court ruled that a father lacked standing to represent his daughter for the "under God" in school; he did not have legal custody of his daughter (the mother didn't want the suit to go forward).

Third party standing is allowed if the injured third party is unlikely to assert his/her rights (some reason to believe the third party can't come to court to protect itself), then the plaintiff who meets the other requirements may represent the claims of the third party.

4) No generalized grievances are allowed.

A cause of action is not a generalized grievance because many people (or everyone) are affected by the injury.

The plaintiff must not be suing solely as a citizen or as a taxpayer.

Lacked standing, his only injuries are a citizen to taxpayers being spent in violation.

Plaintiff is suing as a citizen (or general taxpayer) → generalized grievance → no standing.

Exception: Taxpayers may challenge government expenditures according to a federal statute as violating the establishment clause.

Supreme court has held that the establishment clause was a limit on Congress spending power.

Narrow exception: Supreme Court has held that taxpayers don't have standing for government expenditures of property to religious places (just money) under a specific federal statute.

Flast v. Cohn (1968): federal government adopted a statute that provided for direct federal financial aid for parochial school.

Flast had standing: majority opinion by Chief Justice Earl Warren, the holding established a "double nexus" test which a taxpayer must satisfy to have standing.

> 1ˢᵗ: he must "establish a logical link" between (e.g., taxpayer) status and the type of legislative enactment being challenged,
>
> 2ⁿᵈ: a plaintiff must show that the challenged enactment exceeds specific constitutional limitations upon the exercise of the taxing and spending power and *not* simply that the enactment is generally beyond the powers delegated to Congress by Article I, Section 8.

Only when both nexuses have been satisfied may the petitioner have standing to sue.

Jurisdiction of Federal Courts In General

Subject Matter Jurisdiction

The Constitution limits the subject matter jurisdiction of the federal courts to:

(1) suits between citizens of different states with an amount <u>over</u> $75,000 (Diversity Jurisdiction),

(2) suits involving a federal question (Subject Matter Jurisdiction),

(3) cases involving ambassadors,

(4) admiralty and maritime jurisdiction, and

(5) cases where the United States is a party.

Congress has implemented the constitutional provision by imposing additional restrictions on the jurisdiction which federal courts are permitted to exercise, such as the amount-in-controversy requirement.

Subject matter jurisdiction may not be conferred by agreement or consent of the litigants.

The defense of lack of subject matter jurisdiction may be raised at any point in the trial, and may even be first raised on appeal.

Federal Question Jurisdiction

The Meaning of "Arising Under"

A right or immunity created by the Constitution or federal law must be an essential element of the plaintiff's cause of action for the federal district court to have "arising under" jurisdiction.

The fact that the defendant can raise federal law as an affirmative defense in his answer will not confer this type of jurisdiction.

Federal Question Must Appear in the Complaint

The federal question or constitutional issue must be properly pleaded in the complaint.

The anticipation of a defense based on federal law is insufficient to confer federal question jurisdiction on the court.

Concurrent and Exclusive Federal Jurisdiction

Absent congressional intent to confer exclusive jurisdiction on the federal courts, both federal and state courts have jurisdiction to try claims based upon federal law.

Congress has granted the federal courts exclusive jurisdiction in:

> bankruptcy proceedings,
>
> patent,
>
> copyright cases,
>
> actions against foreign consuls,
>
> admiralty and maritime cases,
>
> antitrust cases,
>
> cases under the Securities Exchange Act of 1934, and
>
> actions where the United States is a party.

Diversity Jurisdiction

The Requirement of Complete Diversity

Congress has not conferred on the federal district courts all the jurisdiction of cases between citizens of different states that the constitution allows it to confer.

To have jurisdiction the lawsuit must have complete diversity between the parties on each side of the controversy, whereby each plaintiff must be from a state different from that of each defendant, or one must be a citizen of a state and the other an alien.

The exception to this rule is an action called statutory interpleader, where parties on both sides of the controversy can be citizens of the same state as long as two different states are represented among all of the parties.

For determining whether the statutory requirements for jurisdiction are met, diversity is determined as of the date the action is commenced; it need not have existed when the cause of action arose.

If the defendant impleads a third party whose citizenship is the same as the plaintiff, diversity is not destroyed.

However, while a defendant may be brought in by a third party complaint, by a party which has the same citizenship as the plaintiff, the plaintiff may not then amend the complaint to add such a person as a party defendant.

Citizenship

Citizenship of a natural person for purposes of determining diversity means the state of that party's domicile.

A person's original domicile is the domicile of his parents.

When he reaches adulthood, a person can change domicile by being physically present in a place which he determines to be his fixed and permanent residence.

Domicile can subsequently be changed by physical presence in the new domicile with the intent to remain there indefinitely.

The citizenship of a corporation for diversity purposes is:

(1) the state of incorporation and

(2) the state in which it has its principal place of business.

Where a partnership, labor union, or other unincorporated association is a party, the citizenship of each member is considered in determining diversity.

If the estate of a deceased person is a party, the citizenship of the decedent is controlling for diversity purposes.

The citizenship of the executor or administrator is irrelevant.

In action on behalf of a trust, the citizenship of the trustee (not that of the beneficiary) controls.

For diversity purposes in class actions, the citizenship of the named representatives of the class controls.

Realignment or Substitution of Parties

Diversity may be created or destroyed by a realignment of the parties according to their real interest in the dispute.

If a party is named as a plaintiff and is, in reality, a defendant, he will be classified as a defendant when determining if complete diversity exists.

The citizenship of the original party governs when there is a substitution of parties because of death, incompetence, or succession to a public office.

Amount-In-Controversy Requirement

The plaintiff's complaint determines the amount in controversy.

For a federal court to have jurisdiction in a diversity suit, the amount in controversy, as measured by the damages the plaintiff is seeking in good faith to collect at the time the suit is commenced, must be greater than $75,000.

Actual recovery of less than $75,000 does not retroactively destroy jurisdiction.

The dollar value for the amount in controversy requirement of injunctive relief is the value of the right to be protected or the extent of the injury to be prevented.

Aggregation of Claims

A single plaintiff suing a single defendant may aggregate his claims to achieve the jurisdictional amount.

Thus, a claim for personal injury and a claim for property damages could be added together to reach more than $75,000.

If a single plaintiff has claims against several defendants, she can aggregate her claims only if the defendants are jointly liable.

Thus, if D1 and D2 were joint tortfeasors and the plaintiff's total claim was more than $75,000 against both, the fact that the right of contribution might reduce the total amount paid by either tortfeasor to equal to or less than $75,000 is not relevant for jurisdiction purposes.

The claims of several plaintiffs against a single defendant cannot be aggregated except where several plaintiffs have an undivided right, title, or interest in the claim.

The claims of each member of the class in a class action cannot aggregate their claims, thus making it less likely that class action cases based upon state causes of action can be brought in federal court.

Jurisdictional Amount in Counterclaims

If the jurisdictional amount is satisfied by the plaintiff's complaint, a compulsory counterclaim which does not meet the jurisdictional amount is permitted.

However, the amount of a counterclaim cannot be aggregated with the plaintiff's claim to satisfy the amount-in-controversy requirement.

Supplemental Jurisdiction

Rules for Supplemental Jurisdiction

A federal district court generally has supplemental jurisdiction over any claims related to the claim upon which federal jurisdiction is founded which form part of the same case or controversy.

Thus, a claim under state antitrust law could be brought in the federal court as a count in the same complaint which alleges a claim under the federal antitrust law.

The federal district court has the discretion to exercise supplemental jurisdiction under 28 U.S.C. 1367 (*Gibbs*) if:

(1) the claim raises a novel or complex issue of state law,

(2) the state law claim substantially predominates over any claim(s) over which the court has original jurisdiction,

(3) the district court has dismissed all claims over which it had original jurisdiction, or

(4) exceptional circumstances and compelling reasons exist for the court to decline jurisdiction.

The federal court can try a state claim which was brought under supplemental jurisdiction even if the count which was brought under the federal claim is dismissed.

Exceptions to Supplemental Jurisdiction

1367(b) is an exception to 1367(a): no supplemental jurisdiction if the jurisdiction was a diversity case. If:

1) jurisdiction establishing a claim is diversity claim, 2nd claim cannot be brought even if part of same case or controversy.

2) would remove supplemental jurisdiction if claim establishing subject matter jurisdiction is a diversity action.

Reason for exceptions to supplemental jurisdiction is because 1367(b) should not undermine the complete diversity rule & Strawbridge.

1367(c): federal district court can decide not to exercise supplemental jurisdiction if:

1) it raises a complicated question of state law,

2) the claim substantially predominates over the claim or claims over which the district court has original jurisdiction,

3) the district court has dismissed all claims over which it has original jurisdiction, or

4) in exceptional circumstances, there are other compelling reasons for declining jurisdiction.

Removal Jurisdiction

Prerequisites to Removal – Federal Subject Matter

If the plaintiff could have brought the action in federal court originally, the defendant may remove a civil action brought in a state court to the federal district court.

A federal question raised in defense or counterclaim is not a basis for removal.

The court will look only to the complaint to determine if federal question jurisdiction is present.

The pleadings determine the question of federal jurisdiction which gives to the right to remove as of the time of filing the petition for removal.

However, if diversity is the basis for federal jurisdiction, the diversity must have existed both when the original action was filed in state court, and when the petition for removal was filed.

Only the Defendant Can Remove

A plaintiff, once he has filed suit in a state court cannot change his mind and remove that case to federal court.

The right to remove is vested only in the defendant.

Diversity cases are not removable if any of the defendants are citizens of the state in which such action is brought.

For example, if P of state A sues D of state B in a state B state court, in a case which presents no federal question, then B may not remove the case to federal court.

A suit involving a federal question is removable even by a resident defendant.

Separate and Independent Claim

If an otherwise non-removable state claim is joined with a removable separate and independent federal claim in the state court action, the entire case may be removed to the district court.

In its discretion, the federal court may determine all issues or may remand the non-removable claims if state law predominates.

Procedure for Removal

Plaintiff may bring suit in the court of their choice so long as jurisdiction and venue are proper.

However, removal is an exception, since it provides the defendant with an option to remove a case from state to federal court.

Only the defendant can remove a case.

All defendants must agree to remove the case (i.e., unanimity).

Note, there are strict limitations in the statute and case law as to which cases may be removed and to which court.

Removal is a one-way street: only goes from state to federal.

The defendant must file a verified petition for removal in the federal court within 30 days after the case becomes removable and must serve all parties in the state court with that petition.

The proper venue for a removed action is the federal district in which the state action is pending.

28 USC 1447 (c): a motion to remand the case from any defect (other than subject matter jurisdiction) must be made within 30 days after the notice of removal has been filed.

However, a motion to remand may be brought for lack of subject matter jurisdiction at any time during litigation before a final judgment is entered.

Once a case has been removed to federal and remanded back to state the motion to remand cannot be appealed.

Plaintiff can file a motion to remand based on the federal court lacking subject matter jurisdiction OR requirements for proper removal were NOT followed.

28 USC 1446(b): the notice of removal shall be filed within 30 days from the defendant's receipt of the initial complaint.

If the case stated by the initial pleading is not removable, defendant may file a notice of removal at any point during the litigation that the case becomes removable and defendant shall have 30 days to file a notice of removal from the date the case became removable.

28 USC 1446 (d): once a case has been removed from state to federal court, the state court shall proceed no further unless and until the case is remanded.

Any judgments and orders issued by the state court will continue to be in force.

Remand

If the case does not belong in federal court, the federal court can remand from federal to state.

The federal court must remand the case to the state court if, at any time, before final judgment, it appears that the case was removed improvidently and without jurisdiction.

Jurisdiction Over Persons and Property

The issue of personal jurisdiction is present in litigation in federal courts.

Generally, such courts have the same personal jurisdiction as the state courts in the state where the federal court is located.

Congress has the right to extend the jurisdiction of any particular state court.

For example, in statutory interpleader actions jurisdiction extends to the entire United States.

Personal jurisdiction can be based on either of the following four types of relationships between the defendant and the forum state:

Domicile

Consent

Physical Appearance or service on an agent

Minimum contacts

Service of Process and Notice

Federal Rules include delivery of both the summons and complaint.

Every paper must be served on the other side.

Rule 5 governs the delivery of later papers (usually just need to mail).

The complaint is the assertion of legal claims.

A summons is a court issued document asserting power and authority of the court over the defendant.

Rules for first delivery more stringent since because the plaintiff must provide the defendant with adequate notice of the suit.

Even if service proper is proper, the court will likely be sympathetic to the defendant and not enforce the default judgment.

Mullane establishes what is necessary for adequate notice.

Just because newspaper advertisement satisfied the statute, it does not mean it is constitutionally sufficient.

The plaintiff should notify some trustees so they can protect the common interests of all holders.

However, if it is unreasonable to contact all unknown trustees, then a paper advertisement is adequate.

Rule 4(c)(2) permits any person over 18 and not a party to the case to deliver the summons.

Rule 4(d) allows the defendant to waive personal service.

Rule 4(e)(2) permits personal service by leave copies at the usual place of abode with some person of suitable age who resides therein, or delivery to an agent authorized by appointment or by law to receive service of process.

Service to a corporation can be by personal service to an appointed agent, officer, or managing agent.

Venue, Forum Non Conveniens, and Transfer

Purpose and Waiver

Venue rules fix the proper place for the trial of an action over which several courts could exercise jurisdiction.

Venue rules are based on convenience and an effort to distribute cases among various trial courts.

The improper venue must be raised affirmatively by the defendant either in a motion to dismiss or in his answer, or it is waived.

Venue Rules

In both diversity and federal question cases, a proper venue in the federal court exists in any district in which either:

(a) a defendant resides, if all of the defendants reside in the same state, or

(b) a "substantial" part of the events or property which are the basis of the claim took place or can be found, respectively.

In diversity cases, the venue is also proper in any district in which "the defendants are subject to personal jurisdiction at the time the action is commenced."

In federal question cases, the venue is also proper in any district "in which any defendant may be found" but only "if there is no district in which the action may be otherwise brought."

This situation occurs when the defendants do not reside in the same state, and there is no state in which a "substantial" part of the claim arose.

Residence for Venue Purposes

Residence for venue purposes is the state where the plaintiff is a citizen.

Also, some courts also consider venue proper in a state where a second home is located.

An alien may be sued in any district, and thus cannot effectively raise the defense of lack of venue.

The proper venue for a corporation is in any judicial district which can constitutionally assert personal jurisdiction over it.

The venue for an unincorporated association (e.g., a partnership) is wherever it is doing business.

Transfer – Where Venue is Improper

If an action is commenced in the wrong district, the court can dismiss the case according to a motion to dismiss under rule 12 (b) (3).

If it is in the interest of justice, the court may transfer the case to any district in which it could have been brought.

The court can transfer an action where it lacks *in personam* jurisdiction over the defendant to a court which has such jurisdiction.

Where Venue is Proper: For Convenience

Even though the venue is proper in the district where an action is brought, the court may, in its discretion, transfer the suit to any district "where it might have been brought," "for the convenience of parties and witnesses, in the interest of justice." 28 U.S.C. § 1404(a).

The phrase "where it might have been brought" limits transfer to a district where the plaintiff could have brought the action at the time the suit was initiated.

Forum Non conveniens

Forum non conveniens allows dismissal by a court if it would be an unfair or inconvenient forum.

An action will be dismissed for *forum non conveniens* if the appropriate forum is a state court or a court in a foreign country.

Law Applied by Federal Courts

Vertical Choice of Law

In federal court diversity cases, state law applies unless the Constitution or Congressional Statute contradicts this principle.

State law could include statutes, common law, state constitution. If federal common law conflicts w/state common law the state common law applies b/c rules of decision act b/c act says only federal statutes

Swift v. Tyson (1842) held that, if there is a federal common law and state common law and they conflict, the district court follows federal common law because for interpreting "laws of several states" it does not mean state common law; it only means statutes, so state common law will not conflict with federal common law

In the absence of a federal statute or a contrary provision in the Constitution, federal courts must follow state law in diversity cases.

State law was defined to include common law (*Erie*); Erie relies on the 10th amendment.

However, if there is a conflict between a federal statute (or US Constitution) and state law, the federal court in a diversity case must use federal law (i.e., Supremacy Clause).

Congress passed the rules enabling act (i.e., Federal Rules of civil procedure), federal courts generally follow the federal rules in diversity cases even if there are contrary state procedures.

Horizontal Choice of Law

Addresses which law should be applied to different state laws.

> For torts cases, the federal district court will use the state law where the injury occurred.

> For contract cases, the federal district court will use the state law where the contract was signed.

A court in another jurisdiction (federal courts or another state court) looks at the lower court decisions and *predicts* how the state supreme court would rule.

Certification is the process where a federal district court has the state supreme court certify the law by resolving any questions from other lower courts in the jurisdiction.

Federal courts and other state courts can request the state supreme court to answer how they would resolve the law.

Pretrial Procedures

Preliminary Injunctions and Temporary Restraining Orders

A party may seek a preliminary injunction before a trial on the merits of the complaint.

Rule 65(a) requires that a preliminary injunction may not be issued without notice to the adverse party.

A temporary restraining order (TRO) is granted by a court when it is necessary to prevent irreparable injury to a party, and the injury will result before a preliminary injunction hearing can be held.

Interlocutory Injunctions

An injunction is an equitable remedy by which a person is ordered to act or to refrain from acting in a specified manner.

Interlocutory injunctions are granted to maintain the status quo until a trial on the merits may be held.

Pleadings

Rule 3 pertains to the commencement of a civil action by the filing a complaint. Old rules were very strict with pleading and if anything different in court from pleading then case was dismissed (variance).

Notice Pleading do not have to allege all facts, but the facts of the cause of action being alleged need to support the cause of action.

The pleading alleges sufficient facts to put the defendant on notice as to what is the claim against him.

Rule 8 requires that the complaint sets out the allegation of facts in numbered paragraphs.

Rule 8(e)(2) the plaintiff is allowed to plead more than one version of the claim because of the lack of time for discovery of facts and development of applicable legal theories.

Three Requirements for Federal Complaints (Rule 8):

> 1) Jurisdictional allegations—subject matter
>
> 2) A "short and plain statement of the claim showing that the pleader is entitled to relief" (Notice Pleading) – all that is required in the complaint is enough to put the defendant on notice

3) Demand for judgment (i.e., damages).

Special Pleadings (fraud or mistake) are covered by 9 (b): the complaint must identify a specific individual that said what was fraud or mistake, what they said when they said it.

An allegation of fraud needs specificity because it is easy to allege, difficult to defend because the defendant needs to disprove a negative, and it is also a damaging accusation,

In response to a complaint, within 21 days of service of process, Rule 8(b) requires that the defendant prepares an answer (also a pleading) by numbering the responses to the allegation and responding to each averment:

1) Affirmative defense: statute of limitations, would appear in answer, and at the end of the answer would put affirmative defenses and then list them,

    a) Counter-claim: at the end of the answer, would put counter-claims and then list the Answer and Third party complaints.

    b) Bring in other parties as defendants.

    c) A third-party complaint is when the defendant sues another who is not listed in the complaint

    d) Cross-complaint is one defendant suing another defendant.

2) Motion to dismiss: filed alleging lack of grounds of personal, subject matter jurisdiction, or venue.

Rule 12(b) defenses may be raised by either motion or answer:

1) lack of subject matter jurisdiction (can be raised at any time),

2) lack of personal jurisdiction (waivable and must be pleaded in the first response),

3) improper venue (waivable and must be pleaded in the first response),

4) insufficiency of process (waivable and must be pleaded in first response),

5) insufficiency of service of process (waivable and must be pleaded in first response),

6) failure to state a claim (may be raised at any time during the trial), and

7) failure to join an indispensable party (may be raised at any time during the trial).

Counterclaims are a claim against an opposing parting (other side of the v.), filed as part of defendant's answer.

Compulsory counterclaim: arises from the same transaction or occurrence as the plaintiff's claim. Must be filed in the pending case or wave.

Permissive counterclaim: does not arise from the same transaction or occurrence as the plaintiff's claim.

Crossclaims are a claim against a co-party (same side of the v.). A cross-claim filed by one defendant against another will not defeat diversity because the exception to the rule applies only to claims filed by plaintiffs.

Amended and Supplemental Pleadings

Rule 15(a) entitles a party to amend pleading (complaint or answer) once at any time before the responsive pleading is served.

If the pleading is one to which no responsive pleading is permitted, and action has not been placed on the trial calendar, the party may so amend it at any time within 20 days after it was served.

A party shall plead in response to an amended pleading within the time remaining for a response to the original pleading or within 10 days after service of the amended pleading, whichever period may be longer

Plaintiff may still amend a pleading after the defendant filed a motion to dismiss under Rule 12(b)(6) as a motion and not an answer.

The defendant must respond to the amended complaint within 10 days or however much time was left before pleading was amended

Defendant has a right to amend answer because it is a pleading to which no responsive pleading is permitted, and the party has 20 days to correct it.

If either party waits too long to amend, then the party would have to file a motion to ask the court for permission to amend to amend the complaint.

Rule 15(c) addresses the Statute of Limitations and joining a new party or adding a new claim?

Rule 15(c)(2): amendment to add a claim after the statute of limitations expired amendments will relate back only if they flesh out the factual details, change the legal theory, or add another claim arising out of the same transaction, occurrence or conduct

Relation back is denied for those amendments which are based on entirely different facts, transactions and occurrences

Rule 15(c)(3): when an amendment to add a new party after the statute of limitations has run. Only allowed after the statute of limitations expires if the defendant would not be prejudiced and should have known that, but for a mistake, the party would have been named a defendant.

Rule 15(d): supplemental pleadings set forth events occurring after a pleading is filed for events that occurred after the original pleading was filed.

Supplemental pleadings do not include facts that occurred before the original filing but which were discovered after filing.

Supplemental pleadings update the dispute by bringing such new facts to the attention of the court even if they change the relief sought or add additional parties.

Supplemental pleadings are allowed only with the court's permission.

Rule 11 – Ethical Restraints in Pleading

Rule 11 (the veracity of pleadings) requires attorneys (or pro se litigants) to sign all papers (except discovery documents) certifying:

> the paper is not for an improper purpose (e.g., harass, cause unnecessary delay or needlessly to increase the cost of litigation,

> legal contentions are warranted by law or by a nonfrivolous argument for extending modifying, reversing existing law or for establishing new law,

> factual contentions and denials have evidentiary support, and

> the denials of factual contentions are warranted on the evidence.

Rule 11 applies to every pleading, motion, and paper representations to the court.

Certification is continuous, so if an attorney argues a point plead, she is re-certifying the above.

Sanctions (monetary or non-monetary) may be levied to deter repeated bad conduct.

Safe Harbor Rule: if the other party violates rule 11, a motion can be filed for sanctions on the party and request correction before filing the motion with the court.

There is no safe harbor requirement when the court itself initiates sanctions.

A party cannot bring a claim certain they cannot win (challenging a Supreme Court decision).

However, this is not frivolous if there was a turnover or the previous bench decision was narrow.

Must identify what allegations of support are likely from discovery vs. those already supported.

Pretrial Motions

Rule 12 Motions

Rule 12(a)(4): if the pre-answer motion is denied, 14 days to file an answer (unless the court sets different time).

If the pre-answer motion is accepted, an answer may not be required.

After filing the pre-answer motion, there is a delayed duty to answer until the motion is decided.

Relationship of Rule 12(b) and special appearance rule: both require a challenge to personal jurisdiction right away, but Rule 12(b) allows other defenses to be raised at the same time while a special appearance would interpret such an action as consenting to the jurisdiction of the court.

A defendant can make these motions before filing an answer.

Rule 12 (b)(1): dismiss for lack of subject matter jurisdiction – when the court lacks the statutory or constitutional power to adjudicate the case.

Rule 12(b)(4): object to process (e.g., the summons).

Rule 12(b)(5): insufficient service (e.g., manner the summons was served).

Rule 12 (b)(6): goes to merits of the case (i.e., failure to state a claim) that even facts true law does not provide a remedy.

Then, the plaintiff can probably amend the complaint.

Rule 12 (b)(6) is the modern version of demurrer: even if all facts as pled are true, the law supplies no relief.

The court will only look at the complaint and assume facts are true and ask what remedy is available; if none, then motion granted

Rule 12(b)(7): failure to join an indispensable party (i.e., can't adjudicate without violating the rights of a third party).

Many of the above deficiencies are curable (e.g., the court can instruct the plaintiff to serve properly or add the 3rd party).

Motions do not suspend discovery. However, motion can be made to stay discovery until motion decided.

So, if motion made for lack of personal jurisdiction, proceed through discovery until the motion is decided.

Most jurisdictions require a brief (i.e., reasons for motion) with the pre-answer motions.

Removal is not a responsive pleading.

After removal, all pre-answer motions available are still at the beginning of the suit.

277

Joinder

Rule 8 governs counterclaims: pleadings for all claims for relief to includes counterclaims and cross-claims.

Joinder of claims for parties:

1) Some common question of law or fact.

2) Arising from the same transaction or occurrence.

Rule 13(a) compulsory counterclaim: from the same set of events.

Rule 13(b) permissive counterclaim: if arising from different events.

Rule 13(b): once a defendant has been sued with a crossclaim, the defendant can invoke compulsory and permissive counterclaims.

Rule 13(h): additional parties to a crossclaim if the claims are from the same facts.

Rule 18(a): both plaintiff or defendant asserting a claim, may join claims, even if unrelated to underlying facts, against an opposing party.

However, once a proper crossclaim is done, additional unrelated crossclaim can be added without violating subject matter jurisdiction.

Rule 18(b): joinder of contingent claims. A party may join two claims even though one of them is dependent on the disposition of the other.

Rule 19 pertains to joinder of parties: requires certain defendants must be ordered by the court to be added into a suit.

This motion for joinder may be raised in a pre-answer motion.

Rule 20(a): joinder of parties. If common question or fact in the occurrence of the action can join the defendant and plaintiffs.

Once proper joinder under Rule 20(a), Rule 18 permits the adding of unrelated claims.

Rule 42(b) authorizes a judge to do separate trials for unrelated claims.

If claim is diversity claim and the joinder of non-diverse party destroys diversity, the court decides if the party is necessary and if so if party is indispensable, and if there is still a remedy for plaintiff (in state court).

Discovery

Automatic disclosure

Discovery is a lawyer-driven process to investigate a claim and compel documents.

Rule 26 (a)(1) pertains to initial disclosures.

Rule 26 requires disclose without waiting for a discovery request.

Opposing counsel must turn over at the beginning of litigation.

1) witnesses that support a position in the case

2) any document that will be used to support the case

3) describe the adversary nature of damages

4) insurance agreements to determine the policy limits

Rule 26 requires parties to disclose all information "then reasonably available" that is not privileged or protected as work product.

However, Rule 26 also has provisions allowing stipulation of the parties (or court order) to modify some disclosure requirements.

Before making disclosures, a party must make a reasonable inquiry into the facts of the case.

Privileges exist as recognition that it is more important to society to protect this communication than reveal this information.

Courts maintain their discretion so at Appellate level the standard for review is an abuse of discretion.

For a good cause shown, a court can also allow discovery of any matter "relevant to the subject matter" involved.

Information need not be admissible to be discoverable if it is "reasonably calculated *to lead to* the discovery of admissible evidence"—evidence might lead you to admissible evidence.

Rule 33 allows a party just to provide access to files, but there could be privileged information in these files.

Common Objections of Discovery

Rule 26 (b)(1) discovery regarding any matter not privileged that is relevant to the claim or defense of any party.

Not all relevant information is admissible but can lead to admissible evidence.

The broader are the pleadings in the complaint, the broader is discovery.

If it is allowed for the other side to look at all documents, privilege and work product are waived.

Rule 26 (b)(2): the court can limit discovery.

Parties can object and get protective orders.

Limitations on discovery include:

1) unduly burdensome

2) cumulative

3) available elsewhere

Rule 26 (b)(3) pertains to documents and tangible things. For example, work product (e.g., notes on documents in preparing for litigation, legal judgments, and strategies) are protected.

Rule 26 (b)(5): have to articulate why using privilege as much as possible without disclosing too much

Discovery Sanctions

Rule 26 (g): discovery (including responses to discovery) must be:

Consistent with the rules and warranted by existing law or good faith extension, modification, or reversal of existing law.

Not interposed for any improper purpose, such as to harass or to cause unnecessary delay or needless increase in the cost of litigation.

Not unreasonable or unduly burdensome or expensive given the needs of the case.

Rule 26 (g)(3): failure to comply with discovery requests can lead to sanctions against attorney and/or party, including payment of opponent's expenses (i.e., attorneys' fees) due to the violation.

Depositions

Rule 30 covers depositions: witness testimony under oath.

Advantages of depositions: uncoached testimony, can ask follow-up questions, and observe a person's actual reaction to the questions.

Disadvantages of depositions: expensive, difficult to plan, have to study the case to do effectively (a reason why depositions are usually taken late in the case).

Sometimes depositions are taken early in the case before the witness knows enough about the case to be aware of what information to hide.

Usually, a witness comes to trial, but when this is not possible, a videotape of the deposition may be used after being screened for objections.

At deposition, objections noted but answers must be given.

Can refuse to answer questions that are privileged.

Rule 30 (d)(4) prohibits harassing or embarrassing questions.

Depositions can be taken from anyone.

Interrogatories

Interrogatories (Rule 33) are written questions (limited to 25 interrogatories, unless the court approves more).

Interrogatories must be answered from anything in possession (i.e., files).

Interrogatories are valuable to determine who depose (i.e., determine the identity of all people that may have information).

Interrogatories are written by lawyers and answered by lawyers under oath.

Interrogatories are used to get basic facts (e.g., names and addresses of witnesses, doctors bills).

Interrogatory are limited in number, so multi-part questions problematic.

No follow up questions are permitted.

Interrogatories are for parties of the suit and not for witnesses.

Often, the sequence is interrogatories first, document requests, then depositions after earlier information is evaluated.

Production of Documents

Rule 34 covers requests for the production of documents.

Sent to parties in the case (if want something from non-party must get subpoena).

Witnesses and documents can be obtained by subpoena.

If in a foreign language, the producing party must translate.

Physical and Mental Exams

Rule 36 covers physical and mental exams: a court order is needed for physical and mental exams of a party.

Personal injury cases will get the physical exam, but they may be limited in their scope.

Cannot get a physical exam for witnesses but can subpoena for these records.

Request for admissions

Rule 36 is request for admissions: to avoid litigating certain points.

Rule 37 (a): when someone fails to comply with a motion to compel.

37 (a)(2)(b): applies in the context of a motion to compel.

A motion is filed after a party believes an opponent has failed to comply with discovery.

Must confer with an opponent before filing.

The court may award fees to the party who successfully pursues or defends against such an action.

Rule 37 (b)(2): does not allow sanctions for interfering with discovery until there is an effort to work it out, since the defendant may resist if the item requested is too burdensome.

Adjudication Without a Trial

Rule 41 covers dismissals.

Voluntary Dismissal

Plaintiff may dismiss an action without a court order by filing:

> i) a notice of dismissal before the opposing party serves either an answer or a motion for summary judgment; or

> ii) a stipulation of dismissal signed by all parties who have appeared.

Unless the notice or stipulation states otherwise, the dismissal is without prejudice.

If the plaintiff previously dismissed any federal- or state-court action based on or including the same claim, a notice of dismissal operates as an adjudication on the merits.

Except as provided in Rule 41(a)(1), an action may be dismissed at the plaintiff's request only by court order, on terms that the court considers proper.

If a defendant has pleaded a counterclaim before being served with the plaintiff's motion to dismiss, the action may be dismissed over the defendant's objection only if the counterclaim can remain pending for independent adjudication.

Unless the order states otherwise, a dismissal under this paragraph is without prejudice.

Involuntary Dismissal

If the plaintiff fails to prosecute or to comply with these rules or court order, a defendant may move to dismiss the action.

Unless the dismissal order states otherwise, a dismissal under this subdivision and any dismissal not under this rule;

> except one for lack of jurisdiction,

> improper venue, or

> failure to join a party under Rule 19

operates as an adjudication on the merits.

Dismissing a Counterclaim, crossclaim or Third-Part Claim

A claimant's voluntary dismissal under Rule 41(a)(1)(A)(i) must be made:

> 1) before a responsive pleading is served; or

> 2) if there is no responsive pleading and before evidence is introduced at a hearing or trial.

If a plaintiff who previously dismissed an action in any court files an action based on or including the same claim against the same defendant, the court:

> 1) may order the plaintiff to pay all or part of the costs of that previous action; and

> 2) may stay the proceedings until the plaintiff has complied.

Pretrial Conference and Order

Pretrial Conferences

The court may hold pretrial conferences as necessary to expedite trial and encourage settlement.

Pretrial Disclosures: At least 30 days before trial, a party must disclose to the other parties and file with the court a list of:

> witnesses to be called at trial,
>
> witnesses that may be called if the need arises,
>
> witnesses whose testimony will be presented by deposition
>
> transcript of pertinent portions of the deposition, and
>
> documents or exhibits she expects to offer if needed.

Evidence or witnesses that would be used solely for impeachment need not be disclosed.

Within 14 days after this disclosure, a party may serve objections to use of the depositions at trial and to the admissibility of disclosed documents and exhibits.

Such objections are waived if not made at this point, except for objections that the evidence is irrelevant, prejudicial, or confusing under Federal Rules of Evidence 402 and 403.

Rule 16(b) scheduling conference: the court must (except in classes of cases exempted by local rule) hold a scheduling conference among the parties or counsel.

The conference may be held by telephone, mail, or suitable means.

The court must, within 90 days after the appearance of a defendant and within 120 days after the complaint has been served on a defendant, enter a scheduling order limiting the time for joinder, motions, and discovery.

Rule 26(f) Conference of Parties when planning for discovery: as soon as practicable, and in any event at least 21 days before a scheduling conference is held or the scheduling order required by Rule 16(b) is due, the parties must confer to consider:

> their claims and defenses,
>
> the possibility of settlement,

> initial disclosures, and

> a discovery plan.

The parties must submit to the court a proposed discovery plan within 14 days after the conference addressing:

> the timing and form of required disclosures,

> the subjects on which discovery may be needed,

> the timing of and limitations on discovery, and

> relevant orders that may be required of the court.

The order may also include dates for pretrial conferences, a trial date, and any other appropriate matters.

A final pretrial conference is held as close to the time of trial as reasonable.

A final pretrial conference is to formulate a plan for the trial, including the admission of evidence.

The final pretrial conference is to be attended by at least one of the lawyers for each side who will be conducting the trial, and by any unrepresented parties.

After a pretrial conference, an order must be entered that controls the subsequent course of events in the case.

Thus, the final pretrial conference order is a blueprint for the trial:

> listing witnesses to be called,

> evidence to be presented,

> factual and legal issues needing resolution.

The final pretrial conference supersedes the pleadings and may be modified only for good cause.

Jury Trials

Right to a Jury Trial – Demand

The right of trial by jury as declared by the Seventh Amendment to the Constitution—or as provided by a federal statute—is preserved to the parties inviolate.

On issue triable of right by a jury, a party may demand a jury trial by:

> 1) serving the other parties with a written demand—which may be included in a pleading—no later than 14 days after the last pleading directed to the issue is served; and
>
> 2) filing the demand per Rule 5(d).

Rules 38 and 39 govern demand for a jury trial.

In its demand, a party may specify the issues that it wishes to have tried by a jury; otherwise, it is considered to have demanded a jury trial on all the issues so triable.

If the party has demanded a jury trial on only some issues, any other party may—within 14 days after being served with the demand or within a shorter time ordered by the court—serve a demand for a jury trial on any other or all factual issues triable by jury.

A party waives the right to a jury trial unless its demand is properly served and filed.

A proper demand may be withdrawn only if the parties consent.

These rules do not create a right to a jury trial on issues in a claim that is an admiralty or maritime claim under Rule 9(h).

Selection and Composition of Juries

Rule 47 addresses selecting jurors.

The court may permit the parties or their attorneys to examine prospective jurors or may itself do so.

If the court examines the jurors, it must permit the parties or their attorneys to make any further inquiry it considers proper, or must itself ask any of their additional questions it considers proper.

28 U.S.C. §1870 requires the court to allow the number of peremptory challenges (e.g., three for civil trials).

During trial or deliberation, the court may excuse a juror for good cause.

Number of jurors, verdict and polling

Rule 48 pertains to the number of jurors, verdict and polling

A jury must begin with at least 6 and no more than 12 members, and each juror must participate in the verdict unless excused.

Unless the parties stipulate otherwise, the verdict must be unanimous and must be returned by a jury of at least 6 members.

After a verdict is returned but before the jury is discharged, the court must on a party's request, or may on its own, poll the jurors individually.

If the poll reveals a lack of unanimity or lack of assent by the number of jurors that the parties stipulated to, the court may direct the jury to deliberate further or may order a new trial.

Instructions to the Jury

At the close of the evidence or at any earlier reasonable time that the court orders, a party may file and furnish to every other party written requests for the jury instructions it wants the court to give.

After the close of the evidence, a party may:

> A) file requests for instructions on issues that could not reasonably have been anticipated by an earlier time that the court set for requests; and

> B) with the court's permission, file untimely requests for instructions on any issue.

The court:

> 1) must inform the parties of its proposed instructions and proposed action on the requests before instructing the jury and before final jury arguments,

> 2) must give the parties an opportunity to object on the record and out of the jury's hearing before the instructions and arguments are delivered, and

> 3) may instruct the jury at any time before the jury is discharged.

Instructions to the Jury for Objections

A party who objects to an instruction or the failure to give an instruction must do so on the record, stating distinctly the matter objected to and the grounds for the objection.

An objection is timely if:

> A) a party objects at the opportunity provided under Rule 51(b)(2), or

> B) a party was not informed of an instruction or action on a request before that opportunity to object, and the party objects promptly after learning that the instruction or request will be, or has been, given or refused.

Instructions to the Jury Preserving a Claim of Error

A party may assign as error:

> A) an error in an instruction given if that party properly objected; or

> B) a failure to give an instruction, if that party properly requested it and—unless the court rejected the request in a definitive ruling on the record—also properly objected.

A court may consider a plain error in the instructions that has not been preserved as required by Rule 51(d)(1) if the error affects substantial rights.

Motions

Pretrial Motions

The sequence of events at trial:

Opening Statements

Plaintiff's case in chief: plaintiff has the burden of proof.

Defendant's case: support position of no liability.

Closing Argument

Deliberation

Summary Judgment

Rule 56 pertains to Summary Judgment.

Motions for Summary Judgment takes place after discovery, uses evidence from discovery & tries to get case disposed of.

Motion granted if evidence does not show that there is any way for jury to find for one party

The question for summary judgment: is there a genuine issue of material fact?

Convincing Clarity Standard—more difficult the case is to prove at trial then the more you need to show to survive summary judgment motion

The moving party for summary judgment must demonstrate an absence of evidence to support the nonmoving party's case.

If the moving party establishes a lack of evidence, non-moving party must present specific facts showing there is a genuine issue for trial.

Summary judgment may be granted on parts of the case.

If the defendant prevails on one element of the case, the plaintiff prevails because the plaintiff has the burden of proof on all elements.

If the plaintiff prevails on one element, that element not at issue at trial.

Plaintiff may plead a case that is legally sufficient (i.e., survives a Rule 12 (b)(6) Motion), but the defendant may have facts that eliminate an essential element.

In such a case, defendant can file a motion for summary judgment and attach admissible evidence and a brief explaining the legal meaning.

Plaintiff has a chance to respond to the motion that shows contradicting evidence to establish a factual dispute requiring a jury.

In some cases, both sides will agree on all facts and will both submit motions for summary judgment to get a ruling on the legal implication of those facts

Rule 56(e) when motion made, adverse party cannot just rely on allegations in the complaint.

If an adverse party does not respond, summary judgment will be granted, if appropriate.

So, if the evidence presented by an opposing party still makes conclusion doubtful then summary judgment is not appropriate.

Summary Judgment is based on the papers before trial (i.e., motions, briefs, and affidavits).

Declaratory Judgment

Rule 57 addresses declaratory judgment (i.e., a binding judgment from a court defining the legal relationship between parties and their rights in a matter before the court).

The existence of another adequate remedy does not preclude a declaratory judgment that is otherwise appropriate.

A court may order a speedy hearing of a declaratory judgment action.

Declaratory Judgment: defined as a mechanism for a party for a party to bring suit to itself to determine its liabilities and rights.

If the party expects to be sued, they can bring the matter to the court to hear its opinion on how it would rule if they were actually sued if they performed in a particular manner.

Courts will only grant declaratory judgments when there is a focused immediate controversy between the parties.

Directed Verdict – Judgment as a Matter of Law (JMOL)

Rule 50: Motions of Judgment as Matter of Law (JMOL) – is a motion made by a party, during the trial, claiming the opposing party has insufficient evidence to reasonably support its case.

Rule 50(a): Directed Verdict – verdict rendered by a jury upon instruction by the judge that they must bring in that verdict because one of the parties has not proved their case as a matter of law (replaces JMOL in federal courts).

Must wait until the non-moving party has presented all evidence:

> must be made before case presented to the jury, and

> must specify the basis for the motion.

A motion for judgment as a matter of law (JMOL) may be made at any time before the case is submitted to the jury.

How can this be balanced with 7th Amendment?

> 1) Right to a jury trial shall be preserved as existed in 1791,

> 2) Juries determine the facts and if there are no facts to decide then not taking anything away from the jury.

Plaintiff cannot make the motion immediately after presenting their case because the defendant has no chance to present case yet, but the defendant could since plaintiff has had their chance to plead their case.

Direct Verdict motion is raised after a party has had an opportunity to present their case.

A plaintiff suing several different defendants because not sure which one is liable, plaintiff puts on evidence that 2 of 3 defendants liable, but nothing about other defendant, third defendant moves for a directed verdict because plaintiff hasn't proved anything for that defendants to be liable and no reasonable jury could find for him.

Court will grant a motion for directed verdict (JMOL) if no reasonable jury could find in favor of the nonmoving party (federal approach).

If the court does not grant a motion for judgment as a matter of law made under Rule 50(a), the court is considered to have submitted the action to the jury subject to the court's later deciding the legal questions raised by the motion.

Why would a judge grant motion before going to the jury?

1). Preserve 7th Amendment by not reexamining jury's findings just renew decision on a motion as a matter of law.

2). Allows a party to fix the problem with the case

Plaintiff can reopen the case to present new evidence to amend oversight.

Standards

Standards of review are the same under Rule 50(a) and Rule 50(b).

Scintilla test – even if only a little evidence to support, then goes to the jury.

Plaintiff's evidence standard – in assessing whether jury can hear case, only look at plaintiff's evidence.

Federal Standards – look at the plaintiff's case in a most favorable light *and* consider all uncontradicted evidence of the defendant (all inferences to favor the plaintiff).

When judgment as a matter of law is reviewed on appeal, it is looked at *de novo*.

However, more deference than usual is given to the lower court which conducted the entire trial.

In a bench trial, motion is made under Rule 52.

Under Rule 52, a fundamentally different argument that evidence has not met the burden of proof (judge is fact finder).

JMOL motion is before the jury so that the other side can address the issues.

JMOL is a judgment because the court heard the merits of the case.

Judgment Notwithstanding Verdict (JNOV)

Rule 50(a) has to be filed *first,* then *after* the verdict, it can be renewed.

Rule 50(b): Judgment notwithstanding the verdict (JNOV).

The difference compared to a Judgment as a Matter of Law (JMOL) / Directed Verdict is that the motion for the Judgment Notwithstanding the Verdict (JNOV) is made *after* the jury renders a verdict.

Judgment notwithstanding the verdict (JNOV): case goes to jury and the jury finds for the other party.

The moving party asks the judge to overrule what the jury concluded.

Standard is whether a reasonable jury could have come out this way.

If a reasonable jury could not have decided as this did, then the judge might enter a JNOV.

Rule: only where there is a complete absence of probative facts to support the conclusion reached does a reversible error appear.

If there is an evidentiary basis for the jury's verdict, the jury is free to disregard whatever facts are inconsistent with its conclusion.

Plaintiff appeals and review is *de novo*; if reversed, then goes to a new jury.

If the plaintiff wins, judge orders a new trial.

If appeals court agrees, case remanded to reinstate the judgment on the original verdict.

If the jury gives excessive damages, the judge can ask the plaintiff to remit some of the damages.

If not, the court orders a new trial on damages.

If damages to low, the court asks the defendant to pay more; a new trial might award more.

Reason for the JNOV is to avoid a new trial.

Scenario 1: Judge grants motion before a jury hears the case (directed verdict); if reversed on appeal, the case must be tried again.

Scenario 2: Motion for directed verdict; judge denies or defers; case goes to jury; defendant renews motion (JNOV) after jury presents finding; judge grants the defendant's motion.

If appealed and reversed, judgment entered on the jury's verdict.

Motions for a New Trial

If procedural problems (jury hearing inadmissible evidence) or clear error, motion for new trial will be sustained.

1) Procedural Issues: if a judge makes a prejudicial mistake like inadmissible evidence, improper jury instructions, improper contacts with the jury, an improper argument to the jury

2) Result clearly wrong

Judge convinced seriously erroneous result

Not deprivation of 7th A. because it just goes to another jury

Piesco (1990) granted summary judgment and then reversed.

A judge granted Rule 59 motion for new trial so no final judgment, no interlocutory appeal allowed.

Must wait for 2nd trial then if disfavorable outcome Plaintiff can appeal the Ruling on the Rule 59 motion and if reversed the first trial judgment will be entered or denied then enter judgment on 2nd trial

The court can give a new trial to just one defendant (e.g., issue of damages).

Also could give remittitur in which plaintiff has the option to take less $ then jury granted or then go to a new trial

Instead of saying no reasonable jury could have come out this way but judge saying that it is against the manifest of evidence.

Juries can draw inferences from the evidence, but they have to be drawn the right way under the law.

If inferences not correctly drawn against manifest of the evidence and new trial can be granted.

Can do partial mistrial – new trial on certain issues.

No later than 28 days after the entry of judgment—or if the motion addresses a jury issue not decided by a verdict, no later than 28 days after the jury was discharged—the movant may file a renewed motion for judgment as a matter of law and may include an alternative or joint request for a new trial under Rule 59.

In ruling on the renewed motion, the court may:

> 1) allow judgment on the verdict, if the jury returned a verdict;
>
> 2) order a new trial; or
>
> 3) direct the entry of judgment as a matter of law.

Granting the Renewed Motion

If the court grants a renewed motion for judgment as a matter of law, it must also conditionally rule on any motion for a new trial by determining whether a new trial should be granted if the judgment is later vacated or reversed.

The court must state the grounds for conditionally granting or denying the motion for a new trial.

Conditional Ruling on a Motion for a New Trial

Conditionally granting the motion for a new trial does not affect the judgment's finality; if the judgment is reversed, the new trial must proceed unless the appellate court orders otherwise.

If the motion for a new trial is conditionally denied, the appellee may assert error in that denial.

If the judgment is reversed, the case must proceed as the appellate court orders.

Findings and Conclusions by the Court

Rule 52 pertains to Findings and Conclusions by the Court.

In an action tried on the facts without a jury or with an advisory jury, the court must find the facts specially and state its conclusions of law separately.

The findings and conclusions may be stated on the record after the close of the evidence or may appear in an opinion or a memorandum of decision filed by the court.

Judgment must be entered under Rule 58.

In granting or refusing an interlocutory injunction, the court must similarly state the findings and conclusions that support its action.

The court is not required to state findings or conclusions when ruling on a motion under Rule 12 or 56 or, unless these rules provide otherwise, on any other motion.

A master's findings, to the extent adopted by the court, must be considered the court's findings.

A party may later question the sufficiency of the evidence supporting the findings, whether or not the party requested findings, objected to them, moved to amend them, or moved for partial findings.

Findings of fact, whether based on oral or other evidence, must not be set aside unless clearly erroneous.

The reviewing court must give due regard to the trial court's opportunity to judge the witnesses' credibility.

Amended or Additional Findings

On a party's motion filed no later than 28 days after the entry of judgment, the court may amend its findings (or make additional findings) and may amend the judgment accordingly.

The motion may accompany a motion for a new trial under Rule 59.

Judgment on Partial Findings

If a party has been fully heard on an issue during a nonjury trial and the court finds against the party on that issue, the court may enter judgment against the party on a claim or defense that, under the controlling law, can be maintained or defeated only with a favorable finding on that issue.

The court may, however, decline to render any judgment until the close of the evidence.

A judgment on partial findings must be supported by findings of fact and conclusions of law as required by Rule 52(a).

Entering Judgment

Judgments NOT on merits: subject matter, jurisdiction, personal jurisdiction, venue, improper service of process, failure to join a party.

Judgments on merits:

> summary judgment,
>
> directed verdict,
>
> Rule 12(b)(6) (get chance to amend complaint), or
>
> dismissal for failure to prosecute.

In a state that treats 12(b)(6) motion as not barring the second suit, then suit brought in Federal Court will apply the same principles.

The court will probably not grant Rule 60(b) relief either since this is just an attempt to avoid res judicata.

Rule 58 pertains to Entering Judgment.

Every judgment and amended judgment must be set out in a separate document, but a separate document is not required for an order disposing of a motion:

> 1) for judgment under Rule 50(b),
>
> 2) to amend or make additional findings under Rule 52(b),
>
> 3) for attorney's fees under Rule 54,
>
> 4) for a new trial under Rule 59,
>
> 5) to alter or amend the judgment under Rule 59; or
>
> 6) for relief under Rule 60.

Subject to Rule 54(b) and unless the court orders otherwise, the clerk must, without awaiting the court's direction, promptly prepare, sign, and enter the judgment when:

> A) the jury returns a general verdict,

B) the court awards only costs or a sum certain, or

C) the court denies all relief.

Subject to Rule 54(b), the court must promptly approve the form of the judgment, which the clerk must promptly enter, when:

A) the jury returns a special verdict or a general verdict with answers to written questions; or

B) court grants other relief not described in this subdivision.

For purposes of these rules, judgment is entered at the following times:

1) if a separate document is not required, when the judgment is entered in the civil docket under Rule 79(a), or

2) if a separate document is required, when the judgment is entered in the civil docket under Rule 79(a), and the earlier of these events occurs:

A) it is set out in a separate document, or

B) 150 days have run from the entry in the civil docket.

A party may request that judgment be set out in a separate document as required by Rule 58(a).

Ordinarily, the entry of judgment may not be delayed, nor the time for appeal extended, in order to tax costs or award fees.

But if a timely motion for attorney's fees is made under Rule 54(d)(2), the court may act before a notice of appeal has been filed and become effective to order that the motion has the same effect under Federal Rule of Appellate Procedure 4 (a)(4) as a timely motion under Rule 59.

Relief from a Judgment or Order

Rule 60. Relief from a Judgment or Order

The court may correct a clerical mistake or a mistake arising from oversight or omission whenever one is found in a judgment, order, or another part of the record.

The court may do so on motion or its own, with or without notice.

However, after an appeal has been docketed in the appellate court and while it is pending, such a mistake may be corrected only with the appellate court's leave.

On motion and just terms, the court may relieve a party or its legal representative from a final judgment, order, or proceeding for the following reasons:

> 1) mistake, inadvertence, surprise, or excusable neglect,

> 2) newly discovered evidence that, with reasonable diligence, could not have been discovered in time to move for a new trial under Rule 59(b),

> 3) fraud (whether intrinsic or extrinsic), misrepresentation, or misconduct by an opposing party,

> 4) the judgment is void,

> 5) the judgment has been satisfied, released, or discharged; it is based on an earlier judgment that has been reversed or vacated, or applying it prospectively is no longer equitable, or

> 6) any other reason that justifies relief.

Claim Preclusion – Res Judicata

Plaintiff cannot bring a second cause of action, based on the same facts and evidence after an original cause of action has already been litigated

Federal Rules of Civil Procedure are very flexible to get the whole case heard *but* very strict about giving a second chance to try the case.

Four requirements:

> 1) Final Judgment

> 2) On the merits

> 3) Claims must be the same

> 4) Parties must be the same

Federal Court for #3 uses claim as same transaction or series of transactions like joinder (same set of historical facts).

Want to present all claims in one lawsuit.

Exception, cases that, by statute, must be heard in the Federal Court (e.g., patent cases)

For example, if the defendant pleads res judicata, will lose because the patent claim could not have brought in state court.

If had ability to sue on the claim in the first suit – res judicata applies.

If the court in 1ˢᵗ suit never reached merits, then no judgment, so res judicata does not apply.

If suit 1 in federal court and suit 2 in state court, suit 2 will be barred if it could have been added under supplemental jurisdiction or did not offer it at all.

However, if did offer the suit and it was denied, it won't be barred.

Then, win or lose, the plaintiff is barred from a second lawsuit on the claim.

If the plaintiff wins, claim merged with judgment.

If the plaintiff lost, claim become barred.

Analysis, same parties as before and claims from the same underlying transaction – focus on underlying events.

If error in 1ˢᵗ case, appealing the first judgment is the approach.

If the defendant sues the plaintiff after plaintiff sued defendant, it is barred if based on same underlying facts.

Compulsory counterclaims, rule based on res judicata.

If a counterclaim is permissive, then not barred.

If crossclaim is permissive, then not barred.

If defendant impleads 3ʳᵈ party, then after case defendant sues 3ʳᵈ party on same underlying facts, it is barred because should have asserted all claims when brought him into the suit as 3ʳᵈ party.

If the plaintiff did not pursue a lawsuit, then barred by failure to prosecute barred by that judgment on dismissal; had a chance to litigate merits and didn't pursue – no 2ⁿᵈ chances.

If default against the defendant – defendant barred because gave up on merits.

If law changes, still cannot litigate because would still be suing on same underlying facts.

Federal Courts: (Majority Rule for State Courts): when it arises from the same cause of action—same transaction, occurrence or event—it is part of the same claim and cannot litigate it again.

Minority Rule (for State Courts): even if one cause of action gives rise to two different claims, the second claim not precluded; claims are different if the nature of the harm done is different (e.g., property damage vs. personal injury).

Possible ways to determine whether subsequent cases involve the same claim:

>Type of damages: used in minority of states

>Single occurrence (federal courts)

>Sameness of evidence: to establish liability

>Common Nucleus of operative facts: restatement definition

Parties are identical or in privity & same configuration: which parties are bound?

Privity: whatever benefits the first plaintiff would get from the first lawsuit would benefit the second plaintiff, so claim precluded (e.g., trustee bring a claim for the benefit of the beneficiary, the beneficiary cannot bring an identical claim against the same defendant.

Class action: person part of class action even though not actually named cannot bring a claim on their own; the legal relationship between litigant and party not a litigant.

Privity: rights were already exhausted because the previous plaintiff already exhausted them; it is like trying the same case again—a case already tried but with the different person standing in)

Same Configuration: plaintiff has to be the same plaintiff in the 2nd case.

Plaintiff has to be the one to sue the defendant in both cases; it is not the same configuration if the defendant initiates suit.

Valid final judgment: valid unless no jurisdiction or venue issues.

Becomes final judgment after trial court is done with the matter.

On the merits – had the opportunity to have the substance heard:

>Summary judgment,

>Judgment as a matter of law (JMOL),

>Judgment notwithstanding the verdict (JNOV).

Dismissed on lack of jurisdiction, cannot impose claim preclusion because the issue was not tried on the merits.

Dismissed because of other elements not due to merits, haven't had a day in court.

Rule 12(6): motion to dismiss for failure to state a claim – when a court dismisses the claim with prejudice (after amended complaint); some states assert it is on the merits because no claim stated.

Issue Preclusion – Collateral Estoppel

Prevents litigation of particular issues that were litigated and determined in the first case.

1st case argues A, B, C, & D, then 2nd case argues A, X, Y, & Z. A cannot be sued again since he was in the prior suit.

Elements:

Was the same issue litigated and determined in the first case?

Was the issue essential to the judgment in the first case?

Was the holding on that issue embodied in a valid, final judgment on the merits?

Is the preclusion being exercised against an appropriate party?

Is the preclusion being asserted by an appropriate party? (mutuality issue)

Appeals and Review – Government as a Party

Appeal as of Right

Rule 4 applies to Appeal as of Right.

In a civil case, except as provided in Rules 4(a)(1)(B), 4(a)(4), and 4(c), the notice of appeal required by Rule 3 must be filed with the district clerk within 30 days after entry of the judgment or order appealed from.

Any party may file the notice of appeal within 60 days after entry of the judgment or order appealed from if one of the parties is:

> i) the United States;

> ii) a United States agency;

> iii) a United States officer or employee sued in an official capacity; or

> iv) a current or former United States officer or employee sued in an individual capacity for an act or omission occurring in connection with duties performed on the United States' behalf (including all instances in which the United States represents that person when the judgment or order is entered or files the appeal for that person).

An appeal from an order granting or denying an application for a writ of error *coram nobis* (i.e., fundamental error or manifest injustice) is an appeal in a civil case for purposes of Rule 4(a).

A notice of appeal filed after the court announces a decision or order – but before the entry of the judgment or order – is treated as filed on the date of and after the entry.

If one party timely files a notice of appeal, any other party may file a notice of appeal within 14 days after the date when the first notice was filed, or within the time otherwise prescribed by this Rule 4(a), whichever period ends later.

Effect of a Motion on a Notice of Appeal

If a party files in the district court any of the following motions under the Federal Rules of Civil Procedure – and does so within the time allowed by those rules – the time to file an appeal runs for all parties from the entry of the order disposing of the last such remaining motion:

> i) for judgment under Rule 50(b);

> (ii) to amend or make additional factual findings under Rule 52(b), whether or not granting the motion would alter the judgment;

> iii) for attorney's fees under Rule 54 if the district court extends the time to appeal under Rule 58;

> iv) to alter or amend the judgment under Rule 59;

> v) for a new trial under Rule 59; or

> vi) for relief under Rule 60 if the motion is filed no later than 28 days after the judgment is entered.

If a party files a notice of appeal after the court announces or enters a judgment –but before it disposes of any motion listed in Rule 4(a)(4)(A) –the notice becomes effective to appeal a judgment or order, in whole or in part, when the order disposing of the last such remaining motion is entered.

A party intending to challenge an order disposing of any motion listed in Rule 4(a)(4)(A), or a judgment's alteration or amendment upon such a motion, must file a notice of appeal, or an amended notice of appeal – in compliance with Rule 3(c) – within the time prescribed by this Rule measured from the entry of the order disposing of the last such remaining motion.

No additional fee is required to file an amended notice.

Motion for Extension of Time

The district court may extend the time to file a notice of appeal if:

> i) a party so moves no later than 30 days after the time prescribed by this Rule 4(a) expires; and

ii) regardless of whether its motion is filed before or during the 30 days after the time prescribed by this Rule 4(a) expires, that party shows excusable neglect or good cause.

A motion filed before the expiration of the time prescribed in Rule 4(a)(1) or (3) may be ex parte unless the court requires otherwise.

If the motion is filed after the expiration of the prescribed time, notice must be given to the other parties per local rules.

No extension under this Rule 4(a)(5) may exceed 30 days after the prescribed time or 14 days after the date when the order granting the motion is entered, whichever is later.

Reopening the Time to File an Appeal

The district court may reopen the time to file an appeal for a period of 14 days after the date when its order to reopen is entered, but only if all the following conditions are satisfied:

A) the court finds that the moving party did not receive notice under Federal Rule of Civil Procedure 77 (d) of the entry of the judgment or order sought to be appealed within 21 days after entry;

B) the motion is filed within 180 days after the judgment or order is entered or within 14 days after the moving party receives notice under Federal Rule of Civil Procedure 77 (d) of the entry, whichever is earlier; and

C) the court finds that no party would be prejudiced.

Entry Defined

A judgment or order is entered for purposes of this Rule 4(a):

i) if Federal Rule of Civil Procedure 58 (a) does not require a separate document when the judgment or order is entered in the civil docket under Federal Rule of Civil Procedure 79 (a); or

ii) if Federal Rule of Civil Procedure 58 (a) requires a separate document when the judgment or order is entered in the civil docket under Federal Rule of Civil Procedure 79(a) and when the earlier of these events occurs:

• the judgment or order is set forth on a separate document, or

- 150 days have run from the entry of the judgment or order in the civil docket under Federal Rule of Civil Procedure 79 (a).

A failure to set forth a judgment or order on a separate document when required by Federal Rule of Civil Procedure 58 (a) does not affect the validity of an appeal from that judgment or order.

Appeals and Review – Criminal Cases

Effect of a Motion on a Notice of Appeal

In a criminal case, a defendant's notice of appeal must be filed in the district court within 14 days after the later of:

i) the entry of either the judgment or the order being appealed; or

ii) the filing of the government's notice of appeal.

When the government is entitled to appeal, its notice of appeal must be filed in the district court within 30 days after the later of:

i) the entry of the judgment or order being appealed; or

ii) the filing of a notice of appeal by any defendant.

A notice of appeal filed after the court announces a decision, sentence, or order – but before the entry of the judgment or order –is treated as filed on the date of and after the entry.

If a defendant timely makes any of the following motions under the Federal Rules of Criminal Procedure, the notice of appeal from a judgment of conviction must be filed within 14 days after the entry of the order disposing of the last such remaining motion, or within 14 days after the entry of the judgment of conviction, whichever period ends later.

The above provision applies to a timely motion:

i) for judgment of acquittal under Rule 29;

ii) for a new trial under Rule 33, but is based on newly discovered evidence, only if the motion is made no later than 14 days after the entry of the judgment; or

iii) for the arrest of a judgment under Rule 34.

A notice of appeal filed after the court announces a decision, sentence, or order – but before it disposes of any of the motions referred to in Rule 4(b)(3)(A) – becomes effective upon the later of the following:

i) the entry of the order disposing of the last such remaining motion; or

ii) the entry of the judgment of conviction.

A valid notice of appeal is effective – without amendment – to appeal from an order disposing of any of the motions referred to in Rule 4(b)(3)(A).

308   Copyright © 2020 Sterling Test Prep. Any duplication is illegal.

Motion for Extension of Time

Upon a finding of excusable neglect or good cause, the district court may – before or after the time has expired, with or without motion and notice – extend the time to file a notice of appeal for a period not to exceed 30 days from the expiration of the time otherwise prescribed by this Rule 4(b).

Jurisdiction.

The filing of a notice of appeal under this Rule 4(b) does not divest a district court of jurisdiction to correct a sentence under Federal Rule of Criminal Procedure 35(a), nor does the filing of a motion under 35(a) affect the validity of a notice of appeal filed before entry of the order disposing of the motion.

The filing of a motion under Federal Rule of Criminal Procedure 35(a) does not suspend the time for filing a notice of appeal from a judgment of conviction.

A judgment or order is entered for purposes of this Rule 4(b) when it is entered on the criminal docket.

Appeal by an Inmate Confined in an Institution

If an institution has a system designed for legal mail, an inmate confined there must use that system to receive the benefit of this Rule 4(c)(1).

If an inmate files a notice of appeal in either a civil or a criminal case, the notice is timely if it is deposited in the institution's internal mail system on or before the last day for filing and:

The notice of appeal must be accompanied by:

> i) a declaration in compliance with 28 U.S.C. § 1746 – or a notarized statement – setting out the date of deposit and stating that first-class postage is being prepaid; or

> ii) evidence (such as a postmark or date stamp) showing that the notice was so deposited and that postage was prepaid; or

The court of appeals exercises its discretion to permit the later filing of a declaration or notarized statement that satisfies Rule 4(c)(1)(A)(i).

If an inmate files the first notice of appeal in a civil case under this Rule 4(c), the 14-day period provided in Rule 4(a)(3) for another party to file a notice of appeal runs from the date when the district court dockets the first notice.

When a defendant in a criminal case files a notice of appeal under this Rule 4(c), the 30-day period for the government to file its notice of appeal runs from the entry of the judgment or order appealed from or from the district court's docketing of the defendant's notice of appeal, whichever is later.

Mistaken Filing in the Court of Appeals

If a notice of appeal in either a civil or a criminal case is mistakenly filed in the court of appeals, the clerk of that court must note on the notice the date when it was received and send it to the district clerk.

The notice is then considered filed in the district court on the date so noted.

Civil Procedure – Quick Facts

American courts: basic principles

1. Every state has its court system.

   The structure of the system, and the types of cases each court within a state court system may hear are generally established by statutes enacted by the **state legislature**.

2. The United States Constitution provides for a **separate federal court system**.

   Article III, §. 1 of the Constitution creates the United States **Supreme Court** and authorizes Congress to create other federal courts below the supreme court.

   Congress has created **federal trial courts** (i.e., federal district courts) and **intermediate appellate courts** (i.e., federal courts of appeals), as well as a few other specialized courts.

3. The structure of the state and federal courts systems are similar.

   The state courts, like the federal system, has a set of trial courts and a state supreme court at the apex of its court system.

   Many state court systems also have intermediate appellate courts analogous to the federal courts of appeals.

4. The **vast majority of disputes** are litigated in state courts.

   Every state has trial courts with **very broad subject matter jurisdiction**.

   Most states also have several specialized (e.g., juvenile) trial courts.

5. The categories of cases that federal courts can hear their "**subject matter jurisdiction**" is quite narrow.

   The broadest categories authorized in article III §. 3 are 1) cases arising under **federal law**, 2) cases between **citizens of different states**, 3) cases between **citizens and aliens**, and 4) **admiralty and maritime cases**.

6. Generally, state courts have **concurrent jurisdiction** over cases that federal courts are authorized to hear.

   For example, cases that arise under federal law usually can be brought in state court, even though general courts are authorized by Article III to hear such cases.

Where a case may be filed in either system, the **plaintiff chooses where to file**.

7. The exception to concurrent jurisdiction is that Congress when it authorizes lower federal courts to hear a particular type of case, may provide that such jurisdiction is "**exclusive of the courts of the states**."

   It has done so for some types of cases including patent and copyright cases.

Diversity Jurisdiction

1. Article III §. 2 of the Constitution authorizes federal courts to hear cases "between citizens of different states" commonly referred to as **diversity jurisdiction**.

2. The constitutional grant in article 3 §. 2 is satisfied as long as there is "**minimal diversity**" between the parties

   Therefore, at least one plaintiff is from a different state than one defendant.

3. Federal district courts do not have diversity jurisdiction just because the constitution authorizes it.

   Congress must convey it to them by statute.

   The diversity statute, 28 USC §. 1332, does not convey all diversity jurisdiction to the federal district courts.

   It imposes an **amount in controversy requirement** (i.e., more than $75,000) – whether the plaintiff. if she prevails at trial, might recover more than $75,000 (e.g., $75,000.01).

   Under the statutory grant, no plaintiff may be from the same state as any defendant (*Strawbridge v. Curtis*) (1806): no party on one side of the controversy may be from the same state as a party on the other side

4. For individuals, federal cases hold that a person is a citizen of the state where she is **domiciled**.

   To establish a domicile a person must reside in a state with the intent to remain indefinitely.

   To be a state citizen for diversity purposes, she must also be a citizen of the United States (or permanent resident).

5. **Corporations are also held to be state citizens** for diversity purposes.

   A corporation is a citizen of the state in which it is incorporated, and of the state of its principal place of business.

Arising-Under Jurisdiction

1. The constitutional grant of arising-under jurisdiction in Article 3 §. 2 is liberally construed.

   So long as a case involves a non-frivolous issue of federal law, whether raised in the original complaint or in a defendant's answer a federal court may be authorized to hear it.

2. The power of Congress to create lower federal courts includes the power to define their jurisdiction by statute.

   Article 3 §. 2 sets the outer limit, but within the scope of Article 3 §. 2 Congress may pick and choose, granting federal trial courts all, some, or none of the jurisdiction authorized by the constitution.

   Thus, Congress has the power to authorize the federal district courts to hear some cases that arise under federal law, but not others.

3. As with diversity jurisdiction, Congress has never granted the full scope of **arising under jurisdiction** to the lower federal courts.

   In the early days of the republic only narrow grant of jurisdiction over claims arising under particular statutes, such as the patent statutes, was granted.

4. Court jurisdiction is considerably more limited than constitutional scope than under 28 USC §. 1331.

   Under *Mottley* (1908), a **well-pleaded complaint rule** instructs the court to look only to the plaintiff's claim in determining whether a case arises under federal law.

5. In the vast majority of cases, the Holmes test works to determine whether a case satisfies the *Mottley* requirement.

   If federal law creates the cause of action the plaintiff seeks to enforce, the federal court has jurisdiction.

   A case may arise under federal law even though the plaintiff seeks recovery on a state law claim.

The supreme court has recognized that sometimes a plaintiff will have to establish an important proposition of federal law to prove an element of a state law claim.

A court may find that cases in this category arise under federal law so that a federal district court has jurisdiction over the case.

6. The statutes granting appellate jurisdiction to the Court are much broader than 28 USC §. 1331. Consequently, many state court cases that involve issues of federal law may be appealed to the supreme court, even though the federal issue in the case was not raised in the plaintiff's complaint so that the case could not have been filed initially in a federal district court.

Removal to Federal Court

1. Many cases that may be brought in federal court may also be filed in state court if the plaintiff prefers.

    If the plaintiff does file such a case in state court, the federal removal statutes allow **defendants to remove** them to federal court.

2. The basic standard for removal in 28 USC §. 1441 allows **cases to be removed to federal court if they could have been filed originally in federal court**.

    The exception is forum rule which bars removal of a diversity case **if any defendant resides in the state in which the suit is brought**.

3. If a removable case is filed in state court, defendants must remove within thirty days, or it will remain in state court.

    If a case becomes removable, they have thirty days after which they know it has become removable.

4. **Removal is automatic**. Even if the defendant removes a non-removable case, it will be pending in federal court once the notice of removal is filed and the state court is notified.

    Any party who believes the case was **improperly removed**, or that is not within the federal court's subject matter jurisdiction, should **move in federal court to remand** the case.

5. Motions to remand for **lack of subject matter jurisdiction** may be made **at any time before final judgment**.

   Motions based on any other problems must be raised within thirty days after removal.

The evolution of personal jurisdiction

1. Under *Pennoyer v. Neff* (1878) which reflected nineteenth-century jurisdictional precepts, courts typically only had ***in personam*** (particular defendant) jurisdiction over a person if she was personally served with the complaint within the forum state.

   Moreover, courts had ***in rem*** (item of property) jurisdiction over property if the property was attached before adjudicating the claim and was located within the forum state.

2. *Pennoyer's* rigid doctrine was ill-equipped to deal with an increasingly mobile society and the increased scope of interstate corporate activity.

   Consequently, the court, in *International Shoe* (1945), shifted its focus from the strict requirement of an in-state presence to allow jurisdiction based on a **defendant's contacts with the state.**

3. Courts have identified several different ways to establish *in personam* jurisdiction.

   If the claim arises out of the defendant's contact, a court has **specific jurisdiction over the defendant.**

   If the claim does not arise out of the defendant's contact, but the defendant has **continuous and systematic contacts with the state**, the court has general jurisdiction.

4. The supreme court has recognized that several other bases for jurisdiction are constitutionally sufficient.

   A person is always subject to **personal jurisdiction where she is domiciled**.

   Also, a defendant who would otherwise not be subject to personal jurisdiction in a state may **waive** her objection or **consent to jurisdiction**.

5. A court may only exercise jurisdiction over a defendant if doing so would satisfy the constitutional requirements for **personal jurisdiction**.

In addition, the legislature of the state must authorize the court to exercise personal jurisdiction, in the states long-arm statute or some other jurisdiction-granting statute or rule.

Long Arm Statutes

1. A court can usually exercise personal jurisdiction only if: 1) a **long arm provision authorizes it** and (2) **personal jurisdiction is constitutional.**

    "Tag" is an exception which appears to exist as part of a court's common law authority even when no long arm provision authorizes it.

2. Courts often have to interpret the scope of the applicable long-arm statute.

Basic Venue

Courts try to **restrict litigation** to those courts that are **convenient** given **the facts** of the case and the **location of the parties.**

Appendix

Court Systems within the United States –
Federal and State Courts

There are two kinds of courts in the USA – federal courts and state courts.

Federal courts are established under the U.S. Constitution by Congress to decide disputes involving the Constitution and laws passed by Congress. A state establishes state and local courts (within states there are also local courts that are established by cities, counties, and other municipalities, which are included here in the general discussion of state courts).

The differences between federal courts and state courts are further defined by jurisdiction.[1] Jurisdiction refers to the kinds of cases that a particular court is authorized to hear and adjudicate (i.e., pronouncement of a legally binding judgment upon the parties to the dispute).

Federal court jurisdiction is limited to the types of cases listed in the Constitution and specifically provided for by Congress. For the most part, federal courts only hear:

- cases in which the United States is a party[2];

- cases involving violations of the U.S. Constitution or federal laws (under federal-question jurisdiction[3]);

- cases between citizens of different states if the amount in controversy exceeds $75,000 (under diversity jurisdiction[4]); and

- bankruptcy, copyright, patent, and maritime law cases.

State courts, in contrast, have broad jurisdiction, so the cases individual citizens are likely to be involved in (e.g., robberies, traffic violations, contracts, and family disputes) are usually heard and decided in state courts. The only cases state courts are not allowed to hear are lawsuits against the United States and those involving certain specific federal laws: criminal, antitrust, bankruptcy, patent, copyright, and some maritime law cases.

In many cases, both federal and state courts have jurisdiction whereby the plaintiff (i.e., the party initiating the suit) can choose whether to file their claim in state or federal court.

Criminal cases involving federal laws can be tried only in federal court, but most criminal cases involve violations of state law and are tried in state court. Robbery is a crime, but what law makes it is a crime? Except for certain exceptions, state laws, not federal laws, make robbery a crime. There are only a few federal laws about robbery, such as the law that makes it a federal crime to rob a bank whose deposits are insured by a federal agency. Examples of other federal crimes are the transport of illegal drugs into the country or across state lines and use of the U.S. mail system to defraud consumers.

Crimes committed on federal property (e.g., national parks or military reservations) are also prosecuted in federal court.

Federal courts may also hear cases concerning state laws if the issue is whether the state law violates the federal Constitution. Suppose a state law forbids slaughtering animals outside of certain limited areas. A neighborhood association brings a case in state court against a defendant who sacrifices chickens in his backyard. When the court issues an order (i.e., an injunction[5]) forbidding the defendant from further sacrifices, the defendant challenges the state law in federal court as an unconstitutional infringement of his religious freedom.

Some kinds of conduct are illegal under both federal and state laws. For example, federal laws prohibit employment discrimination, and the states have added additional legal restriction. A person can file their claim in either federal or state court under the federal law or both the federal and state laws. A case that only involves a state law can be brought only in state court.

Appeals for review of actions by federal administrative agencies are also federal civil cases. Suppose, for example, that the Environmental Protection Agency issued a permit to a paper mill to discharge water used in its milling process into the Scenic River, over the objection of area residents. The residents could ask a federal court of appeals to review the agency's decision.

---

[1] *jurisdiction* – (1) the legal authority of a court to hear and decide a certain type of case; (2) the geographic area over which the court has the authority to decide cases.

[2] *parties* – the plaintiff(s) and defendant(s) in a lawsuit.

[3] *federal-question jurisdiction* – the federal district courts' authorization to hear and decide cases arising under the Constitution, laws, or treaties of the United States.

[4] *diversity jurisdiction* – the federal district courts' authority to hear and decide civil cases involving plaintiffs and defendants who are citizens of different states (or U.S. citizens and foreign nationals) and who meet certain statutory requirements.

[5] *injunction* – a judge's order that a party take or refrain from taking certain action. An injunction may be preliminary until the outcome of a case is determined, or permanent.

How the Federal Courts are Organized

Congress has divided the country into 94 federal judicial districts with each having a U.S. district court. The U.S. district courts are the federal trial courts -- where federal cases are tried, witnesses testify, and juries serve. Each district has a U.S. bankruptcy court which is part of the district court that administers the U.S. bankruptcy laws.

Congress uses state boundaries to help define the districts. Some districts cover an entire state, like Idaho. Other districts cover just part of a state, like the Northern District of California. Congress placed each of the ninety-four districts in one of twelve regional circuits whereby each circuit has a court of appeals. The losing party can petition the court of appeals to review the case to determine if the district judge applied the law correctly. There is also a U.S. Court of Appeals for the Federal Circuit, whose jurisdiction is defined by subject matter rather than by geography. It hears appeals from certain courts and agencies, such as the U.S. Court of International Trade, the U.S. Court of Federal Claims, and the U.S. Patent and Trademark Office, and certain types of cases from the district courts (mainly lawsuits claiming that patents have been infringed).

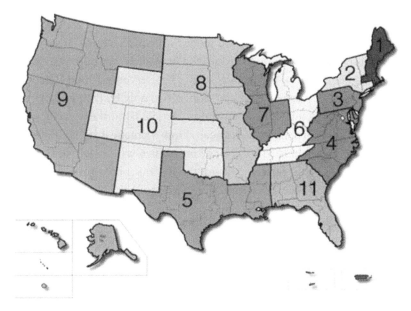

Twelve regional federal circuits

The Supreme Court of the United States, in Washington, D.C., is the highest court in the nation. The losing party can petition in a case in the court of appeals (or, sometimes, in a state supreme court), can petition the

Supreme Court to hear an appeal. However, unlike a court of appeals, the Supreme Court doesn't have to hear the case. The Supreme Court hears only a very small percentage of the cases it is asked to review.

What is judicial independence, and why is it important?

The founders of the United States recognized that the judicial branch must remain independent to fulfill its mission effectively and impartially. Article III of the Constitution protects certain types of judges by providing that they serve "during good behavior" and prohibits the reduction of their salary.

These constitutional protections allow judges to make unpopular decisions without fear of losing their jobs or having their pay cut. For example, the Supreme Court's decision in *Brown v. Board of Education* in 1954 declared racial segregation in public schools to be unconstitutional. This decision was unpopular with large segments of society at that time. Some members of Congress even wanted to replace the judges who made the decision, but this Constitutional protection wouldn't allow them to do so.

What is an Article III judge?

"Article III judge" denotes federal judges who under Article III of the Constitution are enabled to exercise "the judicial power of the United States" without fear of losing their jobs. They serve for "good Behaviour," which means they can be removed from office only by the rarely used process of impeachment and conviction. Article III further provides that their compensation cannot be reduced. From a practical standpoint, almost all of these judges hold office for as long as they wish. "Article III judges" are those on the U.S. Supreme Court, the federal courts of appeals and district courts, and the U.S. Court of International Trade.

Why are some federal judges protected from losing their jobs and having their pay cut?

Federal judges appointed under Article III of the Constitution are guaranteed what amounts to life tenure and unreduced salary so that they won't be afraid to make an unpopular decision. For example, in *Gregg v. Georgia*, the Supreme Court said it is constitutional for the federal and state governments to impose the death penalty if the statute is carefully drafted to provide adequate safeguards. Even though some people are opposed to the death penalty, Article III protections allowed the Judge to make this decision without fear of reciprocity.

The constitutional protection that gives federal judges the freedom and independence to make decisions that are politically and socially unpopular is one of the basic elements of our democracy. According to the Declaration of Independence, one reason the American colonies wanted to separate from England was that King George III "made judges dependent on his will alone, for the tenure of their offices, and the amount and payment of their salaries."

Are there judges in the federal courts other than Article III judges?

Bankruptcy judges and magistrate judges conduct some of the proceedings held in federal courts. Bankruptcy judges handle almost all bankruptcy matters in bankruptcy courts that are technically included in the district courts but function as separate entities. Magistrate judges carry out various responsibilities in the district courts and often help prepare the district judges' cases for trial. They also may preside over criminal misdemeanor trials and may preside over civil trials when both parties agree to have the case heard by a magistrate judge instead of a district judge.

Unlike district judges, bankruptcy and magistrate judges do not exercise "the judicial power of the United States" but perform duties delegated to them by district judges. Bankruptcy and magistrate judges serve for fourteen and eight-year terms, respectively, rather than "during good Behaviour." Bankruptcy judges and magistrate judges don't have the same protections as judges appointed under Article III of the Constitution. Bankruptcy judges, in contrast, may be removed from office by circuit judicial councils, and magistrate judges may be removed by the district judges of the magistrate judge's district.

How many federal judges are there?

Congress authorizes a set number of judge positions, or judgeships, for each court level. Since the 1869 "Circuit Judges Act," Congress has mandated that the Supreme Court would consist of 9 judges. As of 2007, it had mandated 179 court of appeals judgeships and 678 district court judgeships. (In 1950, there were only 65 courts of appeals judgeships and 212 district judgeships). As of 2007, Congress had mandated 352 bankruptcy judgeships and 551 full-time and part-time magistrate judgeships. It is rare that all judgeships are filled at any one time as judges die or retire, causing vacancies until judges are appointed to replace them. In addition to judges occupying these positions, retired judges often continue to perform some judicial work.

How does a person become a federal judge?

Supreme Court justices and the court of appeals and district judges are appointed to office by the President of the United States, with the approval of the U.S. Senate. Presidents most often appoint judges who are members, or at least generally supportive, of their political party, but that doesn't mean that judges are given appointments solely for partisan reasons. The professional qualifications of prospective federal judges are closely evaluated by the Department of Justice, which consults with others, such as lawyers who can evaluate the prospect's abilities. The Senate Judiciary Committee undertakes a separate examination of the nominees. Magistrate judges and bankruptcy judges are not appointed by the President or subject to Congress's approval. The court of appeals in each circuit appoints bankruptcy judges for fourteen-year terms. District courts appoint magistrate judges for eight-year terms.

What are the qualifications for becoming a federal judge?

Although there are almost no formal qualifications for federal judges, there are some strong informal ones. For example, while magistrate judges and bankruptcy judges are required by statute to be lawyers, there is no statutory requirement that district judges, circuit judges, or Supreme Court justices be lawyers. However, there is no legal precedent for a president to nominate someone who is not a lawyer. Before their appointment, most judges were private attorneys, but many were judges in state courts or other federal courts. Some were government attorneys, and a few were law professors.

For judges who are appointed for life, what safeguards ensure that they can do their jobs fairly and capable?

Judges follow the ethical standards set out in the *Code of Conduct for United States Judges*, which contains guidelines to help them avoid situations that might limit their ability to be fair--or that might make it appear to others that their fairness is in question. It tells them, for example, to be careful not to do anything that might cause people to think they would favor one side in a case over another, such as giving speeches that urge voters to pick one candidate over another for public office or asking people to contribute money to civic organizations.

Additionally, Congress has enacted laws telling judges to withdraw or recuse themselves from any case in which a close relative is a party or in which they have any financial interest, even one share of stock. Congress requires judges to file an annual financial disclosure form, so that their stock holdings, board memberships, and other financial interests are a matter of public record.

Congress has also enacted a law that allows anyone to file a complaint alleging that a judge (other than a Supreme Court justice) has engaged in conduct "prejudicial to the effective and expeditious administration of the business of the courts" or that a judge has a mental or physical disability that makes him or her unable to adequately discharge the duties of the office. A complaint is filed with the clerk of the court of appeals of the respective judge's circuit and considered by the chief judge of the court of appeals. If the chief judge believes the complaint deserves attention, the chief judge appoints a special committee of the circuit judicial council to investigate it.

If the committee concludes that the complaint is valid, it may recommend various actions, such as temporarily removing the judge from hearing cases, but it may not recommend that an Article III judge be removed from office. Only Congress may do that, through the impeachment process.

Chief Judges dismiss the great majority of complaints filed under this law because the complaints involve judges' decisions in particular cases. This law may not be used to complain about decisions, even what may appear to be a very wrong decision or very unfair treatment of a party in a case. Parties in a lawsuit who believe the judge issued an incorrect ruling may appeal the case to a higher court, under the rules of procedure.

When do judges retire?

Most federal judges retire from full-time service at around sixty-five or seventy years of age and become senior judges. Senior judges are still federal judges, eligible to earn their full salary and to continue hearing cases if they and their colleagues want them to do so, but they usually maintain a reduced caseload. Full-time judges are known as active judges.

How are cases assigned to judges?

Each court with more than one judge must determine a procedure for assigning cases to judges. Most district and bankruptcy courts use random assignment, which helps to ensure a fair distribution of cases and also prevents "judge shopping," which refers to parties' attempts to have their cases heard by the judge whom they believe will act most favorably. Other courts assign cases by rotation, subject matter, or geographic division of the court. In courts of appeals, cases are usually assigned by random means to temporary three-judge panels.

How Cases Move Through the Federal Courts

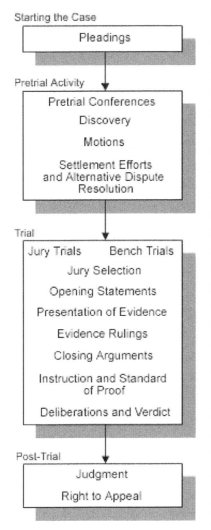

Starting the Case

Pleadings

Pretrial Activity

Pretrial Conferences

Discovery

Motions

Settlement Efforts and Alternative Dispute Resolution

Trial

Jury Trials   Bench Trials

Jury Selection

Opening Statements

Presentation of Evidence

Evidence Rulings

Closing Arguments

Instruction and Standard of Proof

Deliberations and Verdict

Post-Trial

Judgment

Right to Appeal

Civil Cases

A federal civil case begins when a person, or their legal representative, file a paper with the clerk of the court that asserts another person's wrongful act injured the person. In legal terminology, the plaintiff files a *complaint* against the defendant.

The defendant then files an *answer* to the complaint. These written statements of the parties' positions are also called pleadings. In some circumstances, the defendant may file a *motion* instead of an answer; the motion asks the court to take some action, such as dismiss the case or require the plaintiff to explain more clearly what the lawsuit is about.

Jury trials

In a jury trial, the jury decides what happened and to apply the legal standards the judge tells them to apply to reach a verdict. The plaintiff presents evidence supporting its view of the case, and the defendant presents evidence rebutting the plaintiff's evidence or supporting its own view of the case. From these presentations, the jury must decide what happened and applied the law to those facts.

The jury never decides what law applies to the case; that is the role of the judge. For example, in a discrimination case in which the plaintiff alleged that his or her workplace was a hostile environment, the judge would tell the jury the legal standard for a hostile environment. The jury would have to decide whether the plaintiff's description of events was true and whether those events met the legal standard. In a civil case, a trial jury, or petit jury, may consist of six to twelve jurors.

Bench trials

If the parties agree not to have a jury trial and to leave the fact-finding to the judge, the trial is called a bench trial. In either kind of trial, the judge makes sure the correct legal standards are followed. In contrast to a jury trial, in a bench trial, the judge decides the facts and renders the verdict. For example, in a discrimination case in which the plaintiff alleged that his or her workplace was a hostile environment, the judge would determine the legal standard for a hostile environment and would then decide whether the plaintiff's description of events was true and whether those events met the legal standard.

Some kinds of cases always have bench trials. For example, there is never a jury trial if the plaintiff is seeking an injunction, an order from the judge that the defendant does or stop doing something, as opposed to monetary damages. Some statutes also provide that a judge must decide the facts in certain types of cases.

Jury Selection

A jury trial begins with the selection of jurors. Citizens are selected for jury service through a process that is set out in laws passed by Congress and in the federal rules of procedure. First, citizens are called to court to be available to serve on juries. These citizens are selected at random from source lists, in most districts lists of registered or actual voters, which may be augmented by other sources, such as lists of licensed drivers in the judicial district. The judge and the lawyers in each case then choose the persons who will serve on the jury.

To choose the jurors, the judge and sometimes the lawyers ask prospective jurors questions to determine if they will be able to decide the case fairly. This process is called *voir dire*. The lawyers may request that the judge excuse jurors they think may not be impartial, such as those who know a party in the case or who have had an experience that might make them favor one side over the other. These requests for rejecting jurors are *challenges for cause*. The lawyers may also request that the judge excuse a certain number of jurors without giving any reason; these requests are *peremptory challenges*.

Instructions and standard of proof

Following the closing arguments, the judge gives instructions to the jury, explaining the relevant law, how the law applies to the case, and what questions the jury must decide.

How sure do jurors have to be before they reach a verdict? One important instruction the judge gives the jury is the standard of proof they must follow in deciding the case. The courts, through their decisions, and Congress, through statutes, have established standards by which facts must be proven in criminal and civil cases.

In civil cases, in order to decide for the plaintiff, the jury must determine by a *preponderance of the evidence* that the defendant failed to perform a legal duty and violated the plaintiff's rights. A preponderance of the evidence means that, based on all the evidence, the evidence favors the plaintiff more (even if only slightly) than it favors the defendant. If the evidence in favor of the plaintiff could be placed on one side of a scale, and that in favor of the defendant on the other, the plaintiff would win if the evidence in favor of the plaintiff was heavy enough to tip the scale. If the two sides were even, or if the scale tipped for the defendant, the defendant would win.

Judgment

In civil cases, if the jury (or judge) decides in favor of the plaintiff, the result usually is that the defendant must pay the plaintiff money or damages. The judge orders the defendant to pay the decided amount. Sometimes the defendant is ordered to take some specific action that will restore the plaintiff's rights. If the defendant wins the case, however, there is nothing more the trial court needs to do as the case is disposed and the defendant is held not liable

Right to appeal

The losing party in a federal civil case has a right to appeal the verdict of the case to the U.S. court of appeals (or to the state appeals court when the case originated in the state trial court), where the party asks the court of appeals to review the case to determine whether the trial was conducted properly. The grounds for appeal usually are that the federal district (or state) judge made an error, either in the procedure (e.g., admitting improper evidence) or in interpreting the law. The government may appeal in civil cases, as any other party may. Neither party may appeal if there was no trial -- parties settled their civil case out of court.

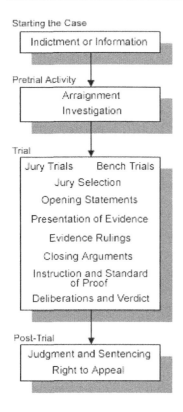

Starting the Case

| Indictment or Information |

Pretrial Activity

| Arraignment |
| Investigation |

Trial

| Jury Trials   Bench Trials |
| Jury Selection |
| Opening Statements |
| Presentation of Evidence |
| Evidence Rulings |
| Closing Arguments |
| Instruction and Standard of Proof |
| Deliberations and Verdict |

Post-Trial

| Judgment and Sentencing |
| Right to Appeal |

Criminal Cases

Indictment or information

A criminal case formally begins with an indictment or information, which is a formal accusation that a person committed a crime. An indictment may be obtained when a lawyer for the executive branch of the U.S. government--the U.S. attorney or an assistant U.S. attorney, also referred to as the prosecutor--presents evidence to a federal grand jury that, according to the government, indicates a person committed a crime. The U.S. attorney tries to convince the grand jury that there is enough evidence to show that the person probably committed the crime and should be formally accused. If the grand jury agrees, it issues an indictment.

A grand jury is different from a trial jury, or petit jury. A grand jury determines whether the person may be tried for a crime; a petit jury listens to the evidence presented at the trial and determines whether the defendant is guilty of the charge. *Petit* is the French word for "small"; petit juries usually consist of twelve jurors in criminal cases. *Grand* is the French word for "large"; grand juries have from sixteen to twenty-three jurors.

Grand jury indictments are most often used for *felonies* (i.e., more serious crimes) such as bank robberies or sales of illegal drugs. Grand jury indictments are not usually necessary to prosecute *misdemeanors* (i.e., less serious crimes) and are not necessary for all felonies. For these crimes, the U.S. attorney issues an information, which takes the place of an indictment. An example of a federal misdemeanor is speeding on a highway in a national park. An information is used when a defendant waives indictment by a grand jury.

Arraignment

After the grand jury issues the indictment, the accused (defendant) is summoned to court or arrested (if not already in custody). The next step is an arraignment, a proceeding in which the defendant is brought before a judge, told of the charges he or she is accused of and asked to plead guilty or not guilty. If the defendant's plea is guilty, a time is set for the defendant to return to court to be sentenced. If the defendant pleads "not guilty," then the time is set for the trial. A defendant may also enter a plea bargain with the prosecution--usually by agreeing to plead guilty to some but not all of the charges or to a lesser charge, in return, the prosecution drops the remaining charges. About nine out of ten defendants in criminal cases plead guilty.

Investigation

In a criminal case, a defense lawyer will conduct a thorough investigation prior to trial, interviewing witnesses, visiting the scene of the crime, and examining any physical evidence. An important part of this investigation is determining whether the evidence the government plans to use to prove its case was obtained legally. The Fourth Amendment to the Constitution forbids unreasonable searches and seizures. To enforce this protection, the Supreme Court has decided that for most purposes, illegally seized evidence cannot be used at trial. For example, if the police seize evidence from a defendant's home without a search warrant, the lawyer for the defendant can ask the court to exclude the evidence from use at trial. The court then holds a hearing to determine whether the search was unreasonable.

If the court rules that key evidence was seized illegally and therefore cannot be used, the government often drops the charges against the defendant. However, if the government already has a strong case and the court rules that the evidence was obtained legally, the defendant may decide to plead guilty rather than go to trial, where a conviction is likely.

Deliberations and verdict

After receiving its instructions from the judge, the jury retires to the jury room to discuss the evidence and to reach a verdict (a decision on the factual issues in the case). A criminal jury verdict must be unanimous, meaning that all jurors must agree that the defendant is guilty or not guilty. If the jurors cannot agree, the judge declares a mistrial, and the prosecutor must then decide whether to ask the court to dismiss the case or have it presented to another jury.

Judgment and sentencing

In federal criminal cases, if the jury (or judge, if there is no jury) decides that the defendant is guilty, the judge sets a date for a sentencing hearing. In federal criminal cases, the jury doesn't decide whether the defendant will go to prison or for how long; the judge does.

In federal death penalty cases, however, the jury does decide whether the defendant will receive a death sentence. Sentencing statutes passed by Congress controls the judge's sentencing decision. Additionally, judges use Sentencing Guidelines, issued by the U.S. Sentencing Commission, as a source of advice as to the proper sentence. The guidelines take into account the nature of the particular offense and the offender's criminal history. A presentence report, prepared by one of the court's probation officers, provides the judge with various types of information about the offender and the offense, including the sentence recommended by the guidelines. After determining the sentence, the judge signs a judgment, which includes the plea, the verdict, and the sentence.

Right to appeal

A defendant who is found guilty in a federal criminal trial has a right to appeal the decision to the U.S. court of appeals, that is, ask the court of appeals to review the case to determine whether the trial was conducted properly. The grounds for appeal usually are that the district judge is said to have made an error, either in a procedure (admitting improper evidence, for example) or in interpreting the law. A defendant who pled guilty may not appeal the conviction. However, a defendant who pled guilty may have the right to appeal his or her sentence.

The government may not appeal if a defendant in a criminal case is found not guilty because the Double Jeopardy Clause of the Fifth Amendment to the Constitution provides that no person shall "be twice put in jeopardy of life or limb" for the same offense. This reflects our society's belief that, even if a second or third trial might finally find a defendant guilty, it is not proper to allow the government to harass an acquitted defendant through repeated retrials. However, the government may sometimes appeal a sentence.

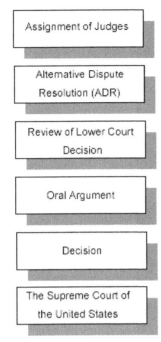

Assignment of Judges

Alternative Dispute Resolution (ADR)

Review of Lower Court Decision

Oral Argument

Decision

The Supreme Court of the United States

Appeals – Civil and Criminal Cases

Assignment of judges

The courts of appeals usually assign cases to a panel of three judges. The panel decides the case for the entire court. Sometimes, when the parties request it, or when there is a question of unusual importance, all the judges on the appeals court assemble *en banc* (however, this is a rare event).

Review of the lower court decision

In making its decision, the panel reviews key parts of the record. The record consists of all the documents filed in the case at trial along with the transcript of the trial proceedings. The panel then learns about the lawyers' legal arguments from the lawyers' briefs. Briefs are written documents that each side submits to explain its case and tell why the court should decide in its favor.

Oral argument

If the court permits oral argument, the lawyers for each side have a limited amount of time (typically between 15 to 30 minutes) to explain their case to the judges (or justices at the highest court in the jurisdiction) in a formal courtroom session. The judges / justices frequently question the attorneys about the relevant law as it applies to the case before them.

If you visit a court of appeals in session, you'll notice how it differs from the federal trial courts. There are no jurors, witnesses, or court reporters. The lawyers for both sides are present, but the parties usually are not present in the courtroom.

Decision

After the submission of briefs and oral argument, the judges discuss the case privately, consider any relevant *precedents* (court decisions from higher courts in prior cases with similar facts and legal issues), and reach a decision. Courts are required to follow precedents. For example, a U.S. court of appeals must follow the U.S. Supreme Court's decisions; a district court must follow the decisions of the U.S. Supreme Court and the decisions of the court of appeals of its circuit. Courts are also influenced by decisions they are not required to follow, such as the decisions of other circuits. Courts also follow their precedents unless they set forth reasons for the change.

At least two of the three judges on the panel must agree on a decision. One of those who agree with the decision is chosen to write an opinion, which announces and explains the decision. If a judge on the panel disagrees with the majority's opinion, the judge may write a dissent, giving his/her reasons for disagreeing. Many appellate opinions are published in books of opinions, called reporters. The opinions are read carefully by other judges and lawyers looking for precedents to guide them in their cases. The accumulated judicial opinions make up a body of law known as *case law*, which is usually an accurate predictor of how future cases will be decided. For decisions that the judges believe are important only to the parties and contribute nothing to the case law, the courts of appeals frequently use short, unsigned opinions that often are not published.

If the court of appeals decides that the trial judge incorrectly interpreted the law or followed incorrect procedures, it reverses the district court's decision. For example, the court of appeals could hold that the district judge allowed the jury to base its decision on evidence that never should have been admitted, and thus the defendant cannot be guilty. Most of the time courts of appeals uphold, rather than the reverse, district court decisions.

Sometimes when a higher court reverses the decision of the district court, it will send the case back (i.e., *remand* the case) to the lower court for another trial. For example, in the famous *Miranda v Arizona* case (1966), the Supreme Court ruled 5-4 that Ernesto Miranda's confession could not be used as evidence because he had not been advised of his right to remain silent or of his right to have a lawyer present during questioning. However, the government did have other evidence against him. The case was remanded for a new trial, in which the improperly obtained confession was not used as evidence, but Miranda was convicted by the other evidence.

The Supreme Court of the United States

The Supreme Court of the United States is the highest court in the nation. It's a different kind of appeals court; its major function is not correcting errors made by trial judges, but clarifying the law in cases of national importance or when lower courts disagree about the interpretation of the Constitution or federal laws.

The Supreme Court does not have to hear every case that it is asked to review. Each year, losing parties ask the Supreme Court to review about 8,000 cases. Almost all these cases come to the Court as petitions for writ of certiorari. The court selects only about 80 – 120 of the most significant cases to review with oral arguments.

The decisions of the Supreme Court establish precedent for the interpretation of the Constitution and federal laws, precedents that all state and federal courts must follow.

The power of judicial review makes the Supreme Court's role in our government vital. Judicial review is the power of any court when deciding a case, to declare that a law passed by a legislature or an action of the executive branch is invalid because it is inconsistent with the Constitution. Although district courts, courts of appeals, and state courts can exercise the power of judicial review, their decisions about federal law are always subject, on appeal, to review by the Supreme Court. When the Supreme Court declares a law unconstitutional, its decision can only be overruled by a later decision of the Supreme Court or amendment to the Constitution. Seven of the twenty-seven amendments to the Constitution have invalidated decisions of the Supreme Court. However, most Supreme Court cases don't concern the constitutionality of laws, but the interpretation of laws passed by Congress.

Although Congress has steadily increased the number of district and appeals court judges over the years, the Supreme Court has remained the same size since 1869. It consists of a Chief Justice and eight associate justices. Like the federal court of appeals and federal district judges, the Supreme Court justices are appointed by the President with the advice and consent of the Senate. However, unlike the judges in the courts of appeals, the Supreme Court justices never sit on panels. Absent recusal, all nine justices hear every case, and a majority ruling decides cases.

The Supreme Court begins its annual session, or term, on the first Monday of October. The term lasts until the Court has announced its decisions in all of the cases in which it has heard an argument that term—usually late June or early July. During the term, the Court, sitting for two weeks at a time, hears oral argument on Monday through Wednesday and then holds private conferences to discuss the cases, reach decisions, and begin preparing the written opinions that explain its decisions. Most decisions, along with their opinions, are released in the late spring and early summer.

THE U.S. NATIONAL ARCHIVES & RECORDS ADMINISTRATION

www.archives.gov

The Constitution of the United States: A Transcription

Note: The following text is a transcription of the Constitution as it was inscribed by Jacob Shallus on parchment (displayed in the Rotunda at the National Archives Museum.) Items that are hyperlinked have since been amended or superseded. The authenticated text of the Constitution can be found on the website of the Government Printing Office.

We the People of the United States, in Order to form a more perfect Union, establish Justice, insure domestic Tranquility, provide for the common defence, promote the general Welfare, and secure the Blessings of Liberty to ourselves and our Posterity, do ordain and establish this Constitution for the United States of America.

Article. I., Section. 1.

All legislative Powers herein granted shall be vested in a Congress of the United States, which shall consist of a Senate and House of Representatives.

Section. 2.

The House of Representatives shall be composed of Members chosen every second Year by the People of the several States, and the Electors in each State shall have the Qualifications requisite for Electors of the most numerous Branch of the State Legislature.

No Person shall be a Representative who shall not have attained to the Age of twenty five Years, and been seven Years a Citizen of the United States, and who shall not, when elected, be an Inhabitant of that State in which he shall be chosen.

Representatives and direct Taxes shall be apportioned among the several States which may be included within this Union, according to their respective Numbers, which shall be determined by adding to the whole Number of free Persons, including those bound to Service for a Term of Years, and excluding Indians not taxed, three fifths of all other Persons. The actual Enumeration shall be made within three Years after the first Meeting of the Congress of the United States, and within

---

every subsequent Term of ten Years, in such Manner as they shall by Law direct. The Number of Representatives shall not exceed one for every thirty Thousand, but each State shall have at Least one Representative; and until such enumeration shall be made, the State of New Hampshire shall be entitled to chuse three, Massachusetts eight, Rhode-Island and Providence Plantations one, Connecticut five, New-York six, New Jersey four, Pennsylvania eight, Delaware one, Maryland six, Virginia ten, North Carolina five, South Carolina five, and Georgia three.

When vacancies happen in the Representation from any State, the Executive Authority thereof shall issue Writs of Election to fill such Vacancies.

The House of Representatives shall chuse their Speaker and other Officers; and shall have the sole Power of Impeachment.

Section. 3.

The Senate of the United States shall be composed of two Senators from each State, chosen by the Legislature thereof, for six Years; and each Senator shall have one Vote.

Immediately after they shall be assembled in Consequence of the first Election, they shall be divided as equally as may be into three Classes. The Seats of the Senators of the first Class shall be vacated at the Expiration of the second Year, of the second Class at the Expiration of the fourth Year, and of the third Class at the Expiration of the sixth Year, so that one third may be chosen every second Year; and if Vacancies happen by Resignation, or otherwise, during the Recess of the Legislature of any State, the Executive thereof may make temporary Appointments until the next Meeting of the Legislature, which shall then fill such Vacancies.

No Person shall be a Senator who shall not have attained to the Age of thirty Years, and been nine Years a Citizen of the United States, and who shall not, when elected, be an Inhabitant of that State for which he shall be chosen.

The Vice President of the United States shall be President of the Senate, but shall have no Vote, unless they be equally divided.

The Senate shall chuse their other Officers, and also a President pro tempore, in the Absence of the Vice President, or when he shall exercise the Office of President of the United States.

The Senate shall have the sole Power to try all Impeachments. When sitting for that Purpose, they shall be on Oath or Affirmation. When the President of the United States is tried, the Chief Justice shall preside: And no Person shall be convicted without the Concurrence of two thirds of the Members present.

Judgment in Cases of Impeachment shall not extend further than to removal from Office, and disqualification to hold and enjoy any Office of honor, Trust or Profit under the United States: but the Party convicted shall nevertheless be liable and subject to Indictment, Trial, Judgment and Punishment, according to Law.

Section. 4.

The Times, Places and Manner of holding Elections for Senators and Representatives, shall be prescribed in each State by the Legislature thereof; but the Congress may at any time by Law make or alter such Regulations, except as to the Places of chusing Senators.

The Congress shall assemble at least once in every Year, and such Meeting shall be on the first Monday in December, unless they shall by Law appoint a different Day.

Section. 5.

Each House shall be the Judge of the Elections, Returns and Qualifications of its own Members, and a Majority of each shall constitute a Quorum to do Business; but a smaller Number may adjourn from day to day, and may be authorized to compel the Attendance of absent Members, in such Manner, and under such Penalties as each House may provide.

Each House may determine the Rules of its Proceedings, punish its Members for disorderly Behaviour, and, with the Concurrence of two thirds, expel a Member.

Each House shall keep a Journal of its Proceedings, and from time to time publish the same, excepting such Parts as may in their Judgment require Secrecy; and the Yeas and Nays of the Members of either House on any question shall, at the Desire of one fifth of those Present, be entered on the Journal.

Neither House, during the Session of Congress, shall, without the Consent of the other, adjourn for more than three days, nor to any other Place than that in which the two Houses shall be sitting.

Section. 6.

The Senators and Representatives shall receive a Compensation for their Services, to be ascertained by Law, and paid out of the Treasury of the United States. They shall in all Cases, except Treason, Felony and Breach of the Peace, be privileged from Arrest during their Attendance at the Session of their respective Houses, and in going to and returning from the same; and for any Speech or Debate in either House, they shall not be questioned in any other Place.

No Senator or Representative shall, during the Time for which he was elected, be appointed to any civil Office under the Authority of the United States, which shall have been created, or the Emoluments whereof shall have been encreased during such time; and no Person holding any Office under the United States, shall be a Member of either House during his Continuance in Office.

Section. 7.

All Bills for raising Revenue shall originate in the House of Representatives; but the Senate may propose or concur with Amendments as on other Bills.

Every Bill which shall have passed the House of Representatives and the Senate, shall, before it become a Law, be presented to the President of the United States; If he approve he shall sign it, but if not he shall return it, with his Objections to that House in which it shall have originated, who shall enter the Objections at large on their Journal, and proceed to reconsider it. If after such Reconsideration two thirds of that House shall agree to pass the Bill, it shall be sent, together with the Objections, to the other House, by which it shall likewise be reconsidered, and if approved by two thirds of that House, it shall become a Law. But in all such Cases the Votes of both Houses shall be determined by yeas and Nays, and the Names of the Persons voting for and against the Bill shall be entered on the Journal of each House respectively. If any Bill shall not be returned by the President within ten Days (Sundays excepted) after it shall have been presented to him, the Same shall be a Law, in like Manner as if he had signed it, unless the Congress by their Adjournment prevent its Return, in which Case it shall not be a Law.

Every Order, Resolution, or Vote to which the Concurrence of the Senate and House of Representatives may be necessary (except on a question of Adjournment) shall be presented to the President of the United States; and before the Same shall take Effect, shall be approved by him, or being disapproved by him, shall be repassed by two thirds of the Senate and House of Representatives, according to the Rules and Limitations prescribed in the Case of a Bill.

Section. 8.

The Congress shall have Power To lay and collect Taxes, Duties, Imposts and Excises, to pay the Debts and provide for the common Defence and general Welfare of the United States; but all Duties, Imposts and Excises shall be uniform throughout the United States;

To borrow Money on the credit of the United States;

To regulate Commerce with foreign Nations, and among the several States, and with the Indian Tribes;

To establish an uniform Rule of Naturalization, and uniform Laws on the subject of Bankruptcies throughout the United States;

To coin Money, regulate the Value thereof, and of foreign Coin, and fix the Standard of Weights and Measures;

To provide for the Punishment of counterfeiting the Securities and current Coin of the United States;

To establish Post Offices and post Roads;

To promote the Progress of Science and useful Arts, by securing for limited Times to Authors and Inventors the exclusive Right to their respective Writings and Discoveries;

To constitute Tribunals inferior to the Supreme Court;

To define and punish Piracies and Felonies committed on the high Seas, and Offences against the Law of Nations;

To declare War, grant Letters of Marque and Reprisal, and make Rules concerning Captures on Land and Water;

To raise and support Armies, but no Appropriation of Money to that Use shall be for a longer Term than two Years;

To provide and maintain a Navy;

To make Rules for the Government and Regulation of the land and naval Forces;

To provide for calling forth the Militia to execute the Laws of the Union, suppress Insurrections and repel Invasions;

To provide for organizing, arming, and disciplining, the Militia, and for governing such Part of them as may be employed in the Service of the United States, reserving to the States respectively, the Appointment of the Officers, and the Authority of training the Militia according to the discipline prescribed by Congress;

To exercise exclusive Legislation in all Cases whatsoever, over such District (not exceeding ten Miles square) as may, by Cession of particular States, and the Acceptance of Congress, become the Seat of the Government of the United States, and to exercise like Authority over all Places purchased by the Consent of the Legislature of the State in which the Same shall be, for the Erection of Forts, Magazines, Arsenals, dock-Yards, and other needful Buildings;—And

To make all Laws which shall be necessary and proper for carrying into Execution the foregoing Powers, and all other Powers vested by this Constitution in the Government of the United States, or in any Department or Officer thereof.

Section. 9.

The Migration or Importation of such Persons as any of the States now existing shall think proper to admit, shall not be prohibited by the Congress prior to the Year one thousand eight hundred and eight, but a Tax or duty may be imposed on such Importation, not exceeding ten dollars for each Person.

The Privilege of the Writ of Habeas Corpus shall not be suspended, unless when in Cases of Rebellion or Invasion the public Safety may require it.

No Bill of Attainder or ex post facto Law shall be passed.

No Capitation, or other direct, Tax shall be laid, unless in Proportion to the Census or enumeration herein before directed to be taken.

No Tax or Duty shall be laid on Articles exported from any State.

No Preference shall be given by any Regulation of Commerce or Revenue to the Ports of one State over those of another: nor shall Vessels bound to, or from, one State, be obliged to enter, clear, or pay Duties in another.

No Money shall be drawn from the Treasury, but in Consequence of Appropriations made by Law; and a regular Statement and Account of the Receipts and Expenditures of all public Money shall be published from time to time.

No Title of Nobility shall be granted by the United States: And no Person holding any Office of Profit or Trust under them, shall, without the Consent of the Congress, accept of any present, Emolument, Office, or Title, of any kind whatever, from any King, Prince, or foreign State.

Section. 10.

No State shall enter into any Treaty, Alliance, or Confederation; grant Letters of Marque and Reprisal; coin Money; emit Bills of Credit; make any Thing but gold and silver Coin a Tender in Payment of Debts; pass any Bill of Attainder, ex post facto Law, or Law impairing the Obligation of Contracts, or grant any Title of Nobility.

No State shall, without the Consent of the Congress, lay any Imposts or Duties on Imports or Exports, except what may be absolutely necessary for executing it's inspection Laws: and the net Produce of all Duties and Imposts, laid by any State on Imports or Exports, shall be for the Use of the Treasury of the United States; and all such Laws shall be subject to the Revision and Controul of the Congress.

No State shall, without the Consent of Congress, lay any Duty of Tonnage, keep Troops, or Ships of War in time of Peace, enter into any Agreement or Compact with another State, or with a foreign Power, or engage in War, unless actually invaded, or in such imminent Danger as will not admit of delay.

Article. II., Section. 1.

The executive Power shall be vested in a President of the United States of America. He shall hold his Office during the Term of four Years, and, together with the Vice President, chosen for the same Term, be elected, as follows

Each State shall appoint, in such Manner as the Legislature thereof may direct, a Number of Electors, equal to the whole Number of Senators and Representatives to which the State may be entitled in the Congress: but no

Senator or Representative, or Person holding an Office of Trust or Profit under the United States, shall be appointed an Elector.

The Electors shall meet in their respective States, and vote by Ballot for two Persons, of whom one at least shall not be an Inhabitant of the same State with themselves. And they shall make a List of all the Persons voted for, and of the Number of Votes for each; which List they shall sign and certify, and transmit sealed to the Seat of the Government of the United States, directed to the President of the Senate. The President of the Senate shall, in the Presence of the Senate and House of Representatives, open all the Certificates, and the Votes shall then be counted. The Person having the greatest Number of Votes shall be the President, if such Number be a Majority of the whole Number of Electors appointed; and if there be more than one who have such Majority, and have an equal Number of Votes, then the House of Representatives shall immediately chuse by Ballot one of them for President; and if no Person have a Majority, then from the five highest on the List the said House shall in like Manner chuse the President. But in chusing the President, the Votes shall be taken by States, the Representation from each State having one Vote; A quorum for this Purpose shall consist of a Member or Members from two thirds of the States, and a Majority of all the States shall be necessary to a Choice. In every Case, after the Choice of the President, the Person having the greatest Number of Votes of the Electors shall be the Vice President. But if there should remain two or more who have equal Votes, the Senate shall chuse from them by Ballot the Vice President.

The Congress may determine the Time of chusing the Electors, and the Day on which they shall give their Votes; which Day shall be the same throughout the United States.

No Person except a natural born Citizen, or a Citizen of the United States, at the time of the Adoption of this Constitution, shall be eligible to the Office of President; neither shall any Person be eligible to that Office who shall not have attained to the Age of thirty five Years, and been fourteen Years a Resident within the United States.

In Case of the Removal of the President from Office, or of his Death, Resignation, or Inability to discharge the Powers and Duties of the said Office, the Same shall devolve on the Vice President, and the Congress may by Law provide for the Case of Removal, Death, Resignation or Inability, both of the President and Vice President, declaring what Officer shall then act as President, and such Officer shall act accordingly, until the Disability be removed, or a President shall be elected.

The President shall, at stated Times, receive for his Services, a Compensation, which shall neither be encreased nor diminished during the Period for which he shall have been elected, and he shall not receive within that Period any other Emolument from the United States, or any of them.

Before he enter on the Execution of his Office, he shall take the following Oath or Affirmation:—"I do solemnly swear (or affirm) that I will faithfully execute the Office of President of the United States, and will to the best of my Ability, preserve, protect and defend the Constitution of the United States."

Section. 2.

The President shall be Commander in Chief of the Army and Navy of the United States, and of the Militia of the several States, when called into the actual Service of the United States; he may require the Opinion, in writing, of the principal Officer in each of the executive Departments, upon any Subject relating to the Duties of their respective Offices, and he shall have Power to grant Reprieves and Pardons for Offences against the United States, except in Cases of Impeachment.

He shall have Power, by and with the Advice and Consent of the Senate, to make Treaties, provided two thirds of the Senators present concur; and he shall nominate, and by and with the Advice and Consent of the Senate, shall appoint Ambassadors, other public Ministers and Consuls, Judges of the supreme Court, and all other Officers of the United States, whose Appointments are not herein otherwise provided for, and which shall be established by Law: but the Congress may by Law vest the Appointment of such inferior Officers, as they think proper, in the President alone, in the Courts of Law, or in the Heads of Departments.

The President shall have Power to fill up all Vacancies that may happen during the Recess of the Senate, by granting Commissions which shall expire at the End of their next Session.

Section. 3.

He shall from time to time give to the Congress Information of the State of the Union, and recommend to their Consideration such Measures as he shall judge necessary and expedient; he may, on extraordinary Occasions, convene both Houses, or either of them, and in Case of Disagreement between them, with Respect to the Time of Adjournment, he may adjourn them to such Time as he shall think proper; he shall receive Ambassadors and other public Ministers; he shall take Care that the Laws be faithfully executed, and shall Commission all the Officers of the United States.

Section. 4.

The President, Vice President and all civil Officers of the United States, shall be removed from Office on Impeachment for, and Conviction of, Treason, Bribery, or other high Crimes and Misdemeanors.

Article III., Section. 1.

The judicial Power of the United States, shall be vested in one supreme Court, and in such inferior Courts as the Congress may from time to time ordain and establish. The Judges, both of the supreme and inferior Courts, shall hold their Offices during good Behaviour, and shall, at stated Times, receive for their Services, a Compensation, which shall not be diminished during their Continuance in Office.

Section. 2.

The judicial Power shall extend to all Cases, in Law and Equity, arising under this Constitution, the Laws of the United States, and Treaties made, or which shall be made, under their Authority;—to all Cases affecting Ambassadors, other public Ministers and Consuls;—to all Cases of admiralty and maritime Jurisdiction;—to Controversies to which the United States shall be a Party;—to Controversies between two or more States;—between a State and Citizens of another State,—between Citizens of different States,—between Citizens of the same State claiming Lands under Grants of different States, and between a State, or the Citizens thereof, and foreign States, Citizens or Subjects.

In all Cases affecting Ambassadors, other public Ministers and Consuls, and those in which a State shall be Party, the supreme Court shall have original Jurisdiction. In all the other Cases before mentioned, the supreme Court shall have appellate Jurisdiction, both as to Law and Fact, with such Exceptions, and under such Regulations as the Congress shall make.

The Trial of all Crimes, except in Cases of Impeachment, shall be by Jury; and such Trial shall be held in the State where the said Crimes shall have been committed; but when not committed within any State, the Trial shall be at such Place or Places as the Congress may by Law have directed.

Section. 3.

Treason against the United States, shall consist only in levying War against them, or in adhering to their Enemies, giving them Aid and Comfort. No Person shall be convicted of Treason unless on the Testimony of two Witnesses to the same overt Act, or on Confession in open Court.

The Congress shall have Power to declare the Punishment of Treason, but no Attainder of Treason shall work Corruption of Blood, or Forfeiture except during the Life of the Person attainted.

Article. IV., Section. 1.

Full Faith and Credit shall be given in each State to the public Acts, Records, and judicial Proceedings of every other State. And the Congress may by general Laws prescribe the Manner in which such Acts, Records and Proceedings shall be proved, and the Effect thereof.

Section. 2.

The Citizens of each State shall be entitled to all Privileges and Immunities of Citizens in the several States.

A Person charged in any State with Treason, Felony, or other Crime, who shall flee from Justice, and be found in another State, shall on Demand of the executive Authority of the State from which he fled, be delivered up, to be removed to the State having Jurisdiction of the Crime.

No Person held to Service or Labour in one State, under the Laws thereof, escaping into another, shall, in Consequence of any Law or Regulation therein, be discharged from such Service or Labour, but shall be delivered up on Claim of the Party to whom such Service or Labour may be due.

Section. 3.

New States may be admitted by the Congress into this Union; but no new State shall be formed or erected within the Jurisdiction of any other State; nor any State be formed by the Junction of two or more States, or Parts of States, without the Consent of the Legislatures of the States concerned as well as of the Congress.

The Congress shall have Power to dispose of and make all needful Rules and Regulations respecting the Territory or other Property belonging to the United States; and nothing in this Constitution shall be so construed as to Prejudice any Claims of the United States, or of any particular State.

Section. 4.

The United States shall guarantee to every State in this Union a Republican Form of Government, and shall protect each of them against Invasion; and on Application of the Legislature, or of the Executive (when the Legislature cannot be convened), against domestic Violence.

Article. V.

The Congress, whenever two thirds of both Houses shall deem it necessary, shall propose Amendments to this Constitution, or, on the Application of the Legislatures of two thirds of the several States, shall call a Convention for proposing Amendments, which, in either Case, shall be valid to all Intents and Purposes, as Part of this Constitution, when ratified by the Legislatures of three fourths of the several States, or by Conventions in three fourths thereof, as the one or the other Mode of Ratification may be proposed by the Congress; Provided that no Amendment which may be made prior to the Year One thousand eight hundred and eight shall in any Manner affect the first and fourth Clauses in the Ninth Section of the first Article; and that no State, without its Consent, shall be deprived of its equal Suffrage in the Senate.

Article. VI.

All Debts contracted and Engagements entered into, before the Adoption of this Constitution, shall be as valid against the United States under this Constitution, as under the Confederation.

This Constitution, and the Laws of the United States which shall be made in Pursuance thereof; and all Treaties made, or which shall be made, under the Authority of the United States, shall be the supreme

Law of the Land; and the Judges in every State shall be bound thereby, any Thing in the Constitution or Laws of any State to the Contrary notwithstanding.

The Senators and Representatives before mentioned, and the Members of the several State Legislatures, and all executive and judicial Officers, both of the United States and of the several States, shall be bound by Oath or Affirmation, to support this Constitution; but no religious Test shall ever be required as a Qualification to any Office or public Trust under the United States.

Article. VII.

The Ratification of the Conventions of nine States, shall be sufficient for the Establishment of this Constitution between the States so ratifying the Same.

The Word, "the," being interlined between the seventh and eighth Lines of the first Page, The Word "Thirty" being partly written on an Erazure in the fifteenth Line of the first Page, The Words "is tried" being interlined between the thirty second and thirty third Lines of the first Page and the Word "the" being interlined between the forty third and forty fourth Lines of the second Page.

Attest William Jackson Secretary, done in Convention by the Unanimous Consent of the States present the Seventeenth Day of September in the Year of our Lord one thousand seven hundred and Eighty seven and of the Independance of the United States of America the Twelfth In witness whereof We have hereunto subscribed our Names, G°. Washington, *Presidt and deputy from Virginia*

Delaware
Geo: Read
Gunning Bedford jun
John Dickinson
Richard Bassett
Jaco: Broom

Maryland
James McHenry
Dan of St Thos.
Jenifer
Danl. Carroll

Virginia
John Blair
James Madison Jr.

North Carolina
Wm. Blount
Richd. Dobbs
Spaight
Hu Williamson

South Carolina
J. Rutledge
Charles Cotesworth
Pinckney
Charles Pinckney
Pierce Butler

Georgia
William Few
Abr Baldwin

New Hampshire
John Langdon
Nicholas Gilman

Massachusetts
Nathaniel Gorham
Rufus King

Connecticut
Wm. Saml. Johnson
Roger Sherman

New York
Alexander Hamilton

New Jersey
Wil: Livingston
David Brearley
Wm. Paterson
Jona: Dayton

Pensylvania
B Franklin
Thomas Mifflin
Robt. Morris
Geo. Clymer
Thos. FitzSimons
Jared Ingersoll
James Wilson
Gouv Morris

Bill of Rights of the United States of America (1791)

The first 10 amendments to the Constitution make up the Bill of Rights. Written by James Madison in response to calls from several states for greater constitutional protection for individual liberties, the Bill of Rights lists specific prohibitions on governmental power. The Virginia Declaration of Rights, written by George Mason, strongly influenced Madison.

One of the many points of contention between Federalists and Anti-Federalists was the Constitution's lack of a bill of rights that would place specific limits on government power. Federalists argued that the Constitution did not need a bill of rights, because the people and the states kept any powers not explicitly given to the federal government. Anti-Federalists held that a bill of rights was necessary to safeguard individual liberty.

Madison, then a member of the U.S. House of Representatives, went through the Constitution itself, making changes where he thought most appropriate. But several Representatives, led by Roger Sherman, objected that Congress had no authority to change the wording of the Constitution itself. Therefore, Madison's changes were presented as a list of amendments that would follow Article VII.

The House approved 17 amendments. Of these 17, the Senate approved 12. Those 12 were sent to the states for approval in August of 1789. Of those 12, 10 were quickly ratified. Virginia's legislature became the last to ratify the amendments on December 15, 1791. These amendments are known as the Bill of Rights.

The Bill of Rights is a list of limits on government power. For example, what the Founders saw as the natural right of individuals to speak and worship freely was protected by the First Amendment's prohibitions on Congress from making laws establishing a religion or abridging freedom of speech. Another example is the natural right to be free from the government's unreasonable intrusion in one's home was safeguarded by the Fourth Amendment's warrant requirements.

Other precursors to the Bill of Rights include English documents such as the Magna Carta[1], the Petition of Right, the English Bill of Rights, and the Massachusetts Body of Liberties.

The Magna Carta illustrates Compact Theory[1] as well as initial strides toward limited government. Its provisions address individual rights and political rights. Latin for "Great Charter," the Magna Carta was written by Barons in Runnymede, England and forced on the King. Although the protections were generally limited to the prerogatives of the Barons, the Magna Carta embodied the general principle that the King accepted limitations on his rule. These included the fundamental acknowledgement that the king was not above the law.

Included in the Magna Carta are protections for the English church, petitioning the king, freedom from forced quarter of troops and unreasonable searches, due process and fair trial protections, and freedom from excessive fines. These protections can be found in the First, Third, Fourth, Fifth, Sixth, and Eighth Amendments to the Constitution.

The Magna Carta is the oldest example of a compact in England. The Mayflower Compact, the Fundamental Orders of Connecticut, and the Albany Plan are examples from the American colonies. The Articles of Confederation was a compact among the states, and the Constitution creates a compact based on a federal system between the national government, state governments, and the people. The Hayne-Webster Debate focused on the compact created by the Constitution.

[1] Philosophers including Thomas Hobbes, John Locke, and Jean-Jacques Rousseau theorized that peoples' condition in a "state of nature" (that is, outside of a society) is one of freedom, but that freedom inevitably degrades into war, chaos, or debilitating competition without the benefit of a system of laws and government. They reasoned, therefore, that for their own happiness, individuals willingly trade some of their natural freedom in exchange for the protections provided by government.

The Bill of Rights

Amendment I

Congress shall make no law respecting an establishment of religion, or prohibiting the free exercise thereof; or abridging the freedom of speech, or of the press; or the right of the people peaceably to assemble, and to petition the government for a redress of grievances.

Amendment II

A well regulated militia, being necessary to the security of a free state, the right of the people to keep and bear arms, shall not be infringed.

Amendment III

No soldier shall, in time of peace be quartered in any house, without the consent of the owner, nor in time of war, but in a manner to be prescribed by law.

Amendment IV

The right of the people to be secure in their persons, houses, papers, and effects, against unreasonable searches and seizures, shall not be violated, and no warrants shall issue, but upon probable cause, supported by oath or affirmation, and particularly describing the place to be searched, and the persons or things to be seized.

Amendment V

No person shall be held to answer for a capital, or otherwise infamous crime, unless on a presentment or indictment of a grand jury, except in cases arising in the land or naval forces, or in the militia, when in actual service in time of war or public danger; nor shall any person be subject for the same offense to be twice put in jeopardy of life or limb; nor shall be compelled in any criminal case to be a witness against himself, nor be deprived of life, liberty, or property, without due process of law; nor shall private property be taken for public use, without just compensation.

Amendment VI

In all criminal prosecutions, the accused shall enjoy the right to a speedy and public trial, by an impartial jury of the state and district wherein the crime shall have been committed, which district shall have been previously ascertained by law, and to be informed of the nature and cause of the accusation; to be confronted with the witnesses against him; to have compulsory process for obtaining witnesses in his favor, and to have the assistance of counsel for his defense.

Amendment VII

In suits at common law, where the value in controversy shall exceed twenty dollars, the right of trial by jury shall be preserved, and no fact tried by a jury, shall be otherwise reexamined in any court of the United States, than according to the rules of the common law.

Amendment VIII

Excessive bail shall not be required, nor excessive fines imposed, nor cruel and unusual punishments inflicted.

Amendment IX

The enumeration in the Constitution, of certain rights, shall not be construed to deny or disparage others retained by the people.

Amendment X

The powers not delegated to the United States by the Constitution, nor prohibited by it to the states, are reserved to the states respectively, or to the people.

Constitutional Amendments 11-27

AMENDMENT XI

Passed by Congress March 4, 1794. Ratified February 7, 1795.

Note: Article III, section 2, of the Constitution was modified by amendment 11.

The Judicial power of the United States shall not be construed to extend to any suit in law or equity, commenced or prosecuted against one of the United States by Citizens of another State, or by Citizens or Subjects of any Foreign State.

AMENDMENT XII

Passed by Congress December 9, 1803. Ratified June 15, 1804.

Note: A portion of Article II, section 1 of the Constitution was superseded by the 12th amendment.

The Electors shall meet in their respective states and vote by ballot for President and Vice-President, one of whom, at least, shall not be an inhabitant of the same state with themselves; they shall name in their ballots the person voted for as President, and in distinct ballots the person voted for as Vice-President, and they shall make distinct lists of all persons voted for as President, and of all persons voted for as Vice-President, and of the number of votes for each, which lists they shall sign and certify, and transmit sealed to the seat of the government of the United States, directed to the President of the Senate; -- the President of the Senate shall, in the presence of the Senate and House of Representatives, open all the certificates and the votes shall then be counted; -- The person having the greatest number of votes for President, shall be the President, if such number be a majority of the whole number of Electors appointed; and if no person have such majority, then from the persons having the highest numbers not exceeding three on the list of those voted for as President, the House of Representatives shall choose immediately, by ballot, the President. But in choosing the President, the votes shall be taken by states, the representation from each state having one vote; a quorum for this purpose shall consist of a member or members from two-thirds of the states, and a majority of all the states shall be necessary to a choice. [And if the House of Representatives shall not choose a President

whenever the right of choice shall devolve upon them, before the
fourth day of March next following, then the Vice-President shall act
as President, as in case of the death or other constitutional disability of
the President. --]* The person having the greatest number of votes as
Vice-President, shall be the Vice-President, if such number be a
majority of the whole number of Electors appointed, and if no person
have a majority, then from the two highest numbers on the list, the
Senate shall choose the Vice-President; a quorum for the purpose shall
consist of two-thirds of the whole number of Senators, and a majority
of the whole number shall be necessary to a choice. But no person
constitutionally ineligible to the office of President shall be eligible to
that of Vice-President of the United States.

Superseded by section 3 of the 20th amendment.

AMENDMENT XIII

Passed by Congress January 31, 1865. Ratified December 6, 1865.

Note: A portion of Article IV, section 2, of the Constitution was
superseded by the 13th amendment.

Section 1.
Neither slavery nor involuntary servitude, except as a punishment for
crime whereof the party shall have been duly convicted, shall exist
within the United States, or any place subject to their jurisdiction.

Section 2.
Congress shall have power to enforce this article by appropriate legislation.

AMENDMENT XIV

Passed by Congress June 13, 1866. Ratified July 9, 1868.

Note: Article I, section 2, of the Constitution was modified by section
2 of the 14th amendment.

Section 1.
All persons born or naturalized in the United States, and subject to the
jurisdiction thereof, are citizens of the United States and of the State
wherein they reside. No State shall make or enforce any law which shall
abridge the privileges or immunities of citizens of the United States; nor
shall any State deprive any person of life, liberty, or property, without due

process of law; nor deny to any person within its jurisdiction the equal protection of the laws.

Section 2.

Representatives shall be apportioned among the several States according to their respective numbers, counting the whole number of persons in each State, excluding Indians not taxed. But when the right to vote at any election for the choice of electors for President and Vice-President of the United States, Representatives in Congress, the Executive and Judicial officers of a State, or the members of the Legislature thereof, is denied to any of the male inhabitants of such State, being twenty-one years of age,* and citizens of the United States, or in any way abridged, except for participation in rebellion, or other crime, the basis of representation therein shall be reduced in the proportion which the number of such male citizens shall bear to the whole number of male citizens twenty-one years of age in such State.

Section 3.

No person shall be a Senator or Representative in Congress, or elector of President and Vice-President, or hold any office, civil or military, under the United States, or under any State, who, having previously taken an oath, as a member of Congress, or as an officer of the United States, or as a member of any State legislature, or as an executive or judicial officer of any State, to support the Constitution of the United States, shall have engaged in insurrection or rebellion against the same, or given aid or comfort to the enemies thereof. But Congress may by a vote of two-thirds of each House, remove such disability.

Section 4.

The validity of the public debt of the United States, authorized by law, including debts incurred for payment of pensions and bounties for services in suppressing insurrection or rebellion, shall not be questioned. But neither the United States nor any State shall assume or pay any debt or obligation incurred in aid of insurrection or rebellion against the United States, or any claim for the loss or emancipation of any slave; but all such debts, obligations and claims shall be held illegal and void.

Section 5.

The Congress shall have the power to enforce, by appropriate legislation, the provisions of this article.

Changed by section 1 of the 26th amendment.

AMENDMENT XV

Passed by Congress February 26, 1869. Ratified February 3, 1870.

Section 1.
The right of citizens of the United States to vote shall not be denied or abridged by the United States or by any State on account of race, color, or previous condition of servitude.

Section 2.
The Congress shall have the power to enforce this article by appropriate legislation.

AMENDMENT XVI

Passed by Congress July 2, 1909. Ratified February 3, 1913.

Note: Article I, section 9, of the Constitution was modified by amendment 16.

The Congress shall have power to lay and collect taxes on incomes, from whatever source derived, without apportionment among the several States, and without regard to any census or enumeration.

AMENDMENT XVII

Passed by Congress May 13, 1912. Ratified April 8, 1913.

Note: Article I, section 3, of the Constitution was modified by the 17th amendment.

The Senate of the United States shall be composed of two Senators from each State, elected by the people thereof, for six years; and each Senator shall have one vote. The electors in each State shall have the qualifications requisite for electors of the most numerous branch of the State legislatures.

When vacancies happen in the representation of any State in the Senate, the executive authority of such State shall issue writs of election to fill such vacancies: *Provided*, That the legislature of any State may empower the executive thereof to make temporary appointments until the people fill the vacancies by election as the legislature may direct.

This amendment shall not be so construed as to affect the election or term of any Senator chosen before it becomes valid as part of the Constitution.

AMENDMENT XIII

Passed by Congress December 18, 1917. Ratified January 16, 1919. Repealed by amendment 21.

Section 1.
After one year from the ratification of this article the manufacture, sale, or transportation of intoxicating liquors within, the importation thereof into, or the exportation thereof from the United States and all territory subject to the jurisdiction thereof for beverage purposes is hereby prohibited.

Section 2.
The Congress and the several States shall have concurrent power to enforce this article by appropriate legislation.

Section 3.
This article shall be inoperative unless it shall have been ratified as an amendment to the Constitution by the legislatures of the several States, as provided in the Constitution, within seven years from the date of the submission hereof to the States by the Congress.

AMENDMENT XIX

Passed by Congress June 4, 1919. Ratified August 18, 1920.

The right of citizens of the United States to vote shall not be denied or abridged by the United States or by any State on account of sex.

Congress shall have power to enforce this article by appropriate legislation.

AMENDMENT XX

Passed by Congress March 2, 1932. Ratified January 23, 1933.

Note: Article I, section 4, of the Constitution was modified by section 2 of this amendment. In addition, a portion of the 12th amendment was superseded by section 3.

Section 1.
The terms of the President and the Vice President shall end at noon on the 20th day of January, and the terms of Senators and Representatives at noon on the 3d day of January, of the years in which such terms

would have ended if this article had not been ratified; and the terms of their successors shall then begin.

Section 2.

The Congress shall assemble at least once in every year, and such meeting shall begin at noon on the 3d day of January, unless they shall by law appoint a different day.

Section 3.

If, at the time fixed for the beginning of the term of the President, the President elect shall have died, the Vice President elect shall become President. If a President shall not have been chosen before the time fixed for the beginning of his term, or if the President elect shall have failed to qualify, then the Vice President elect shall act as President until a President shall have qualified; and the Congress may by law provide for the case wherein neither a President elect nor a Vice President elect shall have qualified, declaring who shall then act as President, or the manner in which one who is to act shall be selected, and such person shall act accordingly until a President or Vice President shall have qualified.

Section 4.

The Congress may by law provide for the case of the death of any of the persons from whom the House of Representatives may choose a President whenever the right of choice shall have devolved upon them, and for the case of the death of any of the persons from whom the Senate may choose a Vice President whenever the right of choice shall have devolved upon them.

Section 5.

Sections 1 and 2 shall take effect on the 15th day of October following the ratification of this article.

Section 6.

This article shall be inoperative unless it shall have been ratified as an amendment to the Constitution by the legislatures of three-fourths of the several States within seven years from the date of its submission.

AMENDMENT XXI

Passed by Congress February 20, 1933. Ratified December 5, 1933.

Section 1.

The eighteenth article of amendment to the Constitution of the United States is hereby repealed.

Section 2.

The transportation or importation into any State, Territory, or possession of the United States for delivery or use therein of intoxicating liquors, in violation of the laws thereof, is hereby prohibited.

Section 3.

This article shall be inoperative unless it shall have been ratified as an amendment to the Constitution by conventions in the several States, as provided in the Constitution, within seven years from the date of the submission hereof to the States by the Congress.

AMENDMENT XXII

Passed by Congress March 21, 1947. Ratified February 27, 1951.

Section 1.

No person shall be elected to the office of the President more than twice, and no person who has held the office of President, or acted as President, for more than two years of a term to which some other person was elected President shall be elected to the office of the President more than once. But this Article shall not apply to any person holding the office of President when this Article was proposed by the Congress, and shall not prevent any person who may be holding the office of President, or acting as President, during the term within which this Article becomes operative from holding the office of President or acting as President during the remainder of such term.

Section 2.

This article shall be inoperative unless it shall have been ratified as an amendment to the Constitution by the legislatures of three-fourths of the several States within seven years from the date of its submission to the States by the Congress.

AMENDMENT XXIII

Passed by Congress June 16, 1960. Ratified March 29, 1961.

Section 1.

The District constituting the seat of Government of the United States shall appoint in such manner as the Congress may direct:

A number of electors of President and Vice President equal to the whole number of Senators and Representatives in Congress to which the District would be entitled if it were a State, but in no event more than the least populous State; they shall be in addition to those appointed by the States, but they shall be considered, for the purposes of the election of President and Vice President, to be electors appointed by a State; and they shall meet in the District and perform such duties as provided by the twelfth article of amendment.

Section 2.

The Congress shall have power to enforce this article by appropriate legislation.

AMENDMENT XXIV

Passed by Congress August 27, 1962. Ratified January 23, 1964.

Section 1.

The right of citizens of the United States to vote in any primary or other election for President or Vice President, for electors for President or Vice President, or for Senator or Representative in Congress, shall not be denied or abridged by the United States or any State by reason of failure to pay any poll tax or other tax.

Section 2.

The Congress shall have power to enforce this article by appropriate legislation.

AMENDMENT XXV

Passed by Congress July 6, 1965. Ratified February 10, 1967.

Note: Article II, section 1, of the Constitution was affected by the 25th amendment.

Section 1.

In case of the removal of the President from office or of his death or resignation, the Vice President shall become President.

Section 2.

Whenever there is a vacancy in the office of the Vice President, the President shall nominate a Vice President who shall take office upon confirmation by a majority vote of both Houses of Congress.

Section 3.

Whenever the President transmits to the President pro tempore of the Senate and the Speaker of the House of Representatives his written declaration that he is unable to discharge the powers and duties of his office, and until he transmits to them a written declaration to the contrary, such powers and duties shall be discharged by the Vice President as Acting President.

Section 4.

Whenever the Vice President and a majority of either the principal officers of the executive departments or of such other body as Congress may by law provide, transmit to the President pro tempore of the Senate and the Speaker of the House of Representatives their written declaration that the President is unable to discharge the powers and duties of his office, the Vice President shall immediately assume the powers and duties of the office as Acting President.

Thereafter, when the President transmits to the President pro tempore of the Senate and the Speaker of the House of Representatives his written declaration that no inability exists, he shall resume the powers and duties of his office unless the Vice President and a majority of either the principal officers of the executive department or of such other body as Congress may by law provide, transmit within four days to the President pro tempore of the Senate and the Speaker of the House of Representatives their written declaration that the President is unable to discharge the powers and duties of his office. Thereupon Congress shall decide the issue, assembling within forty-eight hours for that purpose if not in session. If the Congress, within twenty-one days after receipt of the latter written declaration, or, if Congress is not in session, within twenty-one days after Congress is required to assemble, determines by two-thirds vote of both Houses that the President is unable to discharge the powers and duties of his office, the Vice President shall continue to discharge the same as Acting President; otherwise, the President shall resume the powers and duties of his office.

AMENDMENT XXVI

Passed by Congress March 23, 1971. Ratified July 1, 1971.

Note: Amendment 14, section 2, of the Constitution was modified by section 1 of the 26th amendment.

Section 1.
The right of citizens of the United States, who are eighteen years of age or older, to vote shall not be denied or abridged by the United States or by any State on account of age.

Section 2.
The Congress shall have power to enforce this article by appropriate legislation.

AMENDMENT XXII

Originally proposed Sept. 25, 1789. Ratified May 7, 1992.

No law, varying the compensation for the services of the Senators and Representatives, shall take effect, until an election of Representatives shall have intervened

States' Rights Under the U.S. Constitution

The United States Constitution has articles and amendments that establish constitutional rights.

The provisions providing for rights under the Bill of Rights were originally binding upon only the federal government. In time, most of these provisions became binding upon the states through selective incorporation into the due process clause of the 14th Amendment (i.e., reverse incorporation). When a provision is made binding on a state, a state can no longer restrict the rights guaranteed in that provision.

The 6th Amendment's guarantee of a right to confrontation of witnesses (i.e., Confrontation Clause), and the various rights of the 1st Amendment, guaranteeing the freedoms of speech, the press, government, and assembly.

The 5th Amendment protects the right to grand jury proceedings in federal criminal cases. However, because this right was not selectively incorporated into the due process clause of the 14th Amendment, it is not binding upon the states. Therefore, persons involved in state criminal proceedings as a defendant have no federal constitutional right to grand jury proceedings. Whether an individual has a right to a grand jury becomes a question of state law.

The 10th Amendment to the United States Constitution, which is part of the Bill of Rights, was ratified on December 15, 1791. The Tenth Amendment states the Constitution's principle of federalism by providing that powers not granted to the federal government by the Constitution, nor prohibited to the States, are reserved to the States or the people.

Federalism in the United States

Federalism in the United States is the evolving relationship between state governments and the federal government of the United States. The American government has evolved from a system of dual federalism to one of associative federalism. In "Federalist No. 46," James Madison wrote that the states and national government "are in fact but different agents and trustees of the people, constituted with different powers." Alexander Hamilton, in "Federalist No. 28," suggested that both levels of government would exercise authority to the citizens' benefit: "If their [the peoples'] rights are invaded by either, they can make use of the other as the instrument of redress."[3]

Because the states were preexisting political entities, the U.S. Constitution did not need to define or explain federalism in any one section, but it often mentions the rights and responsibilities of state governments and state officials in relation to the federal government.

The federal government has certain *express powers* (also called *enumerated powers*) which are powers spelled out in the Constitution, including the right to levy taxes, declare war, and regulate interstate and foreign commerce. In addition, the *Necessary and Proper Clause* gives the federal government the *implied power* to pass any law "necessary and proper" for the execution of its express powers. Enumerated powers of the Federal Government are contained in Article I, Section 8 of the United States Constitution.

Other powers—the *reserved powers*—are reserved to the people or the states under the 10th Amendment. The power delegated to the federal government was significantly expanded by the Supreme Court decision in *McCulloch v. Maryland* (1819) and the 13th, 14th and 15th, amendments to the Constitution following the Civil War.

Definitions of Legal Terms

A

Acquittal – a finding that the defendant is not guilty of the charges brought by the government. This finding may be reached by the trial judge either in a case tried before the judge or on a motion for judgment of acquittal made by a defendant or the judge in a jury trial. The jury may make such a finding in a case tried before it.

Active judge – a judge in the full-time service of the court. Compare with **senior judge**.

Administrative Office of the U.S. Courts (AO) – the federal agency responsible for collecting court statistics, administering the federal courts' budget, processing the federal courts' payroll, and performing other administrative functions, under the direction and supervision of the Judicial Conference of the United States.

Admissible – a term used to describe evidence that may be heard by a jury and considered by a judge or a jury in federal civil and criminal cases.

Adversary proceeding – in bankruptcy, a method of handling disputes that may arise during the course of a case. It is a lawsuit within a case and is generally initiated by a complaint and requires a filing fee. The Bankruptcy Rules establish the types of disputes that are considered adversary proceedings. Compare with **contested matter**.

Adversary process – the method courts use to resolve disputes. Through the adversary process, each side in a dispute has the right to present its case as persuasively as possible, subject to the rules of evidence, and an independent fact-finder, either judge or jury, decides in favor of one side or the other.

Alternate juror – a juror who is selected in the same manner as a regular juror and hears the evidence in a case along with the regular jurors, but does not help decide the case unless called upon to replace a regular juror.

Alternative dispute resolution (ADR) – a procedure for settling a dispute outside the courtroom or helping to make the trial more efficient, such as mediation, arbitration, or minitrial. Most forms of ADR are usually not binding on the parties and involve referral of the case to a neutral party. ADR is becoming more common in the federal courts.

amicus curiae – a Latin term meaning "friend of the court." An amicus curiae is a person or organization that is not a party in the case on appeal, has a strong interest in the outcome of the case, and files a brief with the court of appeals called an "amicus brief." This brief may call important legal or factual matters to the court's attention and thus help the court reach a proper decision in the case.

Answer – the formal written statement by a defendant in a civil case that responds to a complaint and sets forth the grounds for defense.

Appeal – a request, usually made after a trial, asking another court (usually the court of appeals) to decide whether the trial court proceeding was conducted properly. To make such a request is "to appeal" or "to take an appeal."

Appellant – the party who appeals a lower court's decision, usually seeking reversal of that decision. Compare with **appellee**.

Appellate court – a court that reviews decisions of lower courts. In the federal courts, the primary appellate courts are the U.S. courts of appeals and the U.S. Supreme Court.

Appellee – the party against whom an appeal is taken and who seeks to protect the judgment or order of the lower court. Compare with **appellant**.

Arbitration – a form of alternative dispute resolution in which an arbitrator (a neutral decision maker) issues a judgment on the legal issues involved in a case after listening to presentations by each party. Arbitration can be binding or nonbinding, depending on the agreement among the parties before the proceeding.

Arraignment – a proceeding in which a person accused of committing a crime is brought into court, told of the charges and asked to plead guilty or not guilty.

Arrest – a law enforcement officer's detaining a person or otherwise leading that person to reasonably believe that he or she is not free to leave.

Article III – the section of the U.S. Constitution that places "the judicial power of the United States" in the federal courts.

Article III judges – judges who exercise "the judicial power of the United States" under Article III of the Constitution. They are appointed by the President, subject to the approval of the Senate. Supreme Court justices, the court of appeals judges, district court judges, and Court of International Trade judges are Article III judges; bankruptcy and magistrate judges are not.

Assistant U.S. attorney (AUSA) – a federal prosecutor who assists the U.S. attorney in the judicial district by prosecuting criminal cases for the federal government and representing the government in civil actions. It is important to distinguish a U.S. attorney from a district attorney (DA), who prosecutes criminal cases for a state, county, or city.

Attorney-client privilege – the doctrine that ensures that communications between an attorney and his or her client remain confidential and that the attorney cannot be compelled to disclose them.

Attorney General – the executive branch official, appointed by the President to head the Justice Department.

Automatic stay – a provision that goes into effect as soon as a bankruptcy case is filed and that stops most creditors from suing or foreclosing against a debtor without prior permission of the bankruptcy court.

B

Bail – the release of a person charged with an offense prior to trial under specified financial or nonfinancial conditions designed to ensure the person's appearance in court when required.

Bankruptcy – federal statutes and judicial proceedings involving persons or businesses that cannot pay their debts and thus seek the assistance of the court in getting a "fresh start." Under the protection of the bankruptcy court and the laws of the Bankruptcy Code, debtors may "discharge" their debts, perhaps by paying a portion of each debt.

Bankruptcy appellate panel (BAP) – in the circuits that have them, a panel of three bankruptcy judges that share the appellate role of the district court in bankruptcy filings.

Bankruptcy court – see **U.S. bankruptcy court.**

Bankruptcy estate – a debtor's assets (money or property) that, unless exempt, must be used to pay creditors in a bankruptcy proceeding.

Bankruptcy judge – a federal judge, appointed by the court of appeals for a fourteen-year term, who has authority to hear matters that arise under the Bankruptcy Code.

Bench trial – a trial without a jury, in which the judge decides the facts. Compare with **jury trial**.

Brief – a written statement submitted by the lawyer for each side that explains the legal and factual arguments why the court should decide in favor of that lawyer's client.

Burden of proof – the level or quality of proof that a party needs to prove his or her case. In civil cases, the plaintiff has the burden of proving his or her case by a preponderance of the evidence, which means the plaintiff's proof must outweigh the defendant's at least slightly for the plaintiff to win; if the two sides are equal, the defendant wins. In criminal cases, the government has the burden of proof, and that burden is much higher: A verdict of guilty requires the government to prove the defendant's guilt beyond a reasonable doubt.

C

Case file – a complete collection of every document in a case.

Case law – the law as laid down in the decisions of the courts; the law in cases that have been decided. Compare with **statute**.

Case management – techniques used to process cases from one stage of the proceeding to another, such as setting deadlines for discovery or scheduling a series of pretrial conferences. Case management calls for different approaches from one case to the next and is the primary responsibility of judges, assisted by lawyers and clerks' office personnel.

Challenge for cause – a lawyer's attempt to prevent a prospective juror from sitting on a jury because, in the lawyer's view, the juror's answers to *voir dire* questions suggest that he or she cannot approach the case impartially. If the judge agrees with the lawyer, the judge will then strike (excuse) the prospective juror for cause. Compare with **peremptory challenge**.

Chambers – the offices of a judge.

Chief judge – the judge who has primary responsibility for the administration of a court, but also decides cases. Chief appellate judges and chief district judges take office according to rules regarding age and seniority; the district judges of the court appoint chief bankruptcy judges. Compare with **Chief Justice**.

Chief Justice – the "first among equals" on the U.S. Supreme Court, who has numerous responsibilities for the administration of the federal judicial system as well as for hearing cases. The President appoints the Chief Justice, with the approval of the Senate, when a vacancy occurs in the office.

Circuit – the regional unit of federal judicial appeals. Congress has divided the federal judicial system into twelve regional circuits (the eleven numbered circuits and the District of Columbia Circuit). In each circuit is a court of appeals to hear appeals from district courts in the circuit, and a circuit judicial council to oversee the administration of the courts of the circuit. See also **district**.

Circuit court – an informal name for a **U.S. court of appeals** (also the name of some state trial courts).

Circuit executive – a federal court employee appointed by a circuit judicial council to assist the chief judge of the circuit and provide administrative support to the courts of the circuit.

Circuit judge – an informal name for a **U.S. court of appeals judge**.

Circuit judicial council – a governing body in each federal circuit created by Congress to ensure the effective and expeditious administration of justice in that circuit. Each council has an equal number of circuit and district court judges; the chief judge of the circuit is the presiding officer.

Civil case – a lawsuit brought by a party (the plaintiff) against another party (the defendant) claiming that the defendant failed to carry out a legal duty owed to the plaintiff and that the defendant's breach of duty caused financial or personal injury to the plaintiff. Usually, the purpose of bringing the case is to get a court order for the defendant to pay for damages suffered by the plaintiff.

Class action – a lawsuit in which one or more members of a large group, or "class," of individuals or other entities sue as "representative parties" on behalf of the entire class. There must be questions of law or fact common to the class, and the district court must agree to "certify the class," thus allowing the action to proceed as a class action.

Clerk of court – an officer appointed by the court to work with the chief judge and other judges in overseeing the court's administration, especially to assist in managing the flow of cases through the court.

Closing arguments – after all the evidence has been presented in a trial, lawyers' presentations summarizing the evidence and attempting to persuade the jury to conclude favorably to their clients. Closing arguments, like **opening statements**, are not themselves evidence.

Community defender organization – a nonprofit defense counsel service organized by a group of lawyers in private practice and authorized by the district court to represent criminal defendants in court who cannot afford to pay for their defense. Compare with **federal public defender organization**.

Complaint – a written statement by the person ("plaintiff") starting a civil lawsuit which details the wrongs allegedly committed against that person by another person ("defendant").

Concurring opinion – see **opinion**.

Condition – a court-imposed requirement that a defendant or offender must abide by in order to remain under community supervision by a pretrial service or probation officer, as an alternative to imprisonment. For example, refraining from the use of illegal drugs is a mandatory condition for everyone under federal supervision; a person who is known to have used illegal drugs in the past may also have regular drug testing as a condition.

Confirmation hearing – (1) in bankruptcy, the court proceeding at which the judge determines whether a debtor's plan of reorganization meets the requirements of the Bankruptcy Code, whether creditors have accepted or rejected the plan, and whether to confirm the plan as presented. (2) the hearing in which Senate Judiciary Committee members question persons nominated by the President to be federal judges.

Contested matter – in bankruptcy, a method of handling disputes that may arise during the course of a case. Contested matters are initiated by motion and generally do not require a filing fee. The Bankruptcy Rules establish the types of disputes that are handled as contested matters. Compare with **adversary proceeding**.

Contract – an agreement between two or more persons that creates an obligation to do or not to do a particular thing.

Counsel – a lawyer or a team of lawyers. The term is often used during a trial to refer to lawyers in a case.

Count – an allegation in an indictment charging a defendant with a crime. An indictment may contain allegations that the defendant has committed more than one crime. The separate allegations are referred to as the counts of the indictment.

Counterclaim – a claim filed by a defendant against the plaintiff in response to the plaintiff's original suit. The defendant becomes the counterclaim plaintiff in the case, and the plaintiff becomes the counterclaim defendant (in addition to their being defendant and plaintiff).

Court – an agency of government authorized to resolve legal disputes. Judges and lawyers sometimes use the term *court* to refer to the judge, as in "the court has read the pleadings."

Court of appeals – see **U.S. court of appeals**.

Court of appeals judge – see **U.S. court of appeals judge**.

Court interpreter – a court employee who orally translates what is said in court from English into the language of a non-English-speaking party or witness and translates that person's testimony into English.

Court reporter – a person who makes a word-for-word record of what is said in a court proceeding and produces a transcript of the proceeding on request.

Courtroom deputy clerk – a court employee who assists the judge by keeping track of witnesses, evidence, and other trial matters, and sometimes by scheduling cases.

Creditor – any person, business, or other entity, such as a government agency, to whom a debtor owes money. In bankruptcy, creditors usually receive a reduced amount because the debtor is unable to pay the full amount owed.

Criminal case – a case prosecuted by the government, on behalf of society at large, against an individual or organization accused of committing a crime. If the defendant is found guilty, the sentence (or punishment) is often imprisonment.

Criminal Justice Act (CJA) – a federal statute designed to implement the Sixth Amendment right to counsel in criminal cases by providing court-appointed attorneys to represent defendants who cannot afford to pay for an attorney's services. Some district courts order these defendants to pay to the court at a later date the amount of money it has spent in providing the defendant with a lawyer. Reimbursement may be made a term of the judgment at sentencing, or a condition of probation or supervised release.

Criminal record – a record listing a defendant's previous arrests and convictions. A copy of the defendant's criminal record, if any, must be given to the defense upon request during discovery.

Cross-claim – in a case with more than one defendant, a claim filed by one defendant (the "cross-claim plaintiff") against another (the "cross-claim defendant"). A cross-claim may allege that any injury to the plaintiff was caused by the cross-claim defendant, who should pay any damages to which the plaintiff is entitled, and/or it may allege a separate but related injury to the cross-claim plaintiff caused by the cross-claim defendant.

Cross-examination – questions directed to a witness by a lawyer for any other party, after the direct examination of the witness. The questions focus on matters the witness testified to during direct examination and may be designed to test the witness's credibility. Leading questions (those which suggest, by their wording, how the attorney would like the witness to answer) may be asked on cross-examination. Compare with **direct examination**.

D

Damages – money that a defendant pays a plaintiff in a civil case that the plaintiff has won, to compensate the plaintiff for loss or injury.

Deadlocked jury – a jury that is unable to agree upon a verdict (also called a **hung jury**). A deadlocked jury results in a mistrial.

Debtor – a person or business that owes money to another person or business. In bankruptcy, the debtor usually repays a reduced amount because of inability to pay the full amount owed.

Debtor-in-possession (DIP) – in bankruptcy, the manager of a debtor business in a Chapter 11 reorganization that continues to operate and control the business after the bankruptcy petition is filed unless the court orders otherwise.

Default judgment – a judgment against the defendant awarding the plaintiff the relief demanded in the complaint because of the defendant's failure to appear in court. A summons must notify the defendant that failure to appear and defend against the lawsuit promptly will result in the court's entry of a default judgment.

Defendant – (1) in a civil suit, the person complained against; (2) in a criminal case, the person accused of the crime.

Deposition – a frequently used means of obtaining discovery in civil cases, in which the attorney who requested the deposition questions a party, witness, or any person with information about the case, and the person (the deponent) answers under oath.

Deputy clerk – see **courtroom deputy clerk**.

Detention hearing – under the Bail Reform Act, a hearing that may be held in a case involving a defendant who is charged with a serious felony or whose record indicates that he or she may flee or pose a serious risk of danger to the community if released prior to trial. If, after an evidentiary hearing, the magistrate judge who conducts the hearing finds that no pretrial release conditions will reasonably ensure the appearance of the defendant in court, the safety of the community, or the safety of another person, the magistrate judge may order the defendant detained without bail pending trial.

Direct examination – the initial questioning of any witness by the attorney who calls the witness to the stand, to bring out evidence for the fact finder (judge or jury). Compare with **cross-examination**.

Discharge – (1) the payment of a debt or satisfaction of some other obligation; (2) in bankruptcy, a legal device that releases a debtor from monetary obligations; it prevents creditors from trying to collect pre-bankruptcy debts from a debtor after a bankruptcy proceeding is over.

Disclosure statement – in bankruptcy, a statement that gives Chapter 11 creditors information to use in deciding whether to vote to accept or reject a debtor's plan of reorganization.

Discovery – (1) in a civil case, pretrial procedures by which the lawyers representing the parties try to learn as much as they can about their opponents' cases by examining the witnesses, physical evidence, and other information that make up the case; (2) in a criminal case, a meeting of the defendant's attorney and the prosecutor in which the defendant's attorney requests disclosure of certain types of evidence against the defendant. The government may then make a discovery request of the defendant.

Discovery plan – a plan developed at a pre-discovery meeting by the parties in a civil case (or their lawyers) and filed with the court. This plan is required by the Federal Rules of Civil Procedure except in cases exempted by a local rule or court order. The parties discuss their claims and defenses, explore possibilities for settlement, and make or arrange for the disclosures required by the rules.

Dissent – see **opinion**.

District – a geographic region over which a particular U.S. district court has jurisdiction. Congress has divided the country into districts to organize the administration of justice. See also **circuit.**

District court – see **U.S. district court**.

District judge – see **U.S. district judge**.

Diversity jurisdiction – the federal district courts' authority to hear and decide civil cases involving plaintiffs and defendants who are citizens of different states (or U.S. citizens and foreign nationals) and who meet certain statutory requirements.

Docket – a list of court proceedings and filings in chronological order.

E

Early neutral evaluation– a form of alternative dispute resolution in which an experienced, impartial attorney with expertise in the subject matter of the case (a neutral evaluator) gives the parties a nonbinding assessment of the case and may also provide case-planning guidance and assistance with the settlement.

en banc–a French term meaning "on the bench." The term refers to a session in which all of the judges on an appellate court participate in the decision. The judges of the U.S. courts of appeals usually sit in panels of three, but for some important cases, they may sit *en banc*.

Evidence – information in the form of testimony, documents, or physical objects that are presented in a case to persuade the fact finder (judge or jury) to decide the case for one side or the other.

Exclusivity period – in bankruptcy, the time during which only the debtor in a Chapter 11 reorganization can propose a plan of reorganization. The exclusivity period is generally at least the first 120 days after the bankruptcy filing.

Exemption – money or property that is not liquidated as part of the bankruptcy estate.

Exhibit – an item of physical evidence (a document or an object).

Expert witness – a person with specialized training and experience about the particular subject matter who testifies in a case to offer an opinion on an issue in the case based on his or her specialized knowledge.

F

Factfinder – the jury in a jury trial or the judge in a bench trial who weighs the evidence in a case and determines the facts.

Fact witness – a person with knowledge about what happened in a particular case who testifies in the case about what happened or what the facts are.

Federal courts – courts established under the U.S. Constitution. The term usually refers to courts of the federal judicial branch, which include the Supreme Court of the United States, the U.S. courts of appeals, the U.S. district courts (including U.S. bankruptcy courts), and the U.S. Court of International Trade. Congress has established other federal courts in the executive branch, such as immigration courts.

Federal crime – a violation of a criminal law passed by Congress. Federal law enforcement agencies investigate federal crimes and are prosecuted by the U.S. attorney for the judicial district in which the crime occurred.

Federal Judicial Center (FJC) – the federal judicial system's agency for research and education. Its responsibilities include developing and administering education programs and services for judges and other court employees, and undertaking empirical and exploratory research on federal judicial processes, court management, and sentencing, often at the request of the committees of the Judicial Conference of the United States.

Federal public defender organization – as provided for by the Criminal Justice Act, an organization established within a federal judicial district (or more than one district) to represent criminal defendants who can't afford to pay a lawyer. Each organization is supervised by a federal public defender appointed by the court of appeals for the circuit.

Federal-question jurisdiction – the federal district courts' authorization to hear and decide cases arising under the Constitution, laws, or treaties of the United States.

Federal rules – bodies of rules developed by the federal judiciary that spell out procedural requirements. The federal rules are the Federal Rules of Civil Procedure, the Federal Rules of Criminal Procedure, the Federal Rules of Appellate Procedure, the Federal Rules of Evidence, and the Federal Rules of Bankruptcy Procedure. Rules can take effect only after they are forwarded to Congress for review and Congress declines to change them.

Federalism – a principle of our Constitution which gives some functions to the U.S. government and leaves the other functions to the states. The functions of the U.S. (or federal) government involve the nation as a whole and include regulating commerce that affects people in more than one state, providing for the national defense, and taking care of federal lands. State and local governments perform such functions as running the schools, managing the police departments, and paving the streets.

Felony – a crime that carries a penalty of more than a year in prison.

Fine – a form of punishment for a crime, in which the defendant must pay a sum of money to the public treasury.

Final decision – a court's decision that resolves the claims of the parties and leaves nothing further for the court to do but ensure that the decision is carried out. The U.S. courts of appeals have jurisdiction over appeals from final decisions of U.S. district courts.

Foreperson – the juror who presides over the jury's deliberations. The foreperson is either elected by the jurors or selected by the judge, depending on the practice in the particular court.

G

Grand jury – a group of citizens who listen to the government present evidence of criminal activity by an individual or individuals to determine whether there is enough evidence to justify filing an indictment charging the individual or individuals with a crime. Federal grand juries are made up of sixteen to twenty-three persons and serve for about a year, sitting one or two days a week.

Guidelines Manual – the manual published by the U.S. Sentencing Commission, which contains the federal sentencing guidelines, policy statements, and commentary.

Guilty plea – a criminal defendant's admission to the court that he or she committed the offense he or she is charged with and his or her agreement to waive the right to trial. If the court accepts the plea, the case proceeds to sentencing.

Guilty verdict – a verdict convicting a criminal defendant of a charge or charges. When a verdict of guilty is returned, the court orders a presentence investigation of the defendant and sets a sentencing date.

H

habeas corpus – a Latin phrase meaning "that you have the body." A prisoner may file a habeas corpus petition seeking release because he or she is being held illegally.

Hearsay – evidence that is presented by a witness who did not see or hear the incident in question but heard about it from someone else. Hearsay is usually not admissible as evidence in a trial.

Home confinement–- a court-imposed requirement that a defendant or offender being supervised in the community by a pretrial service or probation officer must remain within his or her home, either all the time or during certain hours of the day. Electronic monitoring may be used to verify the person's whereabouts; the person wears an electronic device which contacts the supervising officer if it leaves the permissible area.

Hung jury – a jury that is unable to reach a verdict (also called a **deadlocked jury**). A hung jury results in a mistrial.

I

Impeachment – (1) the process of charging government officials with serious misconduct in office that can lead to their removal; (2) the process of calling the credibility of a witness into question, as in "impeaching the testimony of a witness."

Imprisonment – a term in prison served by an offender as part of a federal criminal sentence.

Indictment–the formal charge issued by a grand jury stating that there is enough evidence that the defendant committed a crime to justify having a trial. Indictments are used primarily for felonies. An indictment may contain allegations that the defendant committed more than one crime. The separate allegations are referred to as the counts of the indictment. Compare with **information**.

Indigent defendant – a defendant who does not have the financial resources to hire an attorney and qualifies for a court-appointed attorney under the Criminal Justice Act.

in forma pauperis – a Latin phrase meaning "as a pauper." A party unable to pay the filing fees and other costs involved in an appeal may file a motion in the district court asking to proceed *in forma pauperis*. If the motion is granted, the party may proceed with the appeal without paying any fees or costs.

Information – a formal accusation by a government attorney that the defendant committed a misdemeanor. Compare with **indictment**.

Initial appearance – following an arrest, the appearance of a defendant before a magistrate judge, who informs the defendant of the nature of the charges against him or her. The defendant is also informed of his or her rights to be represented by counsel, to remain silent, and to have a preliminary examination. The magistrate judge then decides whether to detain the defendant or release him or her on bail.

Injunction – a judge's order that a party take or refrain from taking certain action. An injunction may be preliminary until the outcome of a case is determined, or permanent.

Interim trustee–in bankruptcy liquidations, a person who takes "possession of, preserves, and protects" the debtor's nonexempt property (the property that will be divided among creditors) until the creditors elect a case trustee. See also **case trustee**.

Interlocutory appeal – an appeal from a nonfinal, or interlocutory, district court order, such as an injunction. An interlocutory order is issued during litigation of the case in the district court, not at the end of it. Interlocutory appeals are permitted by statute as an exception to the general policy requiring a final district court decision or order before an appeal is permitted.

Interrogatories–a form of discovery consisting of written questions to be answered in writing and under oath. Interrogatories are submitted to a party in the case by the party seeking discovery.

J

Judge – a governmental official with authority to preside over and decide lawsuits brought to courts.

Judgment – a final order of the court that resolves the case and states the rights and liabilities of the parties.

Judgment as a matter of law – a ruling that not enough credible evidence has been introduced on a particular claim to allow the jury to consider it. The Federal Rules of Civil Procedure give any party the right, at the end of the presentation of an opponent's evidence, to ask the court to enter judgment against the opponent.

Judicial Conference of the United States–the federal courts' administrative governing body. The Chief Justice of the United States chairs the Conference, and it meets twice a year. Much of the Conference's work is done through some twenty committees of judges, which make recommendations to the Conference on various issues.

Judicial Panel on Multidistrict Litigation – the federal agency responsible for considering the transfer of civil cases that are pending in different districts but involve common questions of fact to a single district for coordinated or consolidated pretrial proceedings. The panel consists of seven courts of appeals and district court judges designated by the Chief Justice.

Judicial review – (1) the authority of a court, in a case involving either a law passed by a legislature or an action by an executive branch officer or employee, to determine whether the law or action is inconsistent with the U.S. Constitution, and to declare the law or action invalid if it is inconsistent; although judicial review is usually associated with the U.S. Supreme Court, it can be, and is, exercised by lower courts; (2) a form of appeal to the courts for review of an administrative body's findings of fact or law.

Jurisdiction – (1) the legal authority of a court to hear and decide a certain type of case; (2) the geographic area over which the court has authority to decide cases.

Jury – a group of citizens whose duty is to weigh evidence fairly and impartially and decide the facts in a trial (see **petit jury**) or to decide whether the evidence against a defendant is sufficient to file an indictment charging him or her with a crime (see **grand jury**).

Jury instructions – instructions given by the judge to the jury after all the evidence in a case has been presented, either before or after closing arguments and before the jury begins deliberations. The instructions cover such matters as the responsibilities of the jurors, how the jurors are to go about deciding the case, and the law applicable to the case.

Jury trial – a trial in which a jury decides the facts. Compare with **bench trial**.

Justice Department – the agency of the federal executive branch with responsibilities in a wide range of areas bearing on the administration of justice and enforcement of laws passed by Congress. The Justice Department is responsible for investigating alleged criminal conduct, deciding which cases merit prosecution in the federal courts, and prosecuting those cases. It also represents the U.S. government in many civil actions.

L

Lawsuit – any one of various proceedings in a court of law.

Leading question – a question an attorney asks a witness in a trial which, by its very wording, suggests how the attorney would like the witness to answer. Leading questions are permissible during cross-examination but not during direct examination.

Liquidation–the more traditional type of bankruptcy filing, in which the debtor gives up most of its assets in return for not having to pay most of its debts.

Litigants – see **parties**.

Local rules – rules that govern practice and proceedings in a specific federal court. Local rules can supplement but not contradict the federal rules.

M

Magistrate judge – a judge appointed by a federal district court for an eight-year term. Magistrate judges assist district judges in preparing cases for trial. They may also conduct trials in misdemeanor cases when a defendant agrees to allow a magistrate judge instead of a district judge to preside, and they may conduct civil trials when the parties agree to it.

Mandatory minimum sentence–a statutorily defined minimum term of imprisonment that the court is required to impose on a defendant at sentencing. For example, a defendant convicted of distributing one kilogram or more of a substance containing a detectable amount of heroin must be sentenced to "a term of imprisonment which may not be less than 10 years or more than life" under federal law.

Marshals Service – see **U.S. Marshals Service**.

Master wheel – the list of registered voters in a district, supplemented in some districts with other sources, which is used as a source of prospective jurors. The clerk's office sends a questionnaire to each person on the master wheel.

Mediation–the alternative dispute resolution method most commonly used in the district courts. Mediation is an informal process in which a mediator facilitates negotiations between the parties to help them resolve their dispute.

Misdemeanor – a criminal offense less severe than a felony, generally punishable by a fine only or by imprisonment of less than one year.

Mistrial–- a trial that has been terminated because of some extraordinary event, a fundamental error prejudicial to the defendant, or a jury that is unable to reach a verdict.

Motion – an application to the court for an order of some kind. Some kinds of motions may be filed only within certain time limits, and others may be filed at any stage of a case.

N

nolo contendere **plea** – a plea in which the defendant does not admit guilt, but does waive the right to trial and authorize the court to impose punishment at sentencing. *Nolo contendere* is a Latin term that means "it is not contested." This type of plea is rarely entered. The motivation for entering a *nolo* plea is that unlike a plea of guilty, a *nolo* plea may not be used against the defendant as an admission in a related civil case.

O

Objection – a lawyer's belief, stated to the judge, that something is wrong with a question posed by opposing counsel, the way opposing counsel phrases a question, or the way a witness answers it. If the judge thinks the objection is valid, he or she will **sustain** the objection and tell the witness not to answer or tell the jury to disregard the answer. If there is no basis for the objection, the judge will **overrule** it and let the questioning continue.

Opening statements – before the evidence is presented in a trial, lawyers' presentations to the jury summarizing what they intend to present as evidence. Opening statements, like **closing arguments**, are not themselves evidence.

Opinion – a judge's written explanation of a decision in a case or some aspect of a case. An opinion of the court explains the decision of all or a majority of the judges. A dissenting opinion is an opinion by one or more judges who disagree with the majority. A concurring opinion is an opinion by one or more judges that agree with the decision of the majority but offers further comment or a different reason for the decision. A *per curiam* opinion is an opinion handed down by an appellate court but not signed by an individual judge.

Oral argument – in appellate cases, an opportunity for the lawyers for each side to appear before the judges to summarize their positions and answer the judges' questions.

Order – a decision or direction made by a judicial authority. Judges issue orders in response to motions.

Overrule – (1) a judge's ruling at trial that a lawyer's objection is without merit, and that the questioning or testimony objected to may continue; (2) a court's decision to set aside the authority of a former decision.

P

Panel – (1) in appellate cases, a group of three judges assigned to decide the case; (2) in the process of jury selection, the group of potential jurors from which the jury is chosen; (3) in criminal cases, a group of private lawyers whom the court has approved to be appointed to represent defendants unable to afford to hire lawyers.

Parole – the suspension of a convict's prison sentence and the convict's release from prison, at the discretion of an executive branch agency and conditioned on the convict's compliance with the terms of parole. The Sentencing Reform Act of 1984 abolished federal parole. Offenders whose crimes were committed on or after November 1, 1987, are sentenced by the court under sentencing guidelines established by the U.S. Sentencing Commission and, unlike previous offenders, may not have their sentences reviewed by the U.S. Parole Commission. See also **probation** and **supervised release**

Parties – the plaintiff(s) and defendant(s) in a lawsuit.

per curiam opinion – see **opinion**.

Peremptory challenge –- an attorney's striking (excusing) a person from a panel of prospective jurors during jury selection for a trial without stating any reason. Attorneys have the right to a certain number of peremptory challenges in each case. Peremptory challenges may be made for a variety of reasons, including hunches, but may not be based on race or gender. Compare with **challenge for cause**.

Petition – (1) a document filed in a U.S. court of appeals to commence an appeal of a final decision of a federal agency, board, commission, or officer; (2) a document filed in bankruptcy court to initiate a bankruptcy case.

Petitioner – the party filing a petition in the court of appeals, seeking review of an order issued by a federal agency, board, commission, or officer.

Petition for rehearing – a document filed by a party who lost a case in the U.S. court of appeals to ask the panel to reconsider its decision. If the panel grants the petition, it may ask the parties to file additional briefs and reargue the case.

Petit jury (or **trial jury**) – a group of citizens who hear the evidence presented by both sides at trial in a case and determine the facts in dispute. Federal criminal juries consist of twelve persons, and sometimes additional persons serve as alternate jurors in case one or more of the twelve cannot continue. Federal civil juries consist of six to twelve persons. *Petit* is French for "small," thus distinguishing the trial jury from the larger grand jury (*grand* is French for "large").

Plaintiff – the person who files the complaint in a civil lawsuit.

Plan of reorganization – in bankruptcy, a plan that sets out how a debtor in a Chapter 11 reorganization proposes to repay its creditors.

Plea – in a criminal case, the defendant's statement to the court that he or she is "guilty" or "not guilty" of the charges.

Plea agreement – an agreement between the government and the defendant to resolve a pending criminal case by the defendant's entering a guilty plea rather than going to trial. The prosecutor may agree to dismiss or reduce certain charges, or recommend a certain sentence in return for the defendant's entering a guilty plea and, in some cases, providing information to the prosecutor.

Plea bargain – The process in which the defendant and the prosecutor in a criminal case work out a mutually satisfactory disposition of the case subject to court approval. It usually involves the defendant's pleading guilty to a lesser offense or to only one or some of the counts in a multi-count indictment in return for a lighter sentence than the defendant would have received if convicted of the more serious charges.

Pleadings – in a civil case, the written statements of the parties stating their positions about the case.

Precedent – a court decision in an earlier case with facts and legal issues similar to those in a case currently before a court. Courts are required to follow some precedents. For example, a U.S. court of appeals must follow decisions of the U.S. Supreme Court; a district court must follow decisions of the U.S. Supreme Court and the court of appeals of its circuit. Courts are also influenced by decisions they are not required to follow, such as the decisions of other circuits. Courts also follow their precedents unless they set forth reasons for changing the case law.

Prediscovery meeting – a meeting required by Federal Rule of Civil Procedure 26(f), at which the parties or their attorneys in a civil case discuss their claims and defenses, explore possibilities for settlement, make or arrange for the disclosures required by Rule 26(a), and develop a discovery plan to be filed with the court.

Preliminary examination – a pre-indictment hearing at which the prosecutor must present evidence sufficient to establish probable cause to believe that a federal offense was committed and that the defendant committed it.

Preponderance of the evidence – see **burden of proof**.

Presentence report – a report a probation officer prepares from an investigation of a convicted defendant that the officer conducted at the request of the court. It provides extensive information about the defendant's background, financial condition, criminal offense or offenses, and criminal history for the judge to use in determining an appropriate sentence for the defendant.

Presumption of innocence – the requirement in a criminal trial that the jury presume that the defendant is innocent of all charges. The judge instructs the jury that, before the defendant can be found guilty, the government must overcome the presumption of innocence and convince the jurors that the defendant is guilty beyond a reasonable doubt.

Pretrial conference – (1) in a civil case, a meeting of the judge and lawyers conducted pursuant to Federal Rule of Civil Procedure 16(d) to decide which matters are in dispute and should be presented to the jury, to review evidence and witnesses to be presented, to set a timetable for the case, and sometimes to discuss settlement of the case; (2) in a criminal case, a meeting which the court may conduct, pursuant to Federal Rule of Criminal Procedure 17.1, upon motion of any party or on its own motion, "to consider such matters as will promote a fair and expeditious trial."

Pretrial release conditions – the conditions under which a defendant may be released prior to trial under the Bail Reform Act of 1984. The conditions may be designed to ensure the defendant's appearance in court or the safety of the community.

Pretrial services officer – an officer of the court who collects and verifies information to be used by judges in deciding issues related to defendants' pretrial release and detention. In districts that do not have pretrial services offices, probation officers also serve as pretrial services officers.

Pretrial services report – a report a pretrial services officer prepares that contains information learned through a pretrial services investigation about a defendant's personal history, criminal record, and financial status. The report is given to the U.S. magistrate judge, the prosecutor, and defense counsel for use in deciding issues related to bail.

Privilege against self-incrimination – a person's right to remain silent in the face of accusation or questioning by government agents. Also known as the right to remain silent, the privilege against self-incrimination is contained in the Fifth Amendment of the Constitution. People may invoke the privilege at any time, including immediately after an arrest, at the police station, before the grand jury, and at trial.

pro bono publico – a Latin term meaning "for the good of the public." Some lawyers take on certain kinds of cases pro bono, without expectation of payment; these cases are called "pro bono cases."

pro se – a Latin term meaning "on one's behalf." In courts, it refers to persons who present their cases without lawyers.

Probable cause – the legal standard defining the amount of evidence or information needed to justify a search or an arrest. The Fourth Amendment requires that arrests and searches made by law enforcement officers be justified by probable cause. An arresting officer has probable cause for an arrest only if there is enough reliable information or evidence to support the officer's reasonable belief that a crime has been committed and that the defendant committed it.

Probation – a criminal sentence in which the offender is placed under court supervision for a specified period, but allowed to remain in the community. While on probation the offender is required to report to a probation officer and comply with other court-imposed conditions (compare with supervised release).

Probation officer – an officer of the court who is responsible for conducting presentence investigations of offenders and preparing presentence reports, and is responsible for supervising persons on probation or supervised release.

Proof beyond a reasonable doubt – see **burden of proof**.

Prosecute – to charge a person or organization with a crime and seek to gain a criminal conviction against that person or organization.

Prosecutor – the government lawyer responsible for prosecuting criminal defendants. In federal cases, the prosecutor is the **U.S. attorney** or **assistant U.S. attorney (AUSA)**.

Q

Qualified wheel – the group of potential jurors who are not excused or exempted from the master wheel, and who are thus found eligible to serve. An individual on the qualified wheel may request a hardship excuse to be removed from the qualified wheel. See **master wheel**.

R

Reaffirmation – in bankruptcy, an agreement by a debtor to repay a particular debt even though there is no legal obligation to do so.

Record – all the documents filed in a case and a written account of the trial proceedings.

Record on appeal – the record of a case made as proceedings unfold in the U.S. district court, and assembled by clerks in the district court clerk's office and transmitted to the U.S. court of appeals. It consists of the pleadings and exhibits filed in the case, the written orders entered by the trial judge, a certified copy of the docket entries, and a transcript of the relevant court proceedings. Court of appeals judges review parts of the record, along with briefs presented by the parties, when considering appeals of lower courts' decisions.

Recross-examination – questions directed to a witness by the lawyer who conducted the cross-examination of the witness. Recross-examination follows redirect examination and focuses on matters that were raised for the first time during cross-examination. The questions focus on matters the witness testified to during redirect examination and are designed to test the witness's credibility. Leading questions may be asked on recross-examination, as they may on cross-examination. See also **leading question**.

Recuse – to withdraw or disqualify oneself as a judge in a case because of personal prejudice, conflict of interest, or some other good reason why the judge should not sit in the interest of fairness.

Redirect examination – questions directed to a witness by the lawyer who conducted the direct examination of the witness. Redirect examination follows cross-examination and focuses on matters that were raised for the first time during cross-examination.

Referral order -- an order that assigns a magistrate judge responsibility for handling a variety of pretrial issues in a civil case and for ensuring that the parties adhere to a strict case-preparation schedule. In some courts, it is common for district judges to enter referral orders in newly filed civil cases.

Relief – money damages or any other remedy the plaintiff seeks in a complaint.

Remand – the act of an appellate court sending a case back to a lower court for further proceedings.

Removal – a procedure applicable to most cases in which a federal court has jurisdiction because there is a federal question or diversity (parties who live in different states), but the plaintiff chooses to sue in state court. The federal removal statute allows the defendant to get the case removed to federal court, in part to ensure fairness to out-of-state defendants.

Reorganization – a type of bankruptcy filing in which the debtor gets to keep most, if not all, of its assets but has to pay all or some specified part of its debts according to a plan of reorganization.

Representative party – a party who sues on behalf of the class in a class action. The claims or defenses of the representative party must be typical of the class, and the representative party must protect the interests of the class. See **class action**.

Requests for admission – a form of discovery in which one party asks another to admit or deny the truth of facts or the genuineness of documents.

Requests for production of documents – a form of discovery in which one party requests that another make certain documents and other objects available for inspection and copying.

Restitution – payment by an offender of money or services to the victim of a crime for losses suffered as a result of the crime. Restitution must be ordered as part of the defendant's sentence for certain crimes. It may also be ordered as a condition of probation or supervised release.

Reverse – to set aside a lower court's decision or order and enter a different decision or order. A reversal is often followed by a **remand**.

Revocation of probation or supervised release – a court's order that a probationer or supervised releasee who has violated one or more conditions of probation or supervised release can no longer serve his or her sentence in the community and must be imprisoned.

Right to remain silent – see **privilege against self-incrimination**.

Search warrant – a written court order authorizing a law enforcement officer to search certain premises for specified items and to seize the items described.

S

Senior judge – a judge who has retired from active duty but continues to perform some judicial duties, usually maintaining a reduced caseload. Compare with **active judge**.

Sentence – a judgment of the court imposing punishment upon a defendant for criminal conduct.

Sentencing Commission – see **U.S. Sentencing Commission**.

Sentencing guidelines – uniform policies established by the U.S. Sentencing Commission (USSC) to guide federal judges as they sentence criminal offenders. The first set of sentencing guidelines took effect in 1987, and the USSC amends the guidelines annually.

Sentencing hearing – a court hearing at which a defendant who is convicted of a crime is sentenced. At the hearing, the judge considers the probation officer's recommendations for sentencing, allows the attorneys to state their positions, and gives the defendant an opportunity to make a statement before imposing sentence.

Sequestration – (1) the court's exclusion of witnesses from the courtroom until they testify, so that the testimony of prior witnesses will not influence their testimony; this practice is normally available if counsel request it, but does not apply to parties, who have the right to be present in court throughout the trial; (2) the court's requirement that jurors remain isolated while deliberating on a case because justice requires that they be protected from outside influences.

Service of process – bringing a judicial proceeding to the notice of a person affected by it by delivering to him or her a summons, or notice of the proceeding. See **summons**.

Settlement – an agreement between the parties to a lawsuit to resolve their differences among themselves without having a trial or before the judge or jury renders a verdict in a trial.

Settlement week – a type of alternative dispute resolution in which a court suspends normal trial activity for a week and, aided by volunteer mediators, sends trial-ready cases to mediation sessions held at the courthouse. Cases unresolved during settlement week are returned to the court's regular docket for further pretrial or trial proceedings as needed.

Sidebar (or **sidebar conference**) – a discussion between the judge and lawyers held out of earshot of the jury and spectators.

Speedy Trial Act – a statute that imposes a series of time limits upon a court and prosecutors for carrying out the major events in a criminal case to ensure that the defendant receives a speedy trial.

Staff attorney – a member of the central legal staff of the court of appeals.

Standard of proof – see **burden of proof**.

State courts – courts established by various state governments, including county and local courts.

Statute – a law passed by a legislature. Compare with **case law**.

Statute of limitations – a law setting a fixed period (for example, one year) after which a person may not sue someone for an alleged injury or a government may not prosecute someone for a crime. It prevents legal proceedings from taking place long after the injury or crime occurred, when evidence and witnesses may be hard to find.

Stay – the postponement or halting of a judicial proceeding or judgment. A motion for a stay pending appeal seeks to delay the effect of a district court order or agency order until a U.S. court of appeals decides whether that order is valid.

Stipulate – to enter into a binding agreement on an issue that is not genuinely in dispute. Matters stipulated to in a court case are considered proven, so neither side is required to present evidence on them.

sua sponte – a Latin term meaning "on its responsibility or motion." A *sua sponte* order is an order issued by a court without prior motion by either party.

Subpoena – a court order that requires that a person produce documents or appear at a trial, hearing, or deposition to testify as a witness.

Summary judgment – under Federal Rule of Civil Procedure 56, a court's judgment as a matter of law when the court determines that, after looking at all the evidence in the case, there is no dispute as to the facts. A party may file a motion asking the court to order summary judgment on some or all claims in the case.

Summary jury trial – a form of alternative dispute resolution used late in the pretrial proceedings of cases headed for lengthy jury trials. It provides for a short hearing at which counsel present the evidence to a jury in summary form, with no witnesses, and the jury delivers a nonbinding advisory verdict to be used as a basis for subsequent settlement negotiations.

Summons – a document the plaintiff in a lawsuit must file with the court and serve on the defendant, along with a copy of the complaint, to give the defendant notice of a lawsuit. Federal Rule of Civil Procedure 4 governs the form and content of a summons and explains the different methods that can be used to serve a summons on a defendant so that the defendant learns of the lawsuit.

Supervised release – a criminal sentence in which the offender is placed under court supervision for a specified period, but is allowed to remain in the community. Like offenders placed on probation, offenders placed on supervised release are supervised by probation officers and are required to observe certain conditions of release. The court must order a term of supervised release when it is required to do so by statute and when it orders a sentence of more than one year in prison.

Supreme Court of the United States – the highest federal court in the United States. Its primary function is to clarify the law when lower courts disagree. Its members are appointed by the President and approved by the Senate.

Sustain – to rule at trial that a lawyer's objection to questioning or testimony is valid. When the judge sustains an objection, the questioning or testimony objected to must stop or be modified.

T

Term – the time during which the U.S. Supreme Court sits for the transaction of business, also referred to as a session. Each year's term begins on the first Monday in October and ends when the Court has announced its decisions in all the cases it has heard during the term, usually in late June or early July.

Testimony – evidence presented orally by witnesses during trials or depositions or before grand juries.

Third-Party claim – a claim that a defendant can include in its answer to a complaint, stating that a breach of duty by an entity not a party to the lawsuit gave rise to all or part of the plaintiff's claim. Service of the third-party complaint brings the entity into the suit as a third-party defendant, and the filing defendant becomes a third-party plaintiff.

Transcript – a written, word-for-word record of what was said either in a proceeding, such as a trial or during some other exchange, such as a telephone conversation.

Trial – the proceeding at which parties in a civil case, or the government and the defense in a criminal case, produce evidence for consideration by a fact finder in court. The fact-finder, who may be a judge or a jury, applies the law to the facts as it finds them and decides whether the defendant is guilty in a criminal case or which party should win in a civil case.

Trial court – see **U.S. district court**.

Trial jury – see **petit jury**.

U

Uphold – to allow a lower court's decision to stand as is. After reviewing the lower court's decision, an appellate court may uphold or reverse it. Compare with **reverse**.

U.S. attorney – a lawyer appointed by the President, in each judicial district, to prosecute cases for the federal government and represent the government in civil actions.

U.S. bankruptcy court – a federal court that hears and administers matters that arise under the Bankruptcy Code. Although it is a unit of the district court and technically hears cases referred to it by the district court, for most practical purposes it functions as a separate administrative unit.

U.S. Constitution – the document written by the founders of this country, which establishes the basic structure and functions of the federal government, grants certain specified rights (often called constitutional rights), to the American people, and places limits on the powers and activities of our federal and state governments. The term *U.S. Constitution* also includes its amendments. The first ten amendments to the Constitution are referred to as the Bill of Rights.

U.S. court of appeals – a federal court that reviews decisions of the district court when a party in a case asks it to. Some use *circuit court* to refer to the court of appeals, although technically *circuit court* refers to a federal trial court that functioned from 1789 to the early twentieth century.

U.S. Court of Appeals for the Federal Circuit – a federal court of appeals located in Washington, D.C., whose jurisdiction is defined by subject matter rather than geography. It hears appeals only in certain types of cases, including those involving patent laws and those decided by the U.S. Court of International Trade and the U.S. Court of Federal Claims.

U.S. court of appeals judge – a judge of one of the thirteen U.S. courts of appeals. When a party appeals a district court decision in a case, appeals judges review what happened in the district court to see if the district judge made any mistakes that would require them to change or modify the decision or to order that the case be retried. Court of appeals judges are among the group often referred to as Article III judges, because their power to hear and decide cases stems from Article III of the Constitution, and they thus have irreducible salaries and tenure during good behavior.

U.S. Court of Federal Claims – a special trial court with nationwide jurisdiction which hears cases involving money damages in excess of $10,000 against the United States, including disputes over federal contracts, federal takings of private property for public use, and rights of military personnel.

With the approval of the Senate, the President appoints U.S. Court of Federal Claims judges for fifteen-year terms.

U.S. district court – a federal court with general trial jurisdiction. It is the court in which the parties in a lawsuit file motions, petitions, and other documents and take part in pretrial and other types of status conferences. If there is a trial, it takes place in the district court. Also referred to as a *trial court.*

U.S. district judge – a judge of the federal district courts, appointed by the President, subject to the approval of the Senate. District judges are among the group often referred to as Article III judges, because their power to hear and decide cases stems from Article III of the Constitution, and they thus have irreducible salaries and tenure during good behavior.

U.S. Marshals Service – an agency of the Justice Department charged with providing courtroom security in federal district courts, apprehending federal fugitives, transporting federal prisoners, and supervising the Justice Department's Federal Witness Protection Program.

U.S. Sentencing Commission – an independent commission in the judicial branch of the government established by the Sentencing Reform Act of 1984. Its mission is to develop sentencing policies and practices for use in the federal courts.

U.S. trustee – a person who supervises the administration of bankruptcy cases and trustees and relieves bankruptcy judges of routine administrative matters, such as appointing case trustees, naming creditors' committee members, and conducting meetings of creditors. U.S. trustees are appointed by the Attorney General of the United States for a five-year term.

V

Verdict – a petit jury's or a judge's decision on the factual issues in a case.

voir dire – the process by which judges and lawyers select a petit jury from a panel of citizens eligible to serve. They do this by questioning the members of the panel. *Voir dire* is a French term that means "to speak the truth."

Voluntary filing – a bankruptcy case that the debtor initiates. Compare with **involuntary filing**

W

Waiver – the act of knowingly, intentionally, and voluntarily giving up a right. For example, a defendant who pleads guilty waives the right to a jury trial.

Waiver of service – a procedure under Rule 4 of the Federal Rules of Civil Procedure that gives the plaintiff in a lawsuit the option of requesting in writing that the defendant sign a form waiving service of the summons. The defendant receiving such a request has a duty to avoid the "unnecessary costs" involved in serving a summons, and the rule provides the defendant with the two incentives of lower cost and more time to answer.

Witness – a person called upon by either side in a lawsuit to give testimony before the court.

writ of certiorari – an order by a court requiring that the lower court produce the records of a particular case tried so that the reviewing court can inspect the proceedings and determine whether there have been any irregularities. Almost all parties seeking review of their cases in the U.S. Supreme Court file a petition for a writ of certiorari. The Court issues a limited number of writs, thus indicating the few cases it is willing to hear among the many in which parties request review.

writ of execution – a means of enforcing a judgment in which, at the plaintiff's request, the clerk directs the U.S. marshal to seize the defendant's property, sell it, and deliver to the plaintiff the amount of money necessary to satisfy the judgment.

writ of garnishment – a means of enforcing a judgment in which the defendant's property (e.g., a bank account, wages, or any debt owed to the defendant by someone else) is to be seized and is in the hands of a third person.

writ of habeas corpus – a document filed as a means of testing the legality of a restraint on a person's liberty, usually imprisonment. The writ commands the officials who have custody of a prisoner to bring the prisoner before the court so that the court can determine whether the prisoner is being detained lawfully.

Made in the USA
Middletown, DE
14 January 2020